Power at Work

Rebuilding the Australian union movement

To Bron,
My hero

And to Huw, Ted and Sam
Our future.

Power at Work

Rebuilding the Australian union movement

Michael Crosby

THE FEDERATION PRESS
2005

Published in Sydney by:
    The Federation Press
    PO Box 45, Annandale, NSW, 2038
    71 John St, Leichhardt, NSW, 2040
    Ph (02) 9552 2200 Fax (02) 9552 1681
    E-mail: info@federationpress.com.au
    Website: http://www.federationpress.com.au

First published 2005
Reprinted 2007

National Library of Australia
Cataloguing-in-Publication entry

    Crosby, Michael.
    Power at work: rebuilding the Australian union movement

    Bibliography.
    Includes index.
    ISBN 1 86287 569 3

    1.Labor unions – Australia. @. Labor union members – Australia.
    3. Labor unions – Recognition. 4. Industrial relations – Australia.
    I. Title.

331.880994

Typeset by The Federation Press, Leichhardt, NSW.
    Printed by Southwood Press Pty Ltd, Sydney, NSW.

Foreword

Greg Combet, Secretary, Australian Council of Trade Unions

Michael Crosby is a passionate unionist – a true believer in the social justice cause of the labour movement. He has devoted most of his working life to representing working people.

Over the last ten years Michael has gained a unique insight into Australian unions as a result of his reforming work with the ACTU's Organising Centre.

At a time of unprecedented change and challenge many unions have trusted Michael to shine a light into every nook and cranny of their organisation. He has advised them how to modernise their union and to rebuild their membership.

His experience, and his passion for change, has informed this book. His account of the strategic imperatives confronting Australian unions in the 21st century is the most comprehensive statement of the issues yet written.

Michael's book therefore represents an important contribution to the debate about the future of unions.

Two key dynamics are clouding this future – economic change and a hostile political environment. Michael Crosby makes the case for top to bottom change in unions to address these challenges.

His argument is that unions can no longer rely on institutional support from governments, industrial tribunals, awards or "passive" employers. He argues that unions must direct their resources towards building organisational power in the workplace and the industry.

This in itself is not a new insight. However, experience has demonstrated that organisational renewal is far easier said than done. The value of Michael's work lies in his effort to detail what has worked and what hasn't.

I encourage all people who care about the future of unions, and the labour movement, to read and debate the issues contained in this book.

As ACTU Secretary, and as a colleague, I would like to thank Michael for making the considerable effort to document his experience and his views, and for his long-standing commitment to our cause.

With courage let us all combine
To advance Australia fair.

Australian National Anthem

Everyone has the right to form and to join trade unions
for the protection of his or her interests.

The Universal Declaration of Human Rights, Article 23 (4)

Contents

Part 4 – Building strategic leverage

Part 5 – Driving comprehensive change

Preface

Power at Work is my attempt to map out what Australia's unions have done so far to renew themselves and to define what more needs to be done. We have done an awful lot, much more than Prime Minister John Howard appears to realise. His plan to wind back the power of Australia's workers and turn unions into an unrepresentative rump may well be a monumental mistake.

In crafting his strategy, he appears to be guided by a presumption that Australia's unions are unchanged from the 1970s and 1980s. But the attack is directed at a shifting target. The period since 1995 has seen the most profound change in the union movement's history – at least since the very early part of the 20th century.

In attempting to capture the reform agenda as it has already played out, I am challenging all those exercising leadership in unions, whether leaders, staff or delegates, to look closely at their union and decide whether they have done enough to build its power. I am also seeking to challenge even the reformers with the next steps they need to take to ensure a rebalancing of power between capital and labour.

The book aims to sketch out how to instil an organising philosophy into every part of modern unionism. Only by re-envisioning unions as an expression of the collective power of workers rather than as remote and instrumental third parties can we hope to prosper. The book promotes radical change because that's what's required if we are to create unions that can survive in the environment being crafted for us by our enemies.

The force of the campaign against the Howard legislation in 2005 comes from the fact that we have done nothing more than tell the unvarnished truth about the new law's effects on working people and their families. Our appeal to them has resonated because they have already had a foretaste of the government's radical agenda. The re-regulation of industrial relations in the employers' interest creates for workers the most hostile environment in the western world. Its aim is to allow wages and conditions to fall – particularly in time of recession. Its effect is to instil fear into workers. Its rationale is the lifting of productivity by forcing workers to work longer, harder, for less. Its outcome is to shift the balance of reward even further from those who produce to those who own. But the guarantee that all that will happen is that the law is designed to send union density – the proportion of the workforce organised into unions – into freefall once more. As unionism declines so does the power of workers to bargain collectively, to have a say in how they are treated in the workplace. That means that the test of our success is not whether the Prime Minister's approval rating falls or whether public opinion is wholly on our side –

no matter how gratifying that outcome may be. The test is much tougher. Can we maintain current density and actually grow in spite of the hand that has been dealt us?

I have no doubt that we can. Indeed, many of our unions are well advanced down the path of change. But the change agenda I set out here is not easy and requires high levels of leadership and commitment. Failure is unthinkable. The defeat of unionism and its value system will be a tragedy not just for workers but for the whole country.

Australia has been, since the turn of the 20th century, a market economy striving for egalitarianism. Despite our racist past, our treatment of the Indigenous population, our subordination of women, enshrined at the heart of how we think of ourselves, is the idea that we are a commonwealth – a place where every resident has a right to share in the wealth of the society as a whole. The individualism of America is a foreign concept. We developed the country through the force of collective rather than individual activity. Every benchmark national achievement has had that collective activity at its heart – whether it be our prowess in war, the engineering success of a Snowy Mountains Scheme, Sydney Harbour Bridge or Opera House, our film industry, the development of our universities, the success of our migration program, the development of industry.

Behind the business push for industrial relations reform is a value system based on "Greed is Good" – the transplantation of American individualism to our own country through the individualisation of workplace relations.

Unions must be reformed because they deliver good things to workers. But they must also be renewed so that workers can balance the inherent power of those controlling the means of production. Strong unions are the only way in which workers can have a say in the way they are treated by the society in which they live. Only in that way can a market economy be built which has at its heart the need to provide equal opportunity for all. Only in that way can we preserve our national inheritance – the essence of what it is to be Australian. Workers must build for themselves, power at work.

Michael Crosby
Sydney
August 2005

Acknowledgments

Power at Work represents a fair bit of what I have learned about unions over the last 30 years. What I have written is coloured by my own background, education and all the thousands of interactions I have had over that time. I owe a debt to all those who have been part of that experience.

My mum and dad gave me the thirst for justice at the heart of any good union official's thinking and action. They taught me what it was like to be a member of a family that suffers the poverty and insecurity that comes with casual employment. They also showed me that there is power in the union. It was in my father's lifetime that he and his actor colleagues fought for and won rehearsal pay, travelling allowance, superannuation, repeat and residual fees, Australian content guidelines, access to leading roles in their own country ... it is a very long list.

The Christian Brothers gave me an education without equal both as student and as one of their number. They taught me that the Church stands unambiguously on the side of the poor and the vulnerable and I am immensely proud to be associated with them and their mission. Fr Ted Kennedy inspired me and the rest of the family to stay true to that heritage – and it was his knowing smile that spurred me to take the time off and start writing.

Most of what I learned about the fundamentals of unionism came from representing actors both at Equity and at the International Federation of Actors. Actors are the best union members. Despite having no power as individuals – apart from a very few stars – they stick together with enormous courage and refuse to allow themselves to be sold for the lowest price. And our stars are wonderful, throughout the union's history, standing in solidarity with their colleagues.

Every union official I have worked with over the years has had an impact on me – whether in this country or around the world. There are too many to name but a few I must mention. Uri Windt and Anne Britton were wonderful comrades at Equity. Rolf Rembe, John McGuire and Peter Plouviez to name just a few, taught me an enormous amount about the representation of actors internationally and the essence of unionism.

Tas Bull and Tom MacDonald have had an extraordinary impact on me and on many of the people you will meet in this book. We owe them a great debt of gratitude that they spent their retirement so productively!

The educators who were willing to take a gamble – and a pay cut – in setting up the new organisation, Trade Union Training Australia, are owed a debt by the whole union movement and not just me. Cathy Bloch, Jenny Evans, Don Sutherland, Ann Polis and later Jessie Edney and Kathleen Galvin, worked unbelievably hard to make the organisation a success so that it could play its role in disseminating the organising message. Their example has been followed by the staff at the ACTU Organising Centre – both past and present. The educators and organisers at the Centre have brought many of these ideas to life.

The same can be said for the hundreds of organisers and union leaders I have come into contact with in courses and seminars and over cups of coffee. Workers in this country will win because of you. Two leaders, Mark Butler and Tony Sheldon, are worthy of special note – because they were the first willing to give these ideas a go.

In the same vein we owe a debt to a range of academic thinkers who have turned their minds and talents to the situation of workers. Again there are too many to name but a few need to be acknowledged. John Buchanan has been an inspiring thinker and analyst of workplace trends. No one understands unions as well as David Peetz. His written and verbal analysis and advice on the situation of Australian unions is indispensable. Barbara Pocock's passion for justice comes out in everything that she writes. Kate Bronfenbrenner's work on organising tactics has formed the core of what we have taught at the Organising Centre over many years – and she continues to provide us with her insights on what needs to be done next. David Weil is a legend. We nearly killed him with work on his one visit to Australia in 1996 and he took the time to read the first draft of the book during his short Christmas break (sorry Miriam, Rachel and Alana) and provide me with detailed feedback. John Lund gave me encouragement at just the right moment. Rae Cooper tore the history chapter to shreds and made me go back and look at what really happened.

My thanks too to Braden Ellem and then Ron Callus and the staff at ACIRRT who provided me with a home for two months while I tried to get the first draft down. I particularly liked their raised eyebrows any time they caught me on the phone rather than writing!

Thanks too to Chris Holt at Federation Press for agreeing to publish the book without so much as an outline of what I was writing. I hope your confidence is not misplaced.

Over the past ten years I have been constantly embarrassed at the generosity of America's unionists. Teresa Conrow first taught us organising frameworks and we have stolen her work unashamedly since she first came to the country. Bruce Raynor spent his entire five-day holiday in Sydney talking about nothing but organising and inspired everyone he met. Every official we have invited to the country – or just by accident turned up here – has been cheerfully willing to run seminars, give speeches – do whatever we asked to promote the organising agenda. On our visits to the US the staff of the AFL-CIO have spent an enormous amount of time with us both in briefing us and in arranging meetings with other unionists. Three unions in particular have gone out of their way to help a procession of Australian unionists – SEIU, UNITE and HERE.

Two officials above all the others stand out – Andy Stern and Tom Woodruff. They have never refused a single request – no matter how outrageous. They have inspired us all to do whatever it takes to win.

Greg Combet has been enormously generous to me. He let me take the time off to do the writing and more importantly told me to write what I thought rather than what the ACTU might want written.

Two people have been rock solid collaborators with me in the organising project – Chris Walton and Louise Tarrant. Many of the ideas are theirs and our partnership is marked by an absolute willingness to share those ideas and take them to the next step. The book is as much their work as it is mine.

My family have put up with my obsessions for many years and I just hope that they are prepared to stick with it until the 2012 graph is dead and buried for all time.

If there are errors in the book or you think I have got it wrong – don't blame me – do what union officials have done since time immemorial – blame the ACTU!

Abbreviations

ABS	Australian Bureau of Statistics
ACTU	Australian Council of Trade Unions
AFL-CIO	American Federation of Labor-Congress of Industrial Organizations
AMWU	Australian Manufacturing Workers' Union
APHEDA	Australian People for Health Education and Development Abroad
AWU	Australian Workers' Union
CEPU	Communication, Electrical and Plumbing Union of Australia
CFMEU	Construction, Forestry, Mining and Energy Union
CPSU	Community and Public Sector Union
ETU	The Electrical Trades Union (a division of the CEPU)
FIET	International Federation of Commercial, Clerical, Professional and Technical Employees
Finsec	Finance Sector Union (NZ)
GUFs	Global Union Federations
HERE	Hotel Employees and Restaurant Employees International Union (US)
HSU (NSW)	Health Services Union, NSW Branch
LHMU	Liquor, Hospitality and Miscellaneous Workers Union
MEAA	Media Entertainment and Arts Alliance
MSC	Member Service Centre
MUA	Maritime Union of Australia
NUW (Vic)	National Union of Workers (Victorian Branch)
OEA	Office of the Employment Advocate
PATCO	Professional Air Traffic Controllers (US)
QPSU	Queensland Public Sector Union
SDA	Shop Distributive and Allied Employees Association
SEIU	Service Employees International Union (US)
TUC	Trades Union Congress (UK)
TUTA	Trade Union Training Authority from 1996, Trade Union Training Australia
TWU (NSW)	Transport Workers Union (NSW Branch)
UNI	Union Network International
UNITE	Union of Needletrades Industrial and Textile Employees (US)
WOC	Workplace Organising Committee

1

Introduction

This book is about power. How Australian workers got it, lost much of it and the way in which they can regain it. It's therefore about unions – the only real way in which individual workers have a chance of exercising power.

It's a bit cheeky – a former actors' union official writing a book about how the entire Australian union movement should rebuild its power. It really should be written by a wharfie, a coal miner, a metal worker. After all, blue collar blokes are the iconic unionists – the people whose organisation, whose level of militancy, has been the backbone of Australian union success for much of the 20th century.

But actors are much more like the rest of the workforce today than coal miners. They suffer insecure employment. They are in chronic oversupply. They are roughly equally split between males and females – as is the union movement as a whole. They are not naturally militant class warriors – if there is such a thing anywhere.

When you represent actors you see the potential operation of the market in its purest form. For every job there are ten actors who could do the job perfectly well. Employers are allowed to discriminate for almost any reason. (The filmmaker, Philip Noyce – a great friend to actors – describes how if he had seen Bill Hunter without his beard he would never have hired him to play the lead in Newsfront – because he had a double chin!)[1] Actors are desperate to work and will do almost anything to get the job. Each actor pays an agent to help him or her compete against their colleagues.

How is it that actors get decent minimum wages? Get paid to rehearse the work they are about to do? Receive superannuation? Get treated decently when they are on set? How are they able to protect themselves from unfair dismissal – when their employers are allowed to discriminate for "artistic reasons"? How could these completely powerless labour market players manage to force their employers to give them a share in the income from the sale of their work?

The answer is that the actors formed a union back in 1939. They spent the next 20 or 30 years making it strong. They won a strike in 1944 that gave them a

---

1   Caputo R and Burton, G (eds) *Third Take, Australian Film-makers Talk,* Allen and Unwin, 2002, p 96.

closed shop in theatre. And even now, without a closed shop, there is not an employer in the country who is able to hire a professional actor who is not a financial member of the union.

Actors understand that as an individual they are on their own. They are grist to the very nasty mill of free market competition. Without their union, wages are well and truly in competition. Without their unity, they would be part of a race to the bottom where the half dozen Australian stars – whose marketing potential is in short supply – would do reasonably well and the rest would be hobby actors, desperate for any payment that they could get.

I was the General Secretary of the International Federation of Actors from 1991–1995 and part of my job was to help actors get organised so that they were not crushed by their newly-formed, free labour markets. It was just after the fall of the iron curtain and we were either helping actors in Eastern Europe to form new unions or reform the old "socialist" unions.

I was asked to come and speak to a large group of actors gathered together by the newly re-formed Cultural Workers Union of Russia in the middle of a Moscow winter. I had with me an American actor called Joe Ruskin who specialised in playing baddies in American films. He was an honorary officer with the American Screen Actors Guild. I had Joe play the role of a visiting US film producer making a blockbuster picture in Moscow starring Sean Connery and Mel Gibson and they needed some Russian actors to play opposite them. I started the meeting by picking out half a dozen of the actors to come up and negotiate as individuals with him. (They were actors after all. Why wouldn't they love a role play?)

To put it politely, Joe behaved like any film producer in such a situation. He was a monster. (Out of the blue, he even managed to produce a cigar which he smoked throughout the performance! Inevitably, of course, he managed to blow smoke in the actors' faces.) He tried to screw a good deal from each of those actors. Wages? No, no, expenses were on offer – nothing more. The line that had the whole audience baying for his blood was – and remember these people had invented modern acting:

"Payment? You shouldn't ask for payment. This will be a privilege for you to work alongside these great actors. You will learn so much from them!"

The point of the exercise was of course to show the audience just how little bargaining power they had on their own and how little respect they could get as a result. That part of it certainly worked.

I then took the six people outside and got them to form a union and elect an Equity Deputy. You can guess the rest. They came back in and annihilated Joe with demand after demand. Finally, frustrated, he turned to them and said, "But what is it that you want from me?"

With superb timing, our Russian actor turned to his audience and proclaimed, "For every Russian actor, one Mercedes Benz!"

The whole audience stood and cheered.

That story gives us the core idea behind unionism. As individuals we are exploited. The union is the means by which workers get power. Regulation helps. There are very strong regulations in Russia! But the key is, how well organised are the workers?

Make no mistake. There hasn't been a time in human history when the free operation of the labour market has meant good things for workers. They have had to set up their own organisations to act as a restraint on the unbridled power of the market. Their job is to stop the market operating freely. They ensure that the human beings who are at its base are treated as something more than commodities, human resources, to be sold to the lowest bidder.

The strength of the Australian union movement was formed in the first decade of the 20th century after a decade of utter defeat. They achieved, at that time, sufficient power to be able to ensure that the fair treatment of the Australian workforce was a fundamental element of the Australian settlement. The force of the argument – united we bargain, divided we beg – resulted in a century where workers were generally able to share in the wealth generated by a rich Australia.

I am part of that tradition. I took the power of actors for granted. I could never have conceived of a time where the union might disappear and actors be left to bargain on their own. I made certain that the union fought hard for its members. Many of their employers would have preferred, I am sure, that I was in Hades! But many others had a good relationship with the union and our dealings with each other were founded on a measure of mutual respect. We cared about our industry and its continued ability to employ the union's members. Indeed, I still count a few of those employers as friends.

Despite that, I have become one of the people developing ideas which aim to give power back to workers and to do so where necessary by using techniques borrowed from the most radical of union organisers.

Whether my fellow unionists or I like it or not, we are in a class war – although not one of our choosing. Our enemies – and some of our friends[2] – attack the philosophy of organising set out in this book as a manifestation of an outdated class war mentality.

In Australia, particularly in the 1990s, the whole accommodation between capital and labour unravelled. The business community declared class war on us. John Howard and his colleagues – inspired, financed and egged on by Big Business – determined to destroy the institutional power of unions. They attacked the Industrial Relations Commission, they removed the closed shop, they introduced individual contracts, and they encouraged, indeed bullied

---

2   See Kochan, T, "Restoring Workers Voice: A call for action", paper to a Washington DC conference on the future of organised labour, March 2003; or Taylor, R, *Social democratic trade unionism. An agenda for action,* Catalyst, September 2003.

employers, into "taking on" unions in their effort to "free up" the labour market. They even got down and dirty and helped finance an attack on possibly our strongest union – the Maritime Union of Australia – in an effort to demonstrate the futility of resistance. By driving labour costs down, by increasing the unfettered nature of employer prerogative, by introducing flexibility so great that workers could be asked to do anything, at any time, at any price, they aimed to increase profits – and that was deemed to be the prime measure of success. All this was sold as part of the trickle-down theory of wealth generation. We would be better off, because the new wealth created for the owners of capital would benefit us all.

Not all employers wanted to be caught up in this struggle against unions. But even the well meaning were caught by the shift in ideological temperature. To talk about working cooperatively with unions was to characterise yourself as a relic of the old economy – someone failing to make the shift to Australia's new competitive environment. Once employer aggression in one company led to reductions in their cost of labour, competitive pressure forced other employers to secure matching concessions from unions – whatever they wanted their union relationship to be.

We will see just what impact this had on the power of workers. Unions have lost half the proportion of the workforce that had previously been unionised. In the 1990s union membership numbers declined drastically. Some unions have had to face the prospect that if they changed nothing, bankruptcy was a real possibility.

The impact on workers has been almost immediate. At a time of unprecedented financial prosperity, workers have missed out. Many of the jobs created are low waged and casual. Full employment has been re-defined as 5 per cent. Underemployment is rife. In 2001, 10 per cent of the workforce was underemployed.[3] They wanted to work longer hours but couldn't get them. For the first time in our modern history, we now have a category of working poor – men and women who have jobs but cannot manage to support themselves. Their advocates have become the churches and the charities – just as much as their unions.

The personal cost to workers of their lack of power is well illustrated in Elizabeth Wynhausen's book *Dirt Cheap*.[4] There she lives and works as a low waged worker in a series of jobs. The lives of the workers she meets are unremittingly hard as a result of low wages and casual work but the extraordinary thing for me is their level of fear and lack of hope in a better future.

Whole new sectors of the economy have started to grow which are, by and large, union free. Workers don't have the option of organising themselves to get power.

---

3   Watson, I, et al, *Fragmented Futures*, Federation Press, 2003, p 38.
4   Wynhausen, E, *Dirt Cheap*, Macmillan, 2005.

So what is to be done about all this?

One reaction is to hunker down and hope for better times. Defend what we have and try to ensure that the winds of economic rationalism blow over the strongholds of union membership. For the powerless, perhaps they must accept that in a modern economy, unions will have a smaller part to play. Worldwide competition will mean that workers have to accept the deal that is given them.

Since 1994, a relatively small group of people have pushed an alternative view. Chris Walton was the first of these to be given responsibility for looking at another way of envisioning the future. He had been part of a study tour of the US in 1993 looking for answers to the pressure of an increasingly hostile employment environment. Almost by chance they came across Richard Benzinger who was training young organisers at the Organizing Institute – and then memorably they were introduced to a "Brigade" of office cleaners organised by Stephen Lerner of "Justice for Janitors". These two brief interactions so excited the members of the delegation that they rang Bill Kelty[5] that night and got him stirred up about what might be possible. On their return, Bill gave Chris the job of setting up and running Organising Works – a traineeship set up to train a new generation of union organisers capable of talking to non-members and working with them to extend the frontiers of unionism.

In 1995, I came back to Australia to run the Trade Union Training Authority (TUTA) – as it then was – a government training body which educated delegates and union officials. I knew nothing about organising or the work that Chris was doing. I went to our residential training college to give a talk to a group of delegate trainers. I spoke, I remember, about the need to lift service standards if unions were to have a future. We had to adopt a business model that would guarantee that members would have high levels of satisfaction with their union's service delivery. At the end of the talk, my arguments were then, with clinical precision, cut into tiny little pieces by Kelly Livingstone, a young woman who was a recent graduate of the Organising Works program. She told me in no uncertain terms that we were doomed if we tried to run a better standard of insurance company. Organising workers was the only way we could succeed and the sooner I understood that, the better off we all would be!

I came back to Melbourne a very chastened figure! I didn't like being publicly humiliated and I wanted to know from Chris what the hell he was teaching these crazy radicals.

So began my education.

The book that follows represents what I have learnt – or at least as much of it as I can write down in the three months I have available to me and will fit in one book. The learning comes not just from books – although our academic friends have been extremely helpful. It comes rather from the discussion, debate and experimentation that has gone on both within the Australian union

---

5   ACTU Secretary, 1983–2000.

movement and between us and a range of individual American unionists – in particular, the leaders, staff and members of Service Employees International Union (SEIU), Union of Needletrades Industry and Textile Employees (UNITE) and Hotel Employees and Restaurant Employees (HERE).[6] Above all, the work is a product of the long-standing partnership between Chris, myself and our colleague, Louise Tarrant, Assistant National Secretary of the Liquor, Hospitality and Miscellaneous Workers Union (LHMU).

Much of organising theory is drawn from what we have learnt of the American experience in applying the basic principles to their economy. Some of us resist the idea of looking to America for solutions. Theirs has always been a weaker movement than ours and there is much that we have traditionally deplored about their dominant style of unionism.

Yet the sad fact is that our employers and conservative politicians have borrowed their ideas about appropriate corporate behaviour from America. In workplace after workplace, we show workers American union-busting manuals and they recognise instantly the techniques being used against them.

So we looked to America because, despite the overall failure of their movement to defeat the worst excesses of management ideology, some unions are succeeding – against all the odds. Some are growing and surviving in an environment designed to wipe them out. And some are doing so in areas of the economy that no one could predict would be fertile ground for any kind of organising approach.

We have adapted those ideas and at least in some areas we may have improved on them. As you read through these pages, you will see that we now need to rely on very few US examples of organising innovation. After ten years of Australian experimentation, a range of Australian unions have tried out these ideas and can report for us on whether they work or not.

Knowing what works and actually doing it on a broad scale are two quite different things. Kate Bronfenbrenner showed US unions, as early as 1986, what organising tactics and strategies worked in an American environment. Yet she has recently reported that only three or four unions use these measures in a majority of their campaigns – and even they fail to do everything that is associated with organising success. [7]

There is no union in Australia which has gone as far as the best of the American unions. But there are now a range of unions and union branches which have embraced the approach enthusiastically. They still grapple with how to get the maximum benefit from it but they are in no doubt as to where they must travel to deliver success.

---

6   HERE has recently merged with UNITE to form UNITE HERE.

7   Bronfenbrenner, K and Hickey, R, "Changing to Organize, A National Assessment of Union Strategies in Organizing and Organizers", in R Milkman and K Voss (eds), *The New Union Movement*, ILR Press, 2004, p 19.

In talking about organising unionism we can't limit ourselves to the techniques for getting new members to join or even the benefits of an organising model of unionism – a means of dealing with existing members so that they are active and empowered. Chris and I learnt a hard lesson in the early days of developing a strategy to rebuild the power of our union movement. Concentrating just on the processes by which workers could be persuaded to join a union could only lead to failure.

Between approximately 1910 and the early 1990s Australian unionism built – as we will see – a very successful model of unionism. It depended on high levels of institutional support within a stable structure of employment. Given that both these preconditions are disappearing, focusing solely on the mechanics of organising without dealing with the wider issue of institutional renewal can do nothing but doom our efforts to failure.

As I write, the Howard Government is attempting to drive a whole new raft of industrial relations legislation through the Senate. The ideology of this government will be revealed as never before – because never before have they had the unfettered power to do what they really want. The proposed legislation allows the dismantling of the Award system which will be replaced with a Fair Pay Commission.[8] The right of workers to challenge unfair dismissal is to be removed from any worker employed by an organisation with less than 100 employees. The employment relationship is to be individualised by allowing employers to override any collective agreement or Award and make it a condition of employment that new employees sign an individual agreement subject to a handful of minimum conditions. The ability of workers to ask their union representatives to come to the workplace to represent them is to be severely constrained. Any employee forced to become an independent contractor is to be deprived absolutely of any hope of union representation. The ability of State Industrial Relations Commissions to settle industrial disputes is, for the vast bulk of employees, to be removed.

This legislative agenda means that for workers unprotected by the union collective or the strength of any temporary occupational labour shortage, power has shifted entirely to employers. Most can be sacked for any reason – no matter how arbitrary or unfair. The effective removal of an Award safety net means that workers will be desperately thankful for any increase, no matter how miserly, which rescues them from minimum wages. The requirement of individual contracting or independent contractor status means that employees will be forced to accept anything an employer offers.

It is in that context that this book is written. I provide no critique of the legislation nor do I propose an alternative legislative set of protections. Rather, I take our hostile environment as a given – at least for the moment. My concern is to focus on those elements of our environment which lie within the direct

---

8   The irony is implicit!

control of unions and their officials and members. I aim to outline all the changes necessary to deliver a growing and powerful union movement.

If that is the aim, then techniques for organising new members and the need for an active and empowered existing membership are critical. But to get to that point, we have to look at modes of leadership, bargaining strategy, strategic choice, resourcing, financial management, union education. In short, every element of union behaviour has to be examined.

This book then has a number of functions. I aim once more to sound an alarm on behalf of workers. We are in the process of having our inheritance denied. An inheritance that provided principles of equality, fairness and justice to its citizens. I am trying to map out a vision for the movement that is expansive – that makes unionism something to which every worker can and should aspire. I want to give to those unions conscious of the need for change, a description of an approach that I am convinced can, will and does work. I hope that all unions can use the book as a means of looking at their own situation and reflecting on ways in which they can make themselves stronger – whether or not they fully embrace the philosophy I and my colleagues espouse.

The book is a public document and will therefore be read by interested members of the community – including employers. If the book goes some way to persuading the Australian community that not every economic reform embraced so enthusiastically by those with power serves their own self-interest or the wider good of the society, it will have served an important additional purpose.

Finally, I set out my thoughts on what needs to be done next. Some will see these as impossibly radical and impractical.

I hope that is not the case. In the mid-1990s, when Chris and I started this project, we were dismissed, I suspect, as a bit crazy – interesting stuff, but Australian unions would never go for it. As John Howard and his successors will find, it is dangerous to underestimate the courage and capacity of Australian union leadership. The fact is that union leader after leader has picked these ideas up and given them a go. And they have been successful. My aim in this book is to refine these ideas and to take them to the next level. Some may dismiss them as too radical – but I am confident others will be prepared to embrace them. My hope is that they will work. As they become more and more the norm and as they are developed, so the movement as a whole will change and embrace them.

Part 1
MAKING SENSE OF OUR SITUATION

2

Australian unions –
what is the problem?

Everywhere John Howard goes he lists as one of his achievements the rolling back of union power.[1] In Perth at the beginning of 2004, speaking to a gathering of the party faithful, he boasted that union membership stood at less than 20 per cent of the workforce. His figure was wrong – but only just.

Prior to the 2001 election, when asked what he would regret most if he lost the election, he replied that the biggest blow would be "the thought of the boys and girls at the ACTU making whoopee on election night".

Having achieved absolute power with control of the Senate in 2005, his very first concern has been to drive through Big Business' industrial relations reform agenda. Their key aim is the breaking up of the power of workers to bargain collectively.

Conservative commentators put the issue more politely. When listing Howard's lifetime achievements they talk about his "deregulation of Australia's industrial relations system." That's code for – among other things – wrecking trade unions and their ability to stand up for Australia's working people.

Peter Reith, his first Minister for Workplace Relations, was at least honest about it. In a meeting with Bob Carter of the Transport Industry Association he said:

> An award is a mechanism a union can use to justify its existence. To remove unions you remove the relevance of the award.

Our problem is that even our own Labor Party has noticed our decline in density and power. As one newly-elected Labor Premier said forcefully to a Trades and Labor Council Secretary – "Why should I listen to you! You represent just 19 per cent of the workforce!"

Our enemies constantly labour the point that declines in density represent a decline in significance. The Financial Review puts it this way:

---

1   See for example the speech by Howard to CEDA, 25 February 2004.

In the past two decades trade unions have lost more than half their influence in the workplace and much of their relevance.[2]

Unions in Australia have lost power and our members know it – let alone the politicians from both sides. In surveys commissioned by the Labor Council of NSW, the proportion of respondents who agree that management had more power than unions has steadily increased.[3]

But the best measure of union power is the union density figures issued each March for the previous year by the Australian Bureau of Statistics. (Union density measures the proportion of the workforce organised into unions) The level of density approximates the level of power because the higher the proportion of the workforce that is represented, the more influence we are seen to have.

For most of the 20th century, around 50 per cent of workers were organised into unions. In around 1982, the tide turned and density started to decline. Most importantly, in the 1990s, the decline became freefall. The decade saw the most catastrophic decline in density since the disaster of the 1890s Great Strikes. But for our friends in New Zealand, we would have achieved world's best practice for union decline!

Look at Figure 2.1 and you will see the problem for yourself.

Figure 2.1: Density 1986-2004

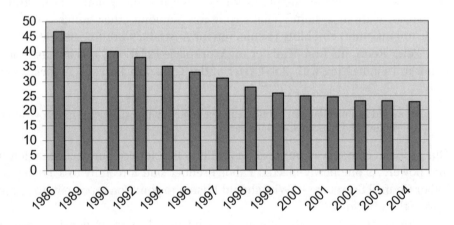

---

2 Editorial, *Australian Financial Review*, 12 March 2004.

3 ACIRRT, 2001 Survey of Community Attitudes.

The interesting thing about the graph of density is that it didn't worry too many union officials – at least until the mid-1990s. I can remember when Peter Berry and Gerry Kitchener of the BWIU[4] published a book called *Can Unions Survive in 1989.*[5] It caused scarcely a ripple. My union was typical I suspect. It was growing quite strongly each year – indeed, I can remember budgeting on achieving 5 per cent growth in membership income every year. What was the problem? Until 1990, membership had been increasing for unions as a whole since the 1900s. Like the church, we thought we were pretty well immortal and our place in the sun guaranteed. It didn't occur to me back then to have a look at whether employment in my industry was growing along with my membership. Were we just keeping pace with or lagging behind employment growth or were we improving our grip on the industry?

The penny really dropped for union leaders at the moment that the numbers of actual members declined. Every one of those members leaving the union represented a loss of income. And we weren't losing members gradually. The membership loss was catastrophic.

Figure 2.2: Union membership 1988-2004

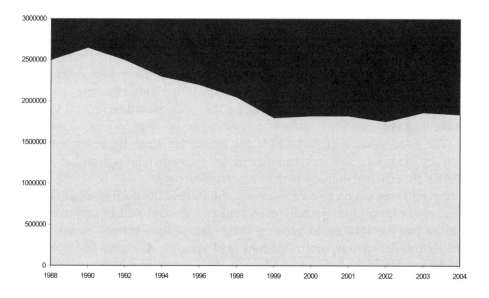

---

4   Building Workers Industrial Union – now one of the constituent parts of the Construction, Forestry Mining and Energy Union.

5   Berry, P and Kitchener, G, *Can Unions Survive?* BWIU (ACT Branch), 1989.

Figure 2.2 charts nine long years of falling income from 1990 to 1999. I calculated that the fall in income as a result of these declines in membership was the equivalent of 3000 organisers losing their job. The total income lost between 1990 and 1999 was in the order of $197 million.[6]

Responses from union leaders varied. Some saw the writing on the wall and started to cut their expenditure – and staff are the main expense for unions. Most did this only as a last resort. They presumed that something would turn up. Some waited for the return of a Labor government. They were reluctant to sack staff.

In most unions after all, it was the staff who had helped get the leader elected and loyalty was owed to them. These Secretaries funded the income shortfall by running down assets.

This process produced what became the famous "scary graph" (Figure 2.3). This is the first of the "scary graphs" that I produced – and they won't mind if I let you know that it was for the Finance Sector Union (FSU).[7] (They asked me to conduct an "Operational Review" of their union which might lay out some ideas for them in how to help them in countering the challenges they faced.)

What I found was that their deficits were caused by a huge drop in membership – a drop that was largely out of their control. The major financial institutions were savagely downsizing, as bank branches were closed across the country, work at head offices was intensified and new technology was introduced.

What the graph showed was that if the union leadership did nothing and changed nothing, their deficits would keep increasing at a constant rate. These losses had to be paid for and that meant that the union's assets kept decreasing. The result was that we could predict the date the union would become insolvent – and most of the officials then working for the union would be around to help turn out the lights.

(The good news is that the FSU got its act together. It cut expenditure drastically, accepting the vast majority of my recommendations and is now a model for the efficient management of union resources.)

The FSU was not on its own. Such was the state of financial management in unions at the time that virtually every union I studied which suffered from declining membership could produce their own unique version of the scary graph. If the deficit was controlled and held steady – the date of insolvency could be put off. If the union had a high level of assets, insolvency would take

---

6   Based on annual dues of $250 per annum and a total staff cost of $60,000 per person employed.

7   Tony Beck, their then National Secretary, deserves credit for being the first Union Secretary to take the risk of letting me near their books. Since then more than a dozen unions in Australia and New Zealand have gone through this review process.

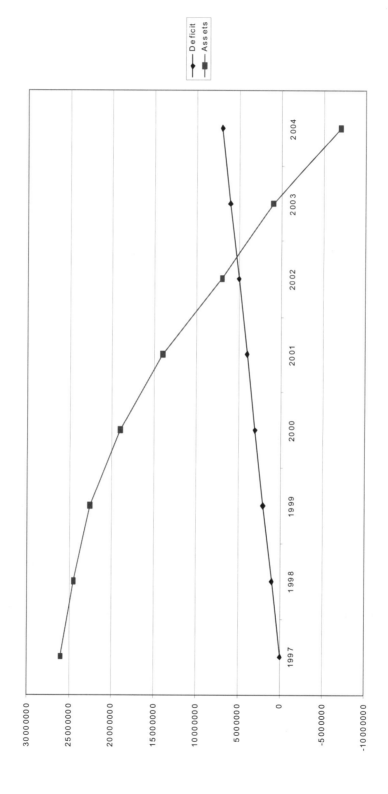

Figure 2.3: The implication of membership decline

longer. In such cases though, there were generally landmark assets that would have to be sold as the financial position worsened. And I could produce a scary graph which would give the approximate date on which that would have to happen if the union continued on its way.

The graphs, the teaching of financial management skills at the Organising Centre's management course for union leaders and all the agitation around union survival seems to have done the trick.

No Australian union has gone bankrupt. This is in contrast to the situation in New Zealand where one of the most powerful unions – the Communications Workers of New Zealand folded as a result of insolvency.

I sat and listened to one of their former officers talk to a group of New Zealand union leaders about attending his union's liquidation sale. He had to bid for the union memorabilia that used hang on their walls – the banners, the photographs of past Executive members and founders of the union, the posters of past campaigns.

This wasn't some sterile money-making corporation that had disappeared. This was the embodiment of generations of New Zealand workers' hopes and effort and achievement.

Telecom New Zealand, the nation's largest employer, is today largely deunionised with virtually every employee on an individual contract. It serves as a negative role model of what is possible for Australia's Telstra.

In Australia, most unions have become adept at coping with decreasing levels of membership income. Most have cut the fat from their operations. Mobile phone costs are controlled, travel expenditure is reined in, staff are retrenched when there is no longer sufficient money to pay for them.

But that doesn't fix the problem.

The problem is a loss of power for Australian workers and their families. There is no point in having a bunch of financially well-managed, rump unions. A union representing a small minority of the whole workforce can't do its job.

The density graph is the key measure of the state of unionism. These are organisations designed to do little else other than express the collective power of workers. If scarcely any worker forms part of that collective, the organisations have little purpose.

At the end of the 1990s, I tried to work out a way to illustrate just where we were heading. I extrapolated what would happen to union density if we changed nothing and density continued to deteriorate at the same average rate of decline. What the graph showed was that the Australian Union Movement would cease to exist in 2012 (Figure 2.4).

The graph and the endpoint of 2012 were designed to give officials and members a jolt – and it succeeded. In three years we would get to American

Figure 2.4: Projected density of union membership

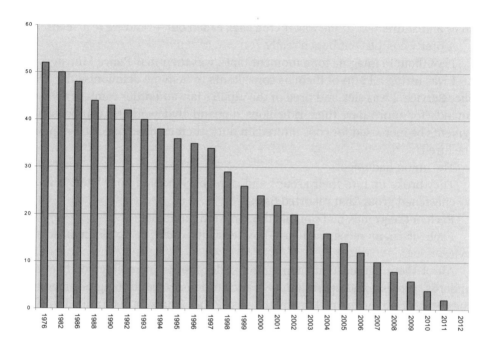

levels of density. In eight years, it would be all over. Most union officials employed at the end of the 1990s would still have been employed at either of these landmark dates.

But was it realistic? After all, won't there always be the strong professional unions or the unions dealing with critical issues like safety for coal miners. Surely these will ensure that at least a rump of unionism will survive, no matter what.

The problem is that in none of the forums where I displayed this graph has anyone said that we can survive no matter what happens to the rest of the union movement. No one was prepared to claim that their occupation or industry couldn't be deunionised – not a single actor, teacher, nurse, coal miner, firefighter or police officer was confident that they could be a union island in a sea of non-unionism. They weren't confident because we had seen just how easy it was to deunionise workforces which we thought were strongholds.

Many of these unions have at least examined the issue of their vulnerability at a theoretical level.

I saw it happen first at a Delegates' Conference of the NSW Police Association. As one of the delegates pointed out to me – "We don't need this stuff on organising. We've got 13,000 members, 40 non-members and we know their names and addresses." (One wag up the back called out – "and we're armed!")

A pretty complacent bunch really.

I got them to imagine for a moment that I was their new Police Minister.

I was hiring all 200 of them as consultants to help me deunionise the NSW Police Service. I was sick and tired of the union's law and order campaigns, their demands for more pay, their ridiculous demand that workers' compensation payments be increased for cops injured on duty, their campaigns for more police to be hired.

The union had to go.

They broke up into their groups and came back half an hour later. It was a very chastened group that reported back.

Each of the groups had roughly the same ten point plan.

Each of them recognised just how easy it would be to deunionise the service.

All of them agreed that their union – despite its incredibly good service standards, professional operation, 98 per cent density, continuing hot member issues – was ripe for the picking by the next Police Minister determined to take them on.[8]

That exercise has now been used with many of the unions that might be thought to be impregnable (I have even used it at a meeting of LO (the Danish peak council of unions) organisers in Denmark.) In many cases, once the strategy for deunionisation is read out, other officials and members point out that the bosses have started to do that already – and then the minds of the officials really concentrate on what needs to be done!

Teacher unions for example are, in most States, very strong, enormously competent outfits. They have delivered good outcomes for members, their opinion is listened to by employers and the community, they have succeeded in making the funding of education a prime electoral issue in virtually every State, they enjoy high rates of density.

Yet when Jeff Kennett[9] in Victoria and Richard Court[10] in Western Australia put their minds to it, they came up with deunionisation strategies that went very close indeed to being effective.

---

8   Just in case any future Police Minister gets any funny ideas, the Association has gone on to build a sophisticated program of activist development to defend itself against any such attack.

9   Premier of Victoria, 1992–1999.

10   Premier of Western Australia, 1993–2001.

The endgame was not played out in either case because Labor governments came to power in the nick of time – but neither union will ever again be overly confident about their impregnability.

No union is safe.

Union density in 2004 stood at 22.7 per cent.[11] That figure, poor as it is, masks the fact that much of that density was concentrated in the public sector. Density in the public sector was 46.4 per cent while in the Private Sector it was just 17.4 per cent.[12]

Remember that at the moment, much of the public sector can be described as a relatively benign environment for unions.

Currently, all State governments are Labor governments and most local councils have not caught the de-unionisation bug – unless they are part of regressive policies like the contracting out episode in Victoria under the Kennett Government. We should recognise how quickly that benign environment can change.

Industry density analysis

It is also misleading to look just at overall union density. The global figure is important for working out what happens at the level of the ACTU or the State Labor Councils.

Politicians are sensitive to just how representative these bodies are.

The media will give added weight to what Greg Combet[13] has to say depending on whether he represents most workers or just a quarter of workers.

It is difficult to imagine that unions will be a dominant force in an industry if they can't claim 50 per cent of an industry's workers as members.

Let's have a look then at industry density.

How many unions can claim to be a dominant force in their industry?

How many workers are safe from the non-union employer down the road competing on the basis of a cheaper wage cost?

How many meet the 50 per cent benchmark?

Table 2.1 shows that just one of these industries meets our test of 50 per cent membership, Electricity, gas and water supply (52.3%). Three industries get above 35 per cent density – Education (44.2%), Government Administration and Defence (37.5 %) and Transport and Storage (36.1%).

---

11 ABS 6310, 18 August 2004.

12 ABS 6310, 17 March 2004.

13 ACTU Secretary, 2000– .

Table 2.1 Trade union membership

Industry	Density 2004 (%)
Agriculture, forestry, fishing	4.7
Mining	17.3
Manufacturing	26
Electricity, gas, water supply	52.3
Construction	23.4
Wholesale Trade	7.8
Retail Trade	16.6
Accommodation, cafes and restaurants	8.1
Transport and storage	36.1
Communication services	28.6
Finance and insurance	17.4
Property and business services	6.7
Government admin and defence	37.5
Education	44.2
Health and community services	29
Culture and recreational services	17.6
Personal and other services	29.6

Source: ABS 6310.0 17 March 2004

The trend in many of the individual ABS categories is lousy. The following graphs depict the trend in density for both blue and white collar sectors. I have isolated out those industries where unions have a substantial base.

The picture is pretty clear. In the vast majority of cases, power has very quickly ebbed away from the unions organising those industries. Not a single one held the density they started with in 1993. After initial setbacks, industries like construction, mining, retail, transport and storage and education appear to have started to bottom out. Health and community services may have begun to do a little better than that. Others, however, appear to be in real trouble. Finance, manufacturing, and communications continue to decline in power, year after year.

Figure 2.5: Blue collar industry density – 1993 to 2004

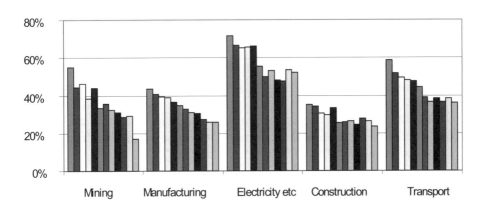

Figure 2.6: White collar industry density – 1993 to 2004

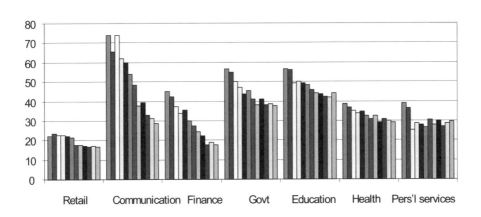

Source: ABS 6310.0 March 2004 and February 2000

The figures are derived from a sample survey conducted by the ABS. In some individual years they may be open to question. Anomalies are thrown up in individual industries each year – based on our own knowledge of what unions have actually managed to achieve in terms of membership growth. But the trend is right. Union density by industry is generally falling – or at best standing still.

Industry density – as measured in fairly broad categories by the ABS, is only an approximation for power. Influence in each industry often depends on where the density is concentrated. The importance of looking at which parts of an industry are organised to get to a realistic estimate of the union's power is discussed later (see p 208).

Young workers

Density within age groups is important. Between 1992 and 1999, union membership among workers aged between 15 and 19 declined at the rate of 4 per cent per annum.

Unionisation among those aged between 20 and 24 declined by, on average, 7.7 per cent per annum. These rates of decline are among the highest of any of the age groups.

That pattern continues whether we break up the data to look at young males, young females, part-time or full-time workers.[14]

The data echoes research from the UK. There, researchers have tracked the level of workers who have never been union members. They found that the percentage of employees who had never been a member of a union grew from 28 per cent to 48 per cent between 1983 and 2001.[15]

In other words, by 2001 "having never joined a union had become a common life event for the cohort of workers born between the mid-1960s and mid-1970s, sharply distinguishing their transition to maturity of those born a decade or so earlier".

There can hardly be a more important issue for the union movement. Left unchecked that trend will mean that we will slowly but surely die out.

Is it the fault of young workers?

Have they bought the individualistic value system of employers and the conservative politicians?

Certainly, many union organisers and activists will say that young workers are harder to sign up to the union. Many of them don't seem to know what a union is and don't want to listen.

There is no evidence that they are less sympathetic to the ideals of the union movement. Hugh McKay reports that young people are heavily predisposed to solving problems in society collectively but they have no hope that collective modes of working have any future.[16]

---

14 ABS, *Employee earnings, benefits and trade union membership,* unpublished data, 2000.

15 Bryson, A and Gomez, R, *Why have workers stopped joining unions?* The Leverhulme Trust Centre for Economic Performance, November 2003.

16 MacKay, Hugh, *Generations, Baby Boomers, their parents and their children,* Macmillan, 1997.

"They see the futility of protest. You can stand in line, and demonstrate about the environment, but nothing happens in reality. They feel impotent to do anything."[17]

Indeed, public opinion polling shows that workers 25 years and under are the most sympathetic to unions.[18]

Our movement will have to work out ways in which we can address this problem and give hope to the next generation of unionists. The problem for the movement and for the working people it aspires to represent is that however we cut it, our power is declining. Density is falling. In almost every sector, strategic weakness can be identified for almost every union affiliated to the ACTU. Every industry has employers seeking to get competitive advantage by driving down wages and conditions and removing the strength of collective representation from the grasp of their workforce. Not a single industry has achieved significant and sustained growth in density. Our resources tend to be concentrated in those industries where we have a significant core of membership. In the booming parts of the economy – services and tourism – we have low density. As a result, the relevant unions have extremely limited resources. They therefore lack the resources to act strategically and build density on the ground floor of the industries that will play an increasingly important role in the development of the Australian economy.

The best that can be said is that our unions have survived.

17 Neer Korn, Director of Heartbeat Trends, quoted in "Big Bother", *Sydney Morning Herald,* 19 June 2004.
18 ACIRRT, *An analysis of the 1996, 1997 and 1999 Newspoll Industrial Relations Survey,* Labor Council of NSW, 1999.

3

What the hell happened to us?

Where did this catastrophic decline in power and membership come from? Did unions wake up one day to find thousands of members at the front door clamouring to resign because they discovered the union was hopeless?

Not at all.

David Peetz, a Professor at Griffith University, has researched reasons for the decline between 1982 and 1997 and you can find his detailed explanation of it in his book, *Unions in a Contrary World*.[1]

Let me outline the argument here in summary form.

We have been declining for a long time – ever since 1982. Over such a long period, we can expect that the reasons for decline are going to vary. One set of influences that knocked us around in one part of that period may be of lesser importance later on. And that is the case here.

Structural change

Peetz estimates that around half of the decline between 1982 and 1992 can be explained by structural change. 'Structural change' basically describes a shift of employment growth from those areas where unions are traditionally strong, to those areas where they are weak.

Let's have a look at how that shift took place during that decade.

Unions are better at organising full-time permanent employees. Because they stay in one place it's easy to contact them. They tend to be in employment for a reasonable period of time so they have the chance to make contact with an organiser, get educated about their rights and do the work involved in organising a union structure in their workplace. The problem is that between 1982 and 1992, employment growth shifted heavily to casual employment. So heavily that Australia has the second highest rate of casual employment in the OECD. Part-time employment is five times the OECD average[2] and one in four

---

1 Peetz, D, *Unions in a Contrary World, The future of the Australian trade union movement*, Cambridge University Press, 1998.
2 Ibid, p 82.

24

employees is casual.[3] The density rate of unionisation among casuals is around 8.6 per cent.[4]

The second element of structural change that affected numbers was the sectors of industry that enjoyed employment growth in this period.

Unions enjoy higher rates of density in the public sector. The Hawke Government cut the public sector back early in its term. That trend eased in the late 1980s but then reaccelerated in the early part of the 1990s. Peetz calculates that 22 per cent of the decline in density between 1982 and 1990 can be explained by this shift of employment from public to private sector.[5]

There was also a change in the rate of employment growth between industries. Unions have been well organised in industries like manufacturing, electricity power generation and transport where there are large concentrations of workers with the ability to stick together and build their collective strength. We have been less well organised in the service sector, with its reliance on lots of smaller firms widely scattered over the whole country. By 1990, of 10 major OECD countries, the share of employment taken by two industry groupings with low density – finance, insurance, real estate, business services on the one hand and wholesale and retail trade, restaurants and hotels on the other – was highest in Australia.[6] That is, low-density industries were unusually important in employment terms in Australia.

Some structural factors don't appear to have much of an impact on density levels – for example, firm size. The perception among unions is that there has been a huge growth in employment in small firms and that has fed through into lower density – because unions find it more difficult to organise smaller workplaces. In fact, the share of employment has fluctuated in these firms on the basis of the business cycle so it doesn't appear that we can explain our long-term decline on the basis of the size of firms.[7]

Similarly, gender appears to have played no part in the decline in density. Interestingly, the traditional gap in male and female density rates appears to have narrowed over the period. Peetz suggests that this is a result of growing union responsiveness to the concerns of women, their location in unions with better delegate structures but above all, their lower reliance on conscripted membership.[8]

If structural change was our big hit before 1992 – what happened after that, when decline really took off?

---

3   The precise figure was 27% in 2003 (ABS 6310.0).
4   ABS 6310.17.
5   Peetz, op cit, p 70.
6   Peetz, ibid, p 82.
7   Peetz, ibid, p 76.
8   Peetz, ibid, p 81.

The institutional break

Peetz points to what he calls an 'institutional break' in union membership – a paradigm shift in the way in which unions were treated by the society in which they operated.

It's not new. As we will see in Chapter 6, the first time this happened was at the end of the 19th century when capital smashed labour on the back of the 1890s depression. The response then was to create a whole new industrial system of arbitration aimed at redressing the imbalance in bargaining power between workers and their employers.

The institutional break that took place in the 1990s started with a change in the ideological environment surrounding industrial relations. During the 1980s, elements of the business community, the driest of the economists and sections of the Liberal Party led by John Howard, constructed an argument that said that the greatest threat to Australia's economic performance was the existence of the system of strong unions and arbitration – the Higgins' legacy. This legacy – which saw the origins of minimum wage-setting – had come from Justice Higgins' 1907 decision in the *Harvester* case[9] that set the minimum wage for a breadwinner, spouse and dependants – "the normal needs of the average employee living in a civilised community". That battle entered the mainstream in 1983 when John Howard said:

> The time has come when we have to turn Mr Justice Higgins on his head.[10]

It is difficult for any vaguely objective person – let alone a trade union member or official – to understand the vehemence, the hatred of trade unions, which motivated these class warriors. Hugh Morgan, now the President of the BCA, said about trade unions and their power:

> [T]he fundamental nature of trade unionism, its subversive challenge to the authority of the State, its jealous dislike and hostility of the family, is increasingly recognised and intuitively understood by more and more Australians ...[11]

John Stone, Secretary to the Treasury under Treasurers Howard and Keating, "described the growth of arbitration to a 'pitch of idiocy ... which has laid so sharp an axe at the roots of our national productive capacity."

The extraordinary thing is that these extremists were utterly successful precisely at the moment when the Accord was in force and Higgins' legacy bore fruit – controlling wages and promoting a modernisation of the Award system so that the levers of macroeconomic power could be opened up. As each of the conservative State governments took office, culminating in the federal Howard

---

9   *Harvester* case, *Ex parte HV McKay* (1907) 2 CAR 1.
10 Quoted in Kelly, Paul, *The End of Certainty*, Allen & Unwin 1994, p 111.
11 Morgan, HM, *The Nature of Trade Union Power*, <www.hrnicholls.com.au>.

Government, it become more and more clear that all the key decision-makers in business, media, politics and the economic bureaucracy accepted that gutting the powers of the Commission and the winding back, if not destruction, of trade unions, was a desirable element of public policy.

Premiers Jeff Kennett in Victoria and Charles Court in WA led the way and did their best to destroy their industrial systems. John Howard couldn't go so far because of his lack of control of the Senate but his *Workplace Relations Act 1996* went in the same direction.[12] Importantly, every single one of these governments legislated against any form of membership compulsion. They created a new right for employees – a right 'not to associate together'.

But they didn't stop with legislative change. They proceeded to act as initiators and cheerleaders of aggressive action against unions. They set out to destroy the Victorian teachers' union – and had some success. Every new teacher was hired on an individual/fixed-term contract – which was subject to performance review – and industrial activity was of course taken into account. Teachers were forbidden to make any public comment – under threat of dismissal. The Victorian government refused to bargain with the union – merely announcing what wage increase would be paid each year. Schools were closed on a wholesale basis. Payroll deduction of union dues was ended just after the ten-week summer holiday started – so that the union was without income and had no chance of getting any until it could contact every teacher in the State when school resumed.

Similar action was taken by the government in Western Australia against the same union.

The role of the federal government in 1998 against the Maritime Union of Australia (MUA) is well understood.[13] The hope was that, by smashing the MUA, the whole union movement would get the message (in the same way that Margaret Thatcher and Ronald Reagan had respectively used the Miners' strike in the UK and the Air Traffic Controllers strike in the US).

But it didn't stop there. Public sector managers had performance standards introduced into their contracts which encouraged them to meet numerical targets for the signing of non-union collective agreements or individual agreements with their employees. The Public Sector Union had its right of access to workplaces reduced and employees became very well aware that union membership was not helpful to a worker's promotion prospects. In some workplaces, promotion became conditional on agreeing to sign an individual agreement. Private sector employers – like the major banks – who agreed with their employees not to introduce individual agreements, were contacted by the Minister

---

12   We are shortly to find out how far he will go now that control of the Senate has shifted to the conservative parties.

13   See Davies, A and Trinca, H, *War on the Waterfront – the battle that changed Australia,* Doubleday/Random House, 2000.

for Workplace Relations and berated. The Royal Commission on the Building Industry was in fact a Royal Commission into the CFMEU, Construction Division. It wasn't really interested in evidence of employer wrongdoing. Anyone who doubts the purpose of that Commission should read Jim Marr's book on the subject.[14]

The overall aim of these policies was to get the whole industrial relations system to shift from a system of collective representation to individual representation. And if that couldn't be achieved in the medium term, then employers were given the ability to strike a non-union 'collective' agreement with their employees.

This governmental action coincided with a fundamental shift in employer behaviour. Industrial Relations Ministers gave employers the green light for overt action against unions and their members. Many of them obeyed enthusiastically.

By 1993, "a survey of 300 firms found that one quarter of firms who had entered into an enterprise agreement sought 'reduced union involvement' as an objective and around one fifth claimed to have achieved it."[15]

Large, high profile companies acted as trail blazers for deunionisation. Conzinc Rio Tinto of Australia (CRA) later to become Rio Tinto, adapted the strategy it had used in New Zealand to smash the unions at the Tiwai Point smelter and applied it at Robe River. It offered extremely generous wage increases to workers, provided that they signed individual agreements. (The employer's consultants were concerned about applying the same strategy, worried that the Australian unions would learn from the actions of their New Zealand counterparts. If only that had happened! Instead the Australian unions used traditional third-party unionism techniques that had no chance of working and union organisation in the iron ore mining industry was smashed.

Similarly at Telstra, the management has mounted a vicious anti-union campaign in an effort to drive labour costs down and reduce the power of its workforce.

Of all these manifestations of an institutional break in membership, the most devastating for unions has been the loss of the closed shop. Peetz estimates that three-quarters of union decline between 1990 and 1995 can be largely explained by the loss of conscripted members.[16]

By contrast, union density in firms where membership was not compulsory has remained steady (between 23 and 26%) throughout the period 1990–1995.[17]

---

14   Marr, J, *First the Verdict,* Pluto Press, 2003.
15   Peetz, op cit, p 106.
16   Peetz, op cit, p 97.
17   Ibid.

Workplace organisation

The final point that Peetz makes in explaining our decline is in relation to the state of our workplace organisation.

Closed shops meant that there wasn't much of it. Just 24 per cent of workplaces had active union delegates and that had dropped by 1995 to just 18 per cent. (And the definition of activity is a low one).[18]

That meant that we were left wide open for employer attack.

Clear signs of trouble for union organisation were if the workplace was subject to any of the following:

- The use of lawyers in bargaining or disputes;

- A change in business strategy;

- A change in ownership;

- A change in senior management;

- Relocation of the workforce;

- An altered site layout;

- The introduction of HRM strategies.

For all of these, Peetz found a strong correlation with union decline – except in the case of HRM strategies where the correlation was relatively weak.[19]

In examining the unionisation performance of firms surveyed in 1990 and then in 1995, the only effective defence he identified was the existence of active delegates who bargained with management.[20] In the face of active delegates, the only employer strategy that was likely to have any success was where the employer "bought" the members out of the union by paying them a large wage increase.[21] And even here the correlation between this tactic and success was weak.

Industrial action helped preserve and build density – but only if it was seen by the workers to be successful. If the action failed, it could lead to significant falls in membership.[22]

So our density declines come from structural change and a paradigm shift in the way that employers and government related to us. Far from the accommodative relationship to which we had grown used, we now faced an environment of unremitting hostility.

---

18   AWIRS 1990 and 1995.
19   Peetz, op cit, p 125.
20   Peetz, ibid, p 121.
21   Peetz, ibid, p 127.
22   Peetz, ibid, p 116.

We were almost uniquely ill equipped to face this challenge. Peetz identified what worked – active delegates' structures and participation in workplace bargaining – whether it was over grievances, enterprise agreements or the way in which the workforce was treated. We didn't have those structures in place to defend the level of density we had built over the preceding 80 years.

But we knew what governments and employers were doing to us from the early 1990s. The environment has existed for 14 or 15 years. Peetz published his book in 1998. We have had his solutions for the last six of those years. Responsibility for reversing the density decline must increasingly rest with us.

We are not helpless. We are not passive actors in our environment. We have the ability to choose to adapt to our environment so that we build organisational strength – even if, for the moment, we can't do much about the economic, social and political environment in which we find ourselves. Just as our forebears in the 1900s picked themselves up off the ground and used their limited resources to win back power, so can we now.

4

Why are unions in Australia the way they are?

In 2000, I spoke at an academic conference on the future of work in Australia.[1] Greg Patmore, a teacher of labour history at Sydney University, got stuck into all the speakers – including me – in no uncertain terms. In the most scathing way he pointed out that every problem we faced, every solution we had proposed, had already been faced and solved at some time in our past. We had to look at our history before doing anything else. We had to learn from the example of those who had gone before us.

I took his lesson to heart. At the very least, the puzzle of what has happened to unionism in Australia starts with us understanding where we came from. As we will find, I think this examination does more than that. It gives us hope that we can repeat what our ancestors achieved – a reconstruction of the power of workers on the back of an historic defeat.

So where do we start? We could start with our convict ancestors – because traces of our anti-authoritarianism can be traced back to the relationship between soldier and prisoner in the history of white settlement. We could begin with the campaign for the eight-hour day – because that was the first time (at least that we remember) that we announced to the world our intention to create a society where working men and women got a fair share of society's wealth. We thought that we had a chance to turn our back on the old-world class-based view of the way things had to be.

As the old Irish folk song told us:

Farewell to your bricks and mortar
Farewell to your dirt and lime
Farewell to your gangway and your gang planks
To hell with your overtime
The good ship Ragamuffin
Is standing in the Bay

---

1   The papers were published as Callus, R and Lansbury, R (eds), *Working Futures, The changing nature of work and employment relations in Australia*, Federation Press, 2002.

> To take old Pat with a shovel on his back
> To the shores of Botany Bay
> ... An 8 hour pay for an 8 hour day
> On the Shores of Botany Bay[2]

As Russell Ward pointed out in *The Australian Legend*,[3] the values of our convict ancestors had a direct influence on the 19th century's development of an Australian bush ethos – they worked alongside the early pastoral workers – and at least the core of their ethos is still alive and well, if under threat.

I want to start at the turn of the 19th century, because the legacy of the union struggles of that period has found itself into every nook and cranny of trade union tradition today. That was the moment when we last organised in the same way as the rest of the world – without the assistance of an arbitration system.

Our earliest unions were the creation of overwhelmingly male "labour aristocrats". Protected by trade certificates, they had built a particular kind of unionism throughout the 19th century. With the protection of their trade and its limited supply of labour they could demand – and at times fight for – fair treatment in the form of an eight-hour day and the right to be paid well enough to afford quite a comfortable living in colonial society. Their unionism wasn't class based – rather they saw a community of interest between the masters – the trades' small employers – and those they employed. After all, it was generally the ambition of every self-respecting tradesman to become a master himself. They saw their union as restrictive in nature, limiting membership to those who truly understood its place as the "collective repository of the skills and 'mystique' which could be passed on to those who received 'the calling'".[4] These workers aimed for both a good life and respectability. They dressed in suits to go to meetings and if you have a look at some of the old photographs of picnic days and union council meetings hanging in union offices to this day, you can see them there, looking very respectable indeed.

The next wave of unionism came with the organisation of the unskilled – the miners, shearers, wharf labourers (or lumpers as they were then known.) The founders of these unions –like WG Spence, the co-founder of the Australian Workers Union – described their unions as part of a "new unionism". In fact, they seem to have modelled themselves quite closely on the kind of unionism that they knew at first hand – the existing craft unions. Indeed, these craft unions played a hand in setting up many of these "new" unions and in providing advice and financial assistance in the process.[5]

---

2   Words supplied by Millie Reidy.
3   Ward, R, *The Australian Legend*, Oxford University Press, 1958.
4   Markey, R, *The Making of the Labor Party in NSW*, UNSW Press, 1988, p 146.
5   Cooper, R, *Making the NSW Union Movement? A study of the organising and recruitment activities of the NSW Labor Council 1900-1910*, IRRC, 1996.

While they were "new" in that they sought to represent those regarded by society as unskilled, they quickly sought to establish job hierarchies and restrict entry to employment wherever this was possible. Many of them limited membership to just part of an industry's workforce and worked side by side with craft unions representing other sectors of employment in the same industry. The benefit policies of the craft unions were replicated with unions like the wharf lumpers, the shearers, the railway workers and the coal miners. Nor were these "new unions" militant class warriors of a kind envisaged by the later Industrial Workers of the World. They fought hard for union recognition but then quickly attempted to settle down to the establishment of a harmonious relationship with their employers. Where that wasn't possible, they employed secondary and consumer boycotts as well as the strike. Indeed, the bush workers felt free to use a form of sabotage, with mysteriously started grass fires, a high incidence of "wet fleeces" in the middle of a drought and high levels of "fleece damage".[6]

Despite all that, they saw the need, right from the very foundation of their unions, to push the respectability of their cause and their leadership.[7]

The new unions shared an overwhelmingly male focus with their craft-based forebears. But the impetus was there to expand the focus of unionisation beyond just men. Attempts were made by the Labor Council's Organising Committee to organise women and they helped form the Tailoresses' Union, the Barmaids and Waitresses' Union, the Laundresses' Union and the Female Workers' Union.[8] But overall, women were left to the mercy of the market during this first period of a rapid growth in union numbers.[9]

Both craft and new unions were politically active and both were involved in the formation of the Labor Party in NSW in 1891.[10] They were also racist. They were among the prime advocates of a White Australia policy and they reflected what was undoubtedly the predominant working-class opinion about Chinese immigration at the time. It would be nice to think that their concern was purely to prevent the undercutting of their rates through the flooding of the labour market with cheap labour but this probably won't wash as an excuse. The Labor Council of NSW, when they were prepared to reject the application of the Australian Shearers Union in Wagga on the basis that they had eight Chinese members[11] or the Melbourne Trades Hall, when it rejected the application of the

---

6   Markey, R, op cit, pp 148-150.

7   Hearn, M and Knowles, H, *One Big Union A history of the Australian Workers Union 1886-1994*, Cambridge University Press, 1996. The authors suggest that one of the prime reasons Temple involved Spence in the newly formed ASU, was to give it respectability.

8   Cooper R, 1996, op cit, pp 32-33.

9   Markey, R, op cit, p 140.

10 Markey, R, ibid, p 171.

11 Markey, R, ibid p 292.

Chinese Furniture Makers Union,[12] gave the game away. It wasn't about unfair competition from non-union workers. It was all about skin colour.

The sad thing about our early history is we find a marvellous firebrand of a leader like Selina Andersen passionately urging Labor Council delegates to organise one night, while taking her place the next as the Chairwoman of the anti-Chinese league.[13] Her language makes clear her racism – warning as she did of the "appalling inroads upon the Industrial, Moral and Social well-being of Australia, made by cheap labour, racial degeneration, and the constant danger of the introduction of leprosy, constituting a standing menace to the status of Australian citizenship ... ."[14]

While much was shared with the craft unions, new unionism was notable for its self-awareness as a force seeking to bind together the whole of working society. Its leaders aimed to achieve the "mass organisation of workers in industries of a common calling, so that an effective, united front could be presented to the capitalist class. They would put an end to the employers' preference for divide and rule".[15] It was that impetus that led to workers in Australia raising the unbelievable sum of £30,000 to send to the striking British dockers[16] – a sum so great that in itself, it is said to have played a part in handing victory to those workers.

This united front of Australian workers was manifest most clearly in the strategy adopted by the Shearers' Unions. As David Temple, the real organising force in the foundation of the Australian Shearers Union said:

"Should the Shearers' Union be affiliated with the Seamen's' and (Wharf) Lumpers' union, and a dispute arose with the Sheepowners, and the seamen and lumpers refused to ship non-union wool, such an enormous pressure would be brought to bear upon the wool growers as would compel them to satisfy demands based upon justice and equity. By such a combination the Unions would have it in their power to insist upon British fair-play, which is all we ask."[17]

It is no accident that the 1880s saw an enormous lift in union membership both within the new unions and in the traditional craft unions. Unions benefited from an economic boom and a shortage of labour which meant that they had real bargaining power over their employers once they achieved collective organisation.

12 Markus, A, "Divided we fall. The Chinese and the Melbourne Furniture Trade Union" in *Labor History* No 26 May 1974, p 10.

13 Cooper, R, 1996, op cit, p 52.

14 Markey, R, *In Case of Oppression, The life and times of the Labor Council of NSW*, Pluto Press, 1994.

15 Hearn, M and Knowles, H, op cit, p 4.

16 Ibid, p 39.

17 Quoted in ibid, p 41.

But just as important in building unionism at the time was the receptivity of the workforce to the idea of collectivism and to the values of the union movement. Ward points out that:

> The phenomenally rapid growth of the (Shearers') union probably sprang more from the bushmen's already existing ethos than from the organising genius and missionary zeal of prominent leaders.[18]

Spence himself wrote:

> Unionism came to the Australian bushman as a religion. It came bringing salvation from years of tyranny. It had in it that feeling of mateship which he understood already, and which always characterised the actions of one 'white man' to another. Unionism extended the idea, so a man's character was gauged by whether he stood true to Union rules or 'scabbed' it on his fellows. The man who never went back on the Union is honored to-day as no other is honoured or respected. The man who fell once may be forgiven, but he is not fully trusted. The lowest term of reproach is to call a man a "scab"... At many a country ball the girls have refused to dance with them, the barmaids have refused them a drink, and the waitresses a meal.[19]

These ideas gripped not just bushworkers – but were communicated to and held by a large part of the Australian workforce. The bush poets and other writers took the opportunity of building the myth of mateship and egalitarianism:

> They tramp in mateship side by side
> The Protestant and Roman
> They call no biped lord or sir
> And touch their hat to no man![20]

On the back of economic boom, skilled organisers like David Temple, leaders like WG Spence, new organisational forms of unionism and a conviction that collectivism was both honourable and effective, Australian workers unionised as never before. By 1890, New South Wales, for example, had 21.5 per cent of workers organised in unions – the highest rate of union density in the world.[21]

The great strikes

That organising impetus came crashing down with the advent of the great strikes. In 1890, the shearers' union tried to get a closed shop in all shearing sheds across the eastern States. In support of their demand they involved the maritime unions in blacking any non-union wool. At the same time the Marine Officers Association applied to join the Trades and Labour Councils. They

---

18   Ward, R, op cit, p 214.
19   Quoted in Ward, R, op cit.
20   Lawson, quoted in Ward, R, op cit, p 246.
21   Markey, R, "A Century of Labour and Labor: New South Wales 1890–1990", in M Easson, (ed) *The Foundation of Labor*, Pluto Press, 1990, p 41.

wanted to get the help of the rest of the movement in their negotiations with shipowners. The employers for their part could not stomach the idea of their officers behaving as trade unionists.

These were strikes about organising. In the middle of a huge economic depression, Capital decided that the time was ripe to determine just how far unionism was to reach in the largest of the Australian enterprises. They fought this battle in ideological terms very familiar to us today. Their cause was the protection of "freedom of contract."

"We have not risked the journey from Europe to let our servants dictate how we are to treat and pay them. Those who don't like it can lump it."[22]

As the *Sydney Morning Herald* centenary historian recalled 40 years later:

"[M]any of the leading shipping centres of the continent, and of Sydney in particular, were in a state of ferment bordering at times almost on revolution. Crowds of strikers and their sympathisers gathered at the Quay and elsewhere, and were not dispersed without bloodshed, and, on one occasion, the reading of the Riot Act. Hundreds of young men, sworn in as special constables, were encamped near the Quay, and, armed and mounted, patrolled the streets for many weeks. Many of the rioters were arrested and imprisoned, and with every fresh arrest and every fresh act of violence, the situation became more sinister."[23]

The concentration of force against the unions was overwhelming. The courts in particular exacted a savage toll. In the first of the strikes, they levied fines and forced the forfeit of wages in 1377 cases, totalling £15,147. Organiser Arthur Rae was fined the enormous sum of £320 and when he couldn't pay was sentenced to two-and-half years in jail.[24] In the second strike in Queensland, 12 unionists were sentenced to three years' hard labour in Rockhampton jail.[25]

The defeat of unionism in the great strikes was not just any defeat. This was a catastrophe. Union density fell to 7 per cent almost overnight. Sydney Trades and Labor Council membership declined to eight consistently financial affiliates with a total of 450 members in 1897-98.[26] Indeed, the employers were so dominant and rubbed labour's nose in the dirt so comprehensively that they provoked a community counter-reaction. The churches, and liberal opinion generally, rejected the total victory of capital over labour. In the early years of the new century, Australian society was ready to accept a redressing of the plainly obvious imbalance of power between labour and capital.

---

22 Quoted in Kisch, E, *Australian Landfall*, Sydney, Macmillan, 1969.

23 Freudenberg, G, "The Great Strike" in Easson, M, *The Foundation of Labor*, Pluto Press, 1990, p 32.

24 Hearn, M and Knowles, H, ibid, p 45.

25 Ibid, p 50.

26 Markey, R, 1994, op cit p 27.

The confidence that had led unions to stand up to the shipowners', steve-dores', miners' and pastoralists' attack on their right to organise had been shattered. They had challenged capital directly and been badly beaten. The whole state apparatus had been turned against them. The army had been called out. Unionists were accused of plotting revolution. Their leaders were gaoled. Parliamentarians sided almost exclusively with their enemies. At a time of economic downturn, the grand march of whole industries to union coverage was stopped dead in its tracks. The combination of state and employer at a time of high unemployment was simply too strong for unions to fight on their own. Workers were slow to come back to a movement that had demonstrated its inability to defend them from a vengeful employer.

Regeneration

Against the backdrop of defeat in the Great Strikes, the idea of arbitration and the Labor Party became powerful ideas indeed.

As the Final Report of the Labour Defence Committee, the body established to handle the strike, put it:

"A still more important lesson, learnt in the hour of defeat is this: That while we must go on ever increasing our capacity for fighting as we have fought before, the time has come when Trade-unionists must use the Parliamentary machinery that in the past has used them ...

The rule that Trades Unionism must steer clear of politics was a golden rule when there was so much work to be done within our present industrial environment. But that time, as we have said before, is drawing to an end, and ere we can radically improve the lot of the worker we must secure a substantial representation in Parliament ..."[27]

And as every Australian unionist knows, that's what happened. We got the Labor Party elected, they introduced arbitration and on the back of that free kick, our membership raced ahead and we spent most of the 20th century sitting back enjoying a union density level of around 50 per cent.

The devil of course, is in the detail.

After all, if modern Australian unionism didn't have a strong body of organised membership, if it was purely the creature of politics and arbitration, how was it that they had the political pull to get a party into power so quickly? How could we get the world's first labour Prime Minister, John Watson, and then a majority Labor Government under Andrew Fisher in 1910, without a well-organised mass base?

Historians Rae Cooper and Ray Markey have closely analysed what was going on in the first decade of the 20th century – at least as far as New South

---

27 Quoted in Freudenberg, G, "The Great Strike" in M Easson (ed), ibid, pp 36-37.

Wales was concerned.[28] What they show is that the unions of the time retrieved a large measure of their power and density by using exactly the same organising skills and tactics that they used in the 1880s. What is also clear is that the advent of arbitration and Labor Party did not herald the surrender of employers to unionisation. Rather, they persisted in anti-union attacks so sophisticated that they have a startlingly familiar resonance for any modern union organiser faced with rampant employer attack.

These conclusions are of real importance in our current struggle to rebuild the power of working people. What we need now is another surge – like the one that took place at the beginning of the 20th century. If the earlier revival came about only as a result of the introduction of an arbitration system meshed with the protection of high tariffs – with its preference clauses, sole representation rights by collective organisations, industry-wide Awards, dispute settling powers and all the rest – then it provides us with a fairly unhelpful model of union renewal. We are unlikely to reinvent such a system any time soon. But if they are right – and the surge had little to do with arbitration and far more to do with the strategies and tactics used by workers themselves to get collective power – then we are entitled to have some considerable hope that we can do the same in this first decade of our own new century.

There is no doubt that the arbitration system as we knew it towards the end of the 20th century came into existence at the beginning of that century. The New South Wales *Industrial Arbitration Act* passed through the Parliament in 1901 – and heard its first case in May 1902.[29] Federally, arbitration became a fundamental plank of the Australian Settlement – alongside protection and a White Australia policy.[30]

Labour held the balance of power from the earliest days of the federal parliament. To govern, Protectionists needed to form an alliance with Labour. An essential condition of labour support was the promotion of arbitration. Labour's parliamentarians were veterans of the Great Strikes and they saw arbitration, and its support for union membership, as critical. Indeed, it is noteworthy that Watson and his colleagues gave up office rather than support an amendment which had the aim of preventing the Arbitration Court from awarding preference in employment to union members.[31] Labor and the Protectionists developed a settlement where industry would develop behind the tariff wall, provided its workers shared in the benefits of that protection.

---

28   See Cooper, R, 1996, op cit, and Markey, R, "Explaining Union Mobilisation in the 1880s and early 1900s" in *Labor History*, Number 83, November 2002.

29   Cooper, R, 1996, op cit, p 40.

30   Kelly, P, *The End of Certainty*, Allen & Unwin, 1992.

31   McMullan, R, *So Monstrous a Travesty, Chris Watson and the world's first labour government,* Scribe, 2004.

Higgins' Harvester judgment, famously setting the basic wage at an amount that was supposed to be sufficient for a man to support a wife and two children, "living in frugal comfort", was in fact a case designed to interpret a provision of the *Excise Tariff (Agricultural Implements) Act* 1906. Protection was granted to the Sunshine Harvester Company provided that they paid their workers a fair wage. Higgins' job was to certify that the wages paid were "fair and reasonable". (Significantly, Sunshine was a company that opposed the organisation of a union for its workforce and made a practice of modelling its activities closely on its American, and fiercely anti-union, competitors.)

But Higgins' judgment was overturned on appeal on constitutional grounds – as were whole sections of the NSW Act.[32] The federal arbitration system had little coverage to begin with as a conservative High Court repeatedly limited its powers. This only changed once the majority Labor Government of 1910 under Andrew Fisher had the chance of making its own more progressive appointments to the High Court. Further, most of the States operated a Wages Board system which didn't necessitate the representation of workers by unions.

The NSW system established in 1901 – which was an arbitration system – became hopelessly clogged with cases as unions rushed to have Awards made. Just one judge sought to deal with every application made to the court. In 1905 the position became vacant and the government took three months to find a replacement! The result was that workers waited for up to four years to have their cases heard. Indeed, the Secretary of the NSW Labor Council Organising Committee reported that they were having difficulty in assisting unions organise – because unions were in "financial difficulties resulting from the legal expenses of arbitration cases".[33]

The granting of preference clauses could not have been responsible for the surge in membership. Preference in the federal system was not granted until 1910 and then usually as a recognition of a fait accompli. The union had used its industrial muscle to get a closed shop and this was then enshrined in the Award.

Further, the reported rate of change in membership – showing increases after arbitration took hold – probably doesn't accurately reflect what was happening on the ground. State Registrars couldn't report union membership accurately early in the century – because registration was largely unnecessary. The surge in membership that appears to follow the introduction of more widespread arbitration mechanisms may well only measure the increased level of reporting of membership, once union registration became a necessity.[34]

Nor did the membership surge take place in a vacuum. Employers – faced with the introduction of an arbitration system that they vehemently opposed –

---

32 Cooper, R, 1996, op cit, p 40.
33 Cooper, R, ibid, p 59.
34 Markey, R, ibid, p 32.

responded quite viciously to the prospect of union resurgence. The list of anti-union tactics will be familiar to modern organisers.

> (Employers) threatened relocation in other States, and circumvented awards by installation of new technology and machinery, replacement of male with (cheaper) female labour, and by the introduction of sub-contracting. They formed and registered bogus unions ... all in competition with existing organisations ... Employers in NSW also deliberately lengthened proceedings with delaying tactics and numerous appeals to the State Supreme Court and the High Court of Australia in the early 1900s.[35]

The main employer organisation set up a £10,000 fund specifically for the purpose of taking appeals to the High Court.[36]

We get a good insight into the tactics used by an individual employer when we look at what was going on at this time inside the McKay Sunshine Harvester Company. Again, the tactics are familiar.

> Management victimised union members and denied union officials entry to the works. In addition, McKay used the issue of tariff protection to develop co-operation between management and workers, in the process encouraging the formation of a 'yellow' union ... Though the union eventually forced the dissolution of the Defence Association, the battle delayed the introduction of a wages board and hampered the union's efforts to advance wages and working conditions at McKay's.[37]

Victimisation of union members was common across a range of industries. Even a member of the Labor Council's Organising Committee itself – a ferryman – had his roster changed "so that he would not take such an active interest in union affairs".[38]

Employers of members of the Masters and Engineers Association fore-shadowed the prescriptions of members of the HR Nicholls society with their multi-faceted deunionisation strategy. They offered workers employment at wages higher than the union rate while also donating £50 to help set up a company union – the Sydney Ferry Employees Mutual Provident Society. As Cooper reports, "The two members who remained with the Masters and Engineers Association, continued to receive the standard union rate of pay, but had been removed from the good ferry runs and were fearful for their jobs. The rest of the employees were reportedly 'even afraid of speaking to a union man'."[39]

---

35   Markey, R, ibid, p 34.
36   Markey, R, ibid, p 35.
37   Cockfield, S, "McKay's Harvester Works and the Continuation of Managerial Control", in *Journal of Industrial Relations*, September 1998, pp 388-89.
38   Cooper, R, 1996, op cit, p 57.
39   Ibid, p 57.

So what does account for the resurgence of union membership – to levels higher than they were prior to the Great Strikes and probably the highest level of density in the world at the time?

The organisers who had been active in the 1880s were still there – although some of the most prominent like Spence had moved into parliament. They set about rebuilding their unions as the economy turned up and the labour market became tighter. The start of the resurgence came as a result of existing unions – with members experienced in the process of organising – rebuilding their membership. A myriad of smaller unions then started to form which maintained momentum for an increase in density beyond previous levels. To a far greater extent, the new century saw unions organising women into unions and the creation of a number of women-only unions.[40]

The organisers of the time were driven by a determination to rid Australian society of "sweated" labour – and women were prime victims of an unregulated market system. As increasing numbers of women entered the labour market, their oppression became more and more obvious – particularly with the involvement of a number of female activists on the Labor Council's Organising Committee. The last three years of the decade saw concerted action aimed at improving the condition of women by helping them to combine together.[41]

With the economic upturn, the institutions of Labor quickly revived and began again their work of driving and supporting organising. For example, the NSW Labor Council's Organising Committee again took on a central role in the support of organising new groups of workers and in encouraging workers to join existing unions.

> During the decade they raised finances for organising drives, arranged recruiting nights and conferences for which they provided speakers and formulated "fair lists" of employers who recognised the appropriate union and paid union wages.[42]

Importantly, the ideology that had made so many workers open to the idea of unionisation in the 1880s was still well and truly present. Workers saw the nation as a "Commonwealth" in fact as well as name and most saw collective action as the means of ensuring that it lived up to its promise. But the defeats of the 1890s provoked union leaders to analyse the reasons for their defeat. Many came to rethink their previous opposition to arbitration and most came to support political action. But they also came to reflect upon the failure of their organising strategy. In seeking to organise the unskilled, new unionism had broken new ground – and to that extent it was indeed "new". But it had replicated in many ways the ethos of the craft unions. Many of these unions had

---

40 Ibid, p 58.

41 Ibid, p 50.

42 Cooper, R, "The Organising Committee of the Labor Council of NSW, 1900-10", in *Labour History*, Number 83, November 2002, p 52.

sought to restrict entry to the key occupations they sought to organise.[43] That strategy had failed. As the Australian Shearers' Union put it:

> Unions should be made as attractive as possible and the chief aim should be to gather as many of the workers as possible into the ranks, instead of raising barricades with a view to keeping them out, which fault many unions have been guilty of in the past.[44]

With the memory of huge numbers of working class men and women moving in to replace striking unionists fresh in their minds, the model of an exclusive craft-based unionism was seen to be inadequate. Unionism had to be expansive in both occupational and industrial scope and in the detail of its organising method. It needed the loyalty and discipline of the whole class.

The result of all this rebuilding activity was a 60 per cent increase in membership (in NSW) between 1903 and 1910.[45]

The evidence appears clear – the surge in membership at the start of the 20th century was not just a function of a new institutional framework. External factors were important. A majority of the population – most employers excluded – had sympathy for the idea that Australia should be an egalitarian country where each was as good as the other. (Of course, none of this applied to anyone without a white skin!) The balance between Capital and Labour was seen to have shifted too far in favour of Capital. Sweatshops were seen by most as unacceptable, rather than an inevitable function of the operation of the market. The economy was reviving from a terrible depression and in particular, employment in urban areas, particularly in manufacturing and among women, was increasing.[46]

But critical to the regeneration of unionism was a determination to build unionism across the whole class, the mobilisation of the labour institutions, the involvement of hundreds of unpaid activists across the country and the skills of the organisers honed over the years of triumph and then defeat.

Taken together, these factors were enough to overcome determined and vicious opposition from employers to the rights of their employees to combine in unions.

The influence of arbitration

The arbitration system did play a part in building and maintaining union density as the century progressed. In giving legislative effect to closed-shop agreements, in putting beyond doubt the issue of union recognition and in

---

43　Markey, op cit, p 148.
44　Cooper, R, 1996, op cit, p 32.
45　Cooper, R, 1996, op cit, p 37.
46　Cooper, R, 1996, op cit, p 39.

taking wages out of competition across whole industries, gains in membership made in an economic upsurge could only with the utmost difficulty be reversed at times of economic weakness. Organising victories were subject to a ratchet effect – once organised, it was quite difficult for employers to deunionise a group of workers. My vaudevillian grandfather, Marshall, and his colleagues in Actors Equity – led by the union's founder, Hal Alexander – organised the actors' strike in 1944 – and won the closed shop in theatre. That settlement has never been seriously challenged. The same was true across industry. As the century wore on, the battle about union recognition in most industries became a non-issue. There was no union/non-union differential. The Commission guaranteed that everyone working in an industry would be paid a rate set as a result of the appropriate union or unions bringing a case to the Commission and having an industry-wide Award made. There was no real incentive for employers to fight the union as the cost to them of unionisation, in terms of their competitive advantage, was minimal.

While full closed shops were rare, clauses that gave preference to union members became common. Where preference clauses existed, the message to workers was clear. In such a workplace you needed to join the union. Zappala estimated that in 1990, approximately two-thirds of union members were employed in workplaces governed by some form of compulsory unionism.[47]

If unions refused to play the game and sought improvements for their members outside the system through strike action, their preference clauses could be suspended or withdrawn, fines could be imposed on them and ultimately they could be deregistered. This very rarely happened.

It was that institutional framework, on a base provided by traditional organising techniques in the first decade of the 20th century, supplemented by the work of organisers as new unions were formed or new employers organised, that led to Australia reaching such high levels of union density throughout most of the century. Membership rose to 50 percent by 1919 – once more the highest in the world – and reached a peak in 1953 of 63 per cent. It hovered around 50 per cent until around 1982, when the decline began.

Given the influence of American organising theory on our current thinking, it is interesting to contrast this experience with that of the US. Their unions struggled for the early part of the 20th century to establish a movement with significant levels of density. They refined and perfected their tradition of organising and developed new organising institutions like the Congress of Industrial Organisations. Their drive to get power for working people culminated in their greatest success during the Second World War when President Roosevelt forced employers to accept the unionisation of major industries in return for a lifting of the threat of strikes. At its peak, using these techniques,

---

47   Zappala, G, *Mapping the Extent of Compulsory Unionism in Australia*, ACIRRT, 1991.

the American movement reached a high of 34 per cent in 1945.[48] At no time was there a social consensus in favour of unionisation and they rarely became strong enough in an industry to entirely take wages out of competition. Employers always had an incentive to destroy their workers' unions.

Secure in our ability to lobby a Labor government at either State or federal level, with our institutional survival more or less assured and with the safety net of the Commission to help even the weakest union provide benefits for its members, unions rarely needed to rely on the radical organising they used prior to and in the decade after the Great Strikes. After all, what was being introduced into Australia was "a new province for law and order". For most of the rest of the century, safe in our density rate of 50 per cent, we could listen with bemusement as visiting American unionists lectured us on the superiority of collective bargaining over a state-sponsored system of arbitration like ours!

So different is our history that some academics have argued that there is in reality no union movement at all in Australia – at least as it is understood internationally. Rather, we have merely created an instrument of the system of arbitration.[49]

This might have been true if we had simply accepted what was given us by the court and its successors. Unions would have been reduced to a collection of lay advocates putting learned arguments to the court, citing precedent and begging the judges to give their members more.

In reality, of course, we were not entirely asleep.

Left to the judges, wages and conditions might have grown over time but it would have been at a snail's pace. Yet, the history of union activity shows that Australian workers' wages and conditions improved dramatically over the course of the century with the one exception of a 10 per cent wage cut during the Depression. It is difficult to believe that what now looks like an inexorable advance in the treatment of workers would have occurred simply due to the brilliance of union advocates and the cleverness of their arguments! In fact, what developed was a highly-sophisticated adaptation of union organisation to the legislative and political environment in which unions found themselves. As Iain Campbell has pointed out, "Collective bargaining led by strong unions provided the underlying dynamic – the vital spirit – in the Award system."[50]

---

48 Freeman, R, *Membership and Earnings Data Book (1983-2001)*, BNA, 2002. This figure looks much lower than the relevant high point for Australia. However, we need to remember that it was by and large 34% of the private sector workforce. US unions only gained the right to organise in most of the public sector some years later. Indeed, in some States and some sectors of the federal public sector – such as the newly created Department of Homeland security – governments still deny workers Freedom of Association.

49 Howard, WA, "Australian Trade Unions in the Context of Union Theory" in *Journal of Industrial Relations*, September 1977, p 255.

50 Campbell, I, *Industrial Relations and Intellectual Challenges: Conceptualising the Recent Changes to Labour Regulation in Australia*, speech, 2001, p 17.

Workers' advancement depended upon the use of "hot shop" activity[51] in a limited number of unions to set precedents, which could then be used by other unions to flow gains to their members.

Unions like the Metal Workers Union, the Transport Workers Union, and the construction unions, all had workplaces with high union density and some workplaces with active, militant delegates and clear strategic leverage. These were typically coordinated to take action around an issue of wide concern to all workers. After strikes were held – generally of relatively short duration – in those areas or workplaces with high levels of militancy and leverage, the court would seek to settle the industrial dispute that was in progress. At least some part of the union's claim was generally won and the settlement was then enshrined in an Award of the court. Once the court had issued its determination in the form of a published decision, it could then be relied on as a legal precedent in other cases brought by other unions over similar issues.

I have placed on the ACTU website[52] a case study written by Tom Macdonald, the former National Secretary of the Building Workers Industrial Union – one of these militant unions responsible for many of the advances spread more widely throughout the workforce. The extract describes the Accident Make Up Pay dispute of 1971.[53]

I think it represents a typical example of the way in which unions organised to get their members united around a key industrial demand. But it also illustrates perfectly the way in which unions could pursue the interests of their members – and then turn those industrial achievements into a precedent that could be spread throughout their own industry and ultimately to the rest of the workforce. That is, a gain in the NSW Building Industry could lead to the winning of precisely the same advance in say, the Actors' Award – with very little industrial activity at all by the actors' union or its members.[54] The labour movement, over a period of years, was able to build a system of nationwide settlements so that all workers were able to share in the gains of the militant few. The only caveat on this was that the Commission might be able to slow the spread of these conditions over a period, depending upon the perceived industrial strength of the other unions or the capacity of the industry to pay.

At the same time, other unions were able to pursue those issues of greatest concern to them. The professional unions in particular – nurses, actors, journalists, teachers, police, firefighters – took advantage of generally determined

---

51 "Hot shops" in Australia refers to workplaces that could be relied on to take strike action in support of the union's industry wide claim.

52 See <www.actu.asn.au/organising/>.

53 McDonald, T and A, *Intimate Union, Sharing a Revolutionary Life*, Pluto Press, 1998.

54 I like this case study because I remember going to the Commission as a young industrial officer to have Accident Make Up Pay flowed into the various actors Awards. At the time I scarcely knew what it was. We certainly didn't have to fight for it!

standards. But they were also able to tailor their Awards to the particular circumstances of their occupations. They too, where they faced trenchant opposition from their employers, organised their own industrial action. The key though was that these were rarely strikes aimed at determining which side could sustain the greatest economic damage and still hold to their position. Rather, these were actions aimed at demonstrating to the court that the union was serious in its claim – it wasn't just asking nicely – and that the claim was made with the backing of the union's membership. It is for that reason that while rates of industrial disputes might have been high, they tended to be of very short duration.

In addition, unions with such high rates of density had real political clout. They were able to use Labor governments in the various States to make breakthroughs in legislative improvements for workers – like workers' compensation or annual leave – which could then be flowed through either the Commission or taken up by other State governments.

In trying to work out what has gone wrong with unions in the light of their precipitous decline over the last 20 years, we can lose sight of their achievements over the rest of the century. The list of union gains is a very long one – and probably unequalled by any other movement in the world, other than those in Scandinavia.

Australian workers – at least those employed in permanent jobs – enjoy high minimum wages and conditions set on the basis of industry Awards– rather than a rock-bottom rate set by government which applies to every industry regardless of its capacity to pay. They receive a minimum of four weeks' annual leave. Many still get a loading when they go on leave. After ten years service they get three months' long service leave. They are all covered by compulsory, employer-funded workers compensation insurance. Every worker receives a guaranteed 9 per cent superannuation contribution in an account which they own and which receives preferential taxation treatment. Every worker gets five days sick leave per year. Women receive 12 months' unpaid maternity leave – although the movement failed to win universal paid maternity leave.

The Prices and Incomes Accord – 1983-1996

The three-pronged approach to advancing the interests of working people – industrial, arbitral and political activity – probably reached its zenith with the operation of the Accord under the Hawke/Keating Labor Governments. Prior to taking office in 1983, leaders in both the political and industrial wings were concerned at the prospect of a wages breakout on the overall economic position. In particular, the leaders of the union which had borne the brunt of leading the movement's wages campaign – the AMWU – had the bitter experience of seeing their incredibly successful wages victory being eroded both by inflation and playing some part at least in rising unemployment in the metal industry. They were determined that there had to be a better way. The Accord was the result.

On the one side unions agreed that they would moderate their wage claims according to a pre-determined target. The hot shops would be controlled. There would be no additional claims beyond the agreed minimum. On the other, the government guaranteed that it would stimulate the economy to ensure a reduction in unemployment as well as an increase in the social wage – most notably in the form of Medicare and compulsory universal superannuation.

The benefits of the Accord were very real – and it was for that reason that virtually every Union Secretary in the country supported it. The feeling at the time was that Labor was engaged in the building of a new kind of Australian economy – one that was open to the world but one that also retained the best of the old order – a strong set of wages and working conditions applicable to every worker. Employers were supposed to become allies in this process, benefiting from lower levels of industrial disputes and higher rates of profitability so that they could invest in the modernisation of the country's productive capacity. The aim was to increase the size of the cake – rather than go back to the bad old days of fighting over a share of the existing cake.

The most obvious problem was that it meant that for 13 years unions were required to moderate the militancy of their 'hot shops'- at least as far as wages were concerned. Left inactive – particularly at a time of profound job redesign – unions lost power. Additionally, we were all far too naive about the good intentions of employers, the depth of their ideological hostility and the commitment of the forces of conservatism to reducing the power of labour. They could not tolerate a system where workers had a say in how the wealth of the nation was created and distributed. The employer class of today had precisely the same set of values as their forebears during the Great Strikes.

For all the effort of the Accord years we were left with a feeling of betrayal, as the Manufacturing Worker's Doug Cameron so eloquently put it:

> We have sought real partnerships and been betrayed.
> We have promoted co-operation and not capitulation.
> We have benchmarked.
> We have introduced teams.
> We have talked endlessly about training and competency with almost no results for the bulk of our members.
> We have innovated.
> We have been flexible.
> We have endured the second tier trade off agenda and the structural efficiency principle.
> We have restructured the Award.
> We have simplified the Award.
> We have strived for "best practice in manufacturing workplaces".
> We have bargained and bargained and bargained.

> None of this has been enough for government or employers. We have been betrayed by employers ... [and] the workers have been abandoned to market forces and the latest fad, such as downsizing, contracting out, re-engineering ...[55]

That bitterness is widely felt, and as we will see in the discussion on partnership, is going to have an effect on future union strategy.

---

55   Cameron, D, Speech to the Australian Industry Group, 31 August 1998.

5

What kind of unions are we?

The history I have described in the previous chapter has shaped the kind of union movement that has evolved. I use the word "evolved" deliberately, because what we ended up with was a brilliant adaptation of a major social institution to its environment. Indeed, the behaviour of unions during the Accord period represented the pinnacle of that evolutionary process. All the levers of power and influence that the system provided were used to the advantage of workers.

The proof of evolutionary success can be seen in the outcomes for workers – four weeks' annual leave, three months' long service leave, Medicare, superannuation and all the rest.

The problem is that the Arbitration environment was coupled with a high level of tariff protection for employers. They were sheltered from competitive pressure. Unions adapted to the requirements of the arbitration system – and that adaptation left us ill equipped for the massive change that hit us in the 1980s and 1990s particularly. We ran the risk of becoming like dinosaurs trying to survive our very own Big Bang.

Let me summarise the privileged position in which we found ourselves.

Many unions didn't have to bother about the fundamental task of persuading non-members to become members. Preference clauses and closed shops meant that membership flowed automatically to the union once a new employee started work. Where resistance was encountered, peer pressure from other workers was often enough to get the new employee to join. In some industries – particularly those involving blue collar employment – the pressure could be quite forceful. Not to join was seen as a rejection of the workplace's collective ethos. You ran the risk of being seen as someone capable of "ratting on your mates".

When the union negotiated a new Award for a workplace or an industry, or extended its coverage, the process would commonly take the form of a mass meeting of the employees and an address by the organiser on the changes to their employment conditions. The employer might then appear and make it clear that he regarded union membership as the norm. The preference clause – while not technically a closed shop – sent the signal to workers that this was now a union shop and if they wanted a quiet life they should join up. This motivation – alongside the ease of payment through payroll deduction arrangements – meant that large numbers of workers could be unionised with minimal effort from the union or its officials.

In other cases, employers could become even more prescriptive. Workers were simply enrolled in payroll deduction schemes and the paperwork – like signing a membership card – was worked out later. Employers had done a deal with the union and they didn't want any more aggravation.

Some employers took the view that it was better for all employees to be in the union – rather than have the possiblity of a more militant minority dominating the union's deliberations. Presumably it was for that reason that in the early 1970s the banking and insurance employers, following the oil clerks' preference decision, approached the unions and offered them membership agreements in 1974 that made membership a condition of employment. That lasted in banking until 1984 and in insurance until the early 1990s.[1]

Further, once members were joined up, the union had a great deal of ability, with minimal effort, to start delivering for them. National Wage Cases meant that every member was guaranteed – more or less – a basic wage increase. Where the pacesetter unions secured an improvement in conditions, this was gradually flowed through the system by other unions making the appropriate application to the Commission.

Further, the protected nature of the economy and the high level of public sector employment meant that wage settlements could be negotiated for an industry without the employer having to worry too much about the pressure of competitive pricing from alternative or foreign suppliers. Most Awards were industry Awards so that wage competition was minimal. Low levels of competitive pressure meant that any increases in costs could be passed on to consumers.

In the public sector, it was common for Awards to be made that would cover huge swathes of workers. Agency bargaining – government department or statutory authority agreements – were virtually unknown.

Individual grievances could be sorted out cheaply and efficiently – and with some regard to the justice of the issue rather than simply the bargaining strength of the union. If talks with the employer broke down, the organiser could take the case to the Commission and have the issue conciliated and then arbitrated. (What a great system for organisers! If you won – it was because of your brilliance as an advocate. If you lost, it was because the arbitrator was irretrievably biased – a bosses' court!)

It has to be said that at the time, we certainly didn't believe that this was a simple system. Conscientious officials worked very hard indeed in manipulating the system to the benefit of their members. The Commission was a complicated and intimidating system. Some skill was required to make sure that workers

---

1   Information supplied by Chris Walton.

benefited from its decisions and all unions experienced the setback of adverse Commission decisions. Employers never seemed to give much indication that they were pushovers and every improvement in conditions seemed to be hard fought.

Members too had very high expectations and their grievances formed a core part of every official's work.

Our current situation throws the whole system in stark contrast. Difficult as it may have seemed at the time, it was union official paradise.

That environment shaped the kind of unions that we were.

Until Organising Works began in 1994 only one union in the whole of Australia had organisers dedicated only to the organising of new members. That union had two of them. Organisers in the American sense of the term scarcely existed. Organising was – as far as it existed at all – the part-time responsibility of people who were called organisers but were in fact largely servicing officers, consumed with meeting the needs of members. Most concentrated little or no time on expanding the reach of the union to non-union areas. Indeed, a very large number of organisers could go through their entire union careers without signing up members in a previously non-unionised site.

The system of arbitration was enormously efficient for unions. Wages were set on the basis of industry-wide Awards. Even quite large unions might administer just a handful of Awards. They needed negotiation on a compre- hensive basis every couple of years and central wage fixation meant that wages were updated across the board following the release of the National Wage Case decision. Except in isolated pockets like my own union – where some of our claims for repeat and residual fees in film and television were outside the Commission's jurisdiction – collective bargaining outside the Commission was unheard of. Few unions bothered with many enterprise-based Awards unless they were gigantic employers or employers with very specific needs.

Members were very rarely mobilised in support of one of their colleagues. If the issue was a broad one, affecting a large section of the workforce, it was rarely settled through direct action in the workplace. More commonly, it was put on the list of things to be negotiated as part of the next revision of the Award.

The Arbitration Commission was at the centre of all union activity. Even the militant pace-setter unions took their industrial action with one eye on the reaction of the Commission to their campaigns. The struggle of the "hot shops" would be wasted if the result of their struggle could not be flowed on to the rest of the union's members – and ultimately the rest of the union movement.

The most fascinating effect of the Commission on unions was on their internal organisation. For most unions, success in the Commission was the pathway to advancement. Union leaders were invariably drawn from the ranks of the advocates. The key skill was not whether a leader could mobilise workers but whether it was possible to persuade an arbitrator that a claim should be granted.

In such a system, industrial officers – the advocates in the Commission – had enormous prestige. (So much so that I recall that in one year when I couldn't afford to pay the organisers a wage increase, I offered them a title change. They would henceforth no longer be known as "organisers" – but rather "industrial officers". My generous offer was accepted eagerly!)

The trappings of a pseudo legal tribunal had the effect of mystifying the role of the union official. Ordinary workers were intimidated by the Commission's formality and the organiser or industrial officer were seen as people apart – capable of understanding what was going on and manipulating the system in the worker's favour. The divide was made even more obvious by the Commission's insistence that advocates wear a suit!

The impact of such a system on the level of workplace organisation is also obvious. As we have seen, in 1990 just 24 per cent of workplaces had active delegates and by 1995, that level had fallen to 18 per cent. That is, the vast majority of workplaces had little or no delegate structure at all.

The reason for this is clear. Unions didn't need delegates. The key relationship was between organiser and member. An intervening link was unnecessary. The organiser could deliver both at the level of individual grievances and in relation to major changes that were required by members to their overall terms and conditions of employment. Workplace action was limited to those parts of the movement that required them – typically the blue collar blokes working in "hot shops" and led by union officials who understood their responsibility to deliver improvements in conditions for the whole movement.

That meant that most unions provided very low member-to-organiser ratios. Some unions I have worked with in recent years are burdened with ratios of as little as 250 members to one organiser. That means that in order to fill his or her day conscientiously, the organiser is nothing more than a professional delegate. The member only has to think of the smallest problem and the organiser will appear on the job to fix it up.

Most unions have ratios of between one organiser to 800 members to a high of 1:1500. Sometimes the ratio is higher – instead of large numbers of organisers, the union has hired large numbers of professional officers who deliver services to members on particular issues across the whole range of membership. Either way, the position is the same. Unions took on the character of insurance companies hiring agents who conscientiously set about the task of delivering on claims set before them.

There were notable exceptions to this picture. Laurie Carmichael, the great Metal Union official and later ACTU Assistant Secretary, told me that when he was involved in the campaign against the Penal Powers – the ability of the courts to levy fines against unions for taking industrial action - the union office consisted of himself and three organisers in Melbourne with another organiser to cover the rest of Victoria and Tasmania. The strength of the union came from their delegates and activists.

The point is that even in his union, once he left, that structure didn't last. The 1980s and the 1990s saw an expansion in the level of union staffing as senior delegates were taken on by unions as full-time officials. I was certainly part of that push. Each year, my prime budgeting concern was to see how I could squeeze the budget to hire more staff. Activism among members was taken as a given rather than specifically resourced and surpluses would have been an embarrassment given the pressing needs of members for more and more from their union.

Given that most strikes were short "demonstration" strikes, unions didn't need to build strike funds or substantial assets. With a few exceptions, the assets that unions have depend on the purchase of CBD-based union offices at a time when such property was cheap. Balance sheets have improved as the prices of these buildings have appreciated. Very few unions have had programs of deliberate accumulation of surpluses. Rather, our leaders have accepted that unions were so secure institutionally that the union's resources could be spent on improving the service given to members.

Institutional security and the development of a settled method of achieving success meant that the management of unions settled into a familiar pattern. Some union leaders became control freaks, supervising every aspect of their officials' work. Had the dispute notification been lodged at the appropriate time? Was it on the correct form? Organisers were given a set pattern of visits to workplaces. Every workplace had to be visited at least once a quarter for a "flying the flag" exercise. If workers didn't receive their visit, the Union Secretary wanted to know why not. These visits were often grievance gathering exercises – providing the organisers with his or her work agenda until the next time a visit was scheduled.

Other leaders were laissez faire managers. They hired what they thought were good people and left them to it. If they had a question, they would ask. Deficient performance would be revealed by complaints from either members or employers.

The system was so clear cut that this approach could work. When a grievance arose there was a set pattern of behaviour that delivered a result. Talk to the member. Talk to the boss. If there was no agreement notify a dispute to the Commission. Get it into conciliation. Try to do a deal. If that didn't work, get the Commissioner to arbitrate.

This hands-off managerial approach was given more weight by the custom of many of the blue collar unions of providing for the direct election of organisers by the general membership. That meant that these organisers then became responsive directly to their electorate – the group of members in the geographic area of workplaces for whom they were responsible. Even if a Secretary or Committee of Management wanted to, the scope for them to control what an elected organiser did was extremely limited. After all, they could argue back that they are elected by the members and they would do what the members wanted. It also meant that these elected officers became very focused in making sure that he (there were very few females in blue collar unions) settled all grievances.

Even appointed union staff, given the protected nature of unionism, held what were in effect "jobs for life". No mechanisms existed for the performance management of staff. It was seen as somehow inimical to traditional union values to dismiss lazy or incompetent staff. That meant that there was some considerable chance that members who may have been conscripted would have their interests represented by someone who simply was not up to the job.

It also needs to be said that one reason for the paucity of active delegate structures was that delegates were seen as potential competitors. Organisers – and indeed some union Secretaries – had a vested interest in making sure that a group of opposition-minded delegates didn't emerge from active representative structures. If delegates existed, they needed to be kept under control.

How is it then that this protected environment didn't lead to a union movement that was supine and corrupt? A movement that provided jobs for union officials in return for compliance with employers and the least improvement in wages and conditions necessary to keep members quiet?

Some unions or union branches at various times in their history fell into that trap. My own union dates its history from 1939 when a group of performers led by a dancer, Hal Alexander, took it over and reformed it. Up until that time, the dominant employer, JC Williamson's, paid the union Secretary £5 a week – on condition that he sign up no members!

Some few unions marketed themselves to employers as the moderate alternative to militant action from competitor unions. That was fine as far as it went. Quite a few very good, conscientious unions used it to effect unionisation of whole swathes of the workforce. They then had the institutional power to deliver real benefits to their members. The problem came when a few became little more than clients of employers whose purpose in life was to hose down member expectations and control the aspirations of their members.

Lazy officials could hide in the system confident that – for as long as the National Wage Case delivered something – they were probably safe from electoral challenge.

Others let power go to their head. The movement is still bedevilled with organisers selected because they are aggressive and overbearing – who think that the force of their argument is helped by the loudness of their voice. Focus group research showed that the public had a preconception of union organisers as big bellied, loud, aggressive individuals[2] – and the stereotype stuck because it had some basis in reality.

One of the most soul-destroying mornings I spent was to sit behind the one-way glass while a researcher was interviewing a focus group of 15 or so non-union workers.[3] These were typical Australian workers – male and female – from working-class suburbs. What was extraordinary was that most of them had been union members at some time in their work history. Most of them told stories of organisers walking into their workplace, going straight past the workers and into the boss' office and then emerging later to announce that a deal had been struck. The union was seen as a bureaucratic force utterly outside the interest of members and liable at any time to do a deal that was disadvantageous to workers. The anger and contempt of these workers for unions was palpable.

I suppose I can defend the action of the organiser. It may be that he or she was not selling the worker out. Perhaps some consultation had taken place over the phone with the workplace delegate. But clearly, these unions had a method of operating that was completely antithetical to an organisation trying to secure the allegiance of its largely conscripted membership.

My mood would have been suicidal if the next focus group hadn't comprised two casual members of the Maritime Union of Australia. This was a mixed group of unionists and non-unionists and the latter started to tell similar stories of union inadequacy. The MUA members set them straight and gave a potted history of the Hungry Mile, what they had achieved on the Sydney docks and the role that members played in those struggles. At the end of the session, these two just about had the group singing "Solidarity Forever"!

For all these abuses, the failures of management, the complacency that was evident, the personal failures of many officials, I nevertheless characterise the Australian movement as overwhelmingly idealistic in nature – committed to the betterment of those it represented.

At no stage in our history did a sizeable part of the movement settle for the status quo. It was a genuinely held part of almost every union's focus to try to improve the position of workers. True, some were incompetent and monumentally unsuccessful but as a rule, the vast majority was committed to progress for their members. Even in unions where the overall strategic direction was questionable, committed officers existed trying to do the best that they could for members. The movement was never forced to make the bargain with employers that became a hallmark of much of the American movement – business unionism. Australian unions always sought to represent all workers and their families – and not just union members. The benefits of unionism were never

---

2   Riley Research Pty Ltd for Labor Council of NSW, Attitudes to Work and Unions, April 1996.

3   This was the research that underpinned the report to Labor Council in 1996.

confined just to those who joined and remained members. Nor did unions limit their concerns solely to the wages and working conditions of their members. Unions were active campaigners on every kind of issue from improved workers' compensation to provision of universal health care. My own union, shortly after its reformation in 1939, became one of the country's first and most active campaigners for a National Opera, National Ballet and National Theatre. Among most unions, opposition to the Vietnam War was a prime area of activity. The radicalised younger generation of that period saw the unions as rock solid allies.

Unions, their leadership and staff, were subject to the at least theoretical discipline of electoral challenge. They were clearly split between Left and Right. Virtually every union was held by one faction or the other and these were warring factions. The Left was a combination of Communist leaders and left-leaning members of the ALP. The Right was a mixture of Catholic unionists and other conservatives. Both felt free to attempt to take control of each other's unions. Indeed, the post-war years were marked in particular by the very aggressive and partially successful campaigning by the Right to wrest control of unions from their communist leaders.

The heat of these battles had the side effect that both sides threw up highly dedicated and inspirational leaders and union officials. They were not in it for the money or the personal exercise of power. Our leaders had no chauffeur-driven cars or huge pay packets. Unions tended to be led and run by people committed to a big idea of one kind or another, both sides infected with a sense of high moral purpose. The threat of takeover by an opposition faction meant that leaders were conscious of the need to make sure that the union delivered for its members.

This factional system had a heavy downside. Unions became intensely tribal and the level of cooperation between unions of either colour was almost non-existent. The natural tendency of unions to bodysnatch from each other was given the additional legitimacy that it was taking members from the opposing faction. Factional warfare meant a huge waste of resources and energy – which might otherwise have been put to the service of members.

I suspect too, that the ideological nature of the struggle for control of unions had some impact on the level of corruption in unions. In Australia, corruption is almost unknown. Criminal involvement in unions is virtually unprecedented, with the exception of the Painters and Dockers in Victoria over a short period. Norm Gallagher of the Builders Labourers Federation in Victoria was convicted of accepting benefits – largely free building materials and labour on his holiday house – from employers. But that is by and large the sum total of the problem. In part this was due to the fact that union negotiated benefits applied to the whole workforce whether union or non-union. The capacity of employers to suborn officials in order to get an advantage for the employer was limited. But it also derived from the fact that the leaders of Australian unions were highly idealistic members of their union and faction. The thought of accepting money from an employer was completely outside their value system.

This has left us with an important legacy. One difference in the public opinion polling in the US and Australia is that in Australia at least, unions are not associated with corruption. Employers and conservative governments don't have that weapon available to them.

The character of the officials concerned, together with the implicit competition between factional opponents, has also meant that unions have been conservative in the way in which they have managed their finances. Australian unions are poor. They have not used their long periods of high, protected density to ramp up the price of membership and accumulate assets. Union fees have been kept low – as we will find in a later chapter – and the income earned has been used to increase year on year the services and support provided to members. We don't have huge asset bases capable of withstanding large shocks – like rapid loss of membership or prolonged industrial attack.

Finally, the ACTU was an incredibly important institution. Central wage-fixing through the Arbitration Commission meant that when government needed to intervene in the wages system, it could talk to the entire union movement by talking to the leadership of the ACTU. This meant that both conservative and Labor governments were in the habit of consulting closely with the ACTU. This process of course, reached its pinnacle in the Accord period when the Secretary of the ACTU became a de facto member of the Cabinet.

Just as importantly, it was at the ACTU that the industrial campaigns of affiliates were coordinated. It was there that the National Wage Case and the other test cases on issues like redundancy payment, were constructed and run – and the results flowed on to every worker in the country almost immediately.

All this gave the peak council enormous authority. Generations of union officials became used to interacting with the ACTU Secretary and understanding that serious consequences followed from failing to secure his support. It also meant that many officials chafed under the control exercised by the ACTU at various times in its history. While they generally went along with the decisions of the Executive, there is no doubt that it became common for many to blame the ACTU for all the ills besetting unions.

The ACTU played another role. Because the Commission had the power to settle disputes, the ACTU had the capacity, on the invitation of a union, to intervene in national disputes. It could and did secure settlements through all manner of backroom wheeling and dealing. Bob Hawke, the ACTU President between 1970 and 1980, built his considerable national reputation on the back of his ability to broker settlements in the most difficult disputes. It was that reputation as a conciliator that made it possible for him to become the country's Prime Minister.

The leadership of the ACTU used its authority – particularly under the Accord with a relatively friendly Labor government – to fundamentally restructure the movement.

The ACTU's Congress policy document, *Future Strategies for the Trade Union Movement* in 1987 warned of the danger of a decline in density and recommended a program for amalgamation along industry lines. The aim was to achieve sufficient economies of scale to enable unions to free up resources to focus on their declining density. From 326 unions, 20 large unions were to emerge from the restructuring process.

This was followed in 1991 with an ACTU Congress decision which threatened to categorise each union into one of three classifications – principal, significant and other. Unions classified as "other" were in practice "on notice" that their future in an industry was limited. Even "significant" unions were to be forced to form a single bargaining unit with the principal union and could only recruit members by agreement with the principal union. These policies were backed up by the ACTU's ability to intervene in the Industrial Relations Commission's demarcation hearings.

The 1991 decision, taken together with a sense that merger was happening and unions risked being left behind if they failed to get on board with their own merger proposals, meant that the 326 unions had reduced to 47 federally-registered unions by 1995.[4] The vast majority of union members are now covered by one of the country's 21 largest unions.

The fact that unions were so involved both in the Arbitration system and the Australian Labor Party meant that there was a continual flow of senior officials from the unions to these two institutions. Talented officials saw it as quite normal to aspire to a career in parliament after leading one of the major unions. As I write, there are three former ACTU Presidents in parliament – two of them in senior shadow Cabinet positions. Others became Arbitration Commissioners or Deputy Presidents at the end of their union careers.

That means that the senior leadership of the movement is young by international standards. The ACTU Executive, in comparison to either the UK or US equivalents, is incredibly young.

There are of course, pros and cons to this. Union members are cynical about union "politicians" seeing time at the union as nothing more than a stepping stone to a good life in Parliament or Commission. We lose valuable experience as a result of some of our most senior officials moving on quite quickly. But it has had the advantage that our leadership is relatively young and open to the possibility of rapid adaptation to our changed environment.

Finally, unions in Australia, I suspect because of the arbitration system, have enjoyed lower levels of public sympathy for their activities than they do in

---

4   Peetz, D, *Unions in a Contrary World, The future of the Australian trade union movement*, Cambridge University Press, 1998, p 133.

other comparable countries.[5] Until the *Industrial Relations Reform Act* of 1993, unions have never had a right to strike. Arbitration was supposed to mean a "new province of law and order" and that meant that disputes were to be settled by the court or Commission. Striking was seen by the public as an attempt by workers to use their collective power to get around the decision of the "independent umpire". And it has to be said that we did ourselves no favours by calling strikes at times that created maximum chaos for consumers. People still talk about mail strikes just before Christmas and beer strikes just before the summer holidays.

The good thing was that during the Accord, unions started to improve their levels of public approval.[6]

So, what does all this mean?

To meet the onslaught of structural change and antagonistic employers and government, the union movement in Australia had:

- Extremely limited assets and virtually no strike funds;

- No organisers – in the true sense of that word;

- Just 18 per cent of workplaces with active delegates;

- A recent history under the Accord of a weakening of the Movement's "hot shops";

- A culture of dependence on organiser action among members;

- A leadership with almost no understanding of open shop organising;

- Little experience of managing long strikes or lock outs;

- An entirely mismatched skill set – the best and the brightest of union officials were trained and expert in advocacy before a tribunal that was shortly to lose its power to deliver much at all to workers;

- A membership made up of 70 per cent union conscripts;

- A membership that was largely unused to being mobilised in its own defence;

- Historically and internationally low levels of public approval.

The strength of the movement was:

- An overwhelmingly young and energetic leadership;

- A culture of passionate idealism in defence of workers – business unionism had never been common in Australia;

---

5   Peetz, ibid, pp 61-62.

6   Peetz, ibid, p 62.

- A strong peak council in the ACTU with a leadership both under Bill Kelty and Greg Combet that has been open to any idea that shows a chance of working;

- A contraction of union membership into 21 major unions with the potential for them to realise economies of scale;

- The absence of any taint of corruption;

- An understanding among most affiliates of their responsibilities to each other;

- The start of an improvement in public attitudes to unions.

Part 2

RETHINKING UNIONISM

6

LHMU South Australia

If you care at all about the idea that workers should have power, and that unions are the way they generally get it, the previous section will have left you pretty depressed. We feel much like our forebears must have felt just after the Great Strikes rolled over them. Our density and power, our membership, our financial capacity, have all taken an enormous hit. The institutional framework which has been so important to us in delivering for workers lies – if not in ruins, then pretty close to it. Our proud history looks set to be unravelled as we lose the ability to protect and extend the system of industrial relations regulation which has been so important to the maintenance of fairness in our society. And above all, our unions are in poor shape to survive in such a hostile environment.

We need to reflect carefully on unionism's fundamentals. What kind of union will it take to be able to succeed in its mission of giving power to the individuals who are our members?

A good place to start is to look at one union that has gone through the process of change and experienced some success. This is no time for an airy fairy theoretical discussion. We need to see with our own eyes that unionism can survive. We need to be able to touch and feel a union that has rethought the fundamentals of unionism and come up with a model that works.

The South Australian Branch of the LHMU is one such union.

I first came across the LHMU in South Australia in 1999 when Mark Butler, their Secretary, invited me to come over and write a report for them on what they needed to do in order to survive.

I remember vividly what the union was like back then.

My overwhelming impression was that they had good people, trying really hard to rescue the union – but nothing much was working. They were shell shocked. People knew that things were bad and when I appeared their thoughts obviously turned to the possibility of retrenchments. (In these circumstances, my job is often to find out how they can balance their budget – and that means I have a reputation as a hatchet man.) Above all, they were desperate to be given hope that they could pull the union out of its terminal decline.

The contrast now couldn't be more marked.

Here is a union bubbling with energy. People know what works and they are getting on with the job of succeeding. Their membership is growing, they have a whole raft of new enthusiastic delegates, their employers know that they should be wary of taking the union on, new staff and delegates are everywhere.

They have come through their trial by fire. Now is the time to start consolidating their power with increased density and good bargaining outcomes.

In mapping out where that change came from, there are lessons for every union in what needs to be done to build a strong union movement.

Mark took over the union almost by accident when the previous long-serving Secretary left suddenly, with no nominated successor waiting in the wings. Mark was a highly competent industrial officer and to that extent was a typical fine product of Australia's old-style unionism. He knew how to appear in the Commission, negotiate a deal, use precedent, cross-examine witnesses. He could also talk to members, get them onside and he was and is respected by his colleagues. He's conscientious and completely dedicated to the interests of his members – ancillary workers in hospitals, aged care staff, child care workers, cleaners, security officers, disability services staff, hospitality workers and workers in a range of manufacturing industry from Bridgestone Tyres, wine makers to baking. It's an open secret that he turned down a safe seat in parliament in order to take on the job of Secretary.

The union he took over was in a mess with, among other things, a million dollar deficit. A hostile conservative government was in power in South Australia and they had busily privatised and outsourced every bit of public sector employment that they could. That meant that the union lost a large chunk of its membership in a very few years. It was losing swathes of its closed-shop membership in hospitality and cleaning, the Adelaide casino used individual contracts to deunionise its workforce and employers were replacing permanent workers with casuals. The union had little if any ability to organise new starts in each of its unionised workplaces – let alone organise new sectors of its coverage.

Everything that was happening in terms of membership decline generally was applicable specifically to this union. In June 1997, their membership was 25,148. By June 1999, membership had dropped to 20,203.

They tried a few things. They moved away from geographic organising and formed industry teams because they thought that people needed to identify with each other beyond their workplaces. By making organisers specialists in each industry they would increase their knowledge of the industry and the connections with the workers that they represented. They talked extensively to the organisers about the need to recruit new members. They started to cut costs wherever they could to try to get the deficits caused by declining union income under control. They even did what most unions steer clear of – they bought smaller cars for the organisers!

None of it worked.

The union was bleeding badly and no matter how much Mark and his leadership talked to the organisers about the need to recruit, they kept losing members. No matter what cost cutting was done, they kept incurring deficits.

Taking a long hard look at the union

At that stage, Mark and his inner circle of Ann Drohan, Chris Field, David DiTroia and Barry Pritchard – met and decided to find an outsider prepared to analyse their union and provide some guidance on what needed to be done.

The financial statements told the story. Their scary graph (Figure 6.1) is below.

There was no need to manufacture a sense of urgency! Something had to be done to halt the exodus of members. They had two or three years before the bank called them in for a serious discussion. And weighing on their minds was the thought that their membership – some of the most vulnerable workers in South Australia – would be left entirely unprotected.

Figure 6.1: Asset/Deficit projection LHMU (SA)

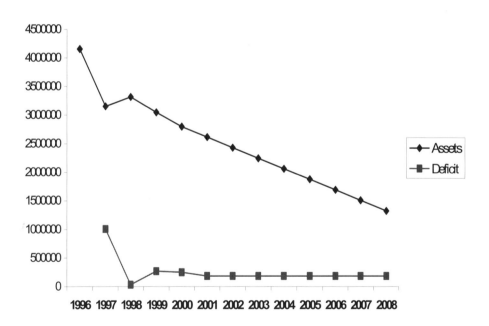

A leadership determined to succeed

The group of leaders surrounding Mark was an extraordinary bunch. Whether Mark set out to gather them together or whether it just happened I am not sure. I do know that they met with me the night after I finished consulting with their staff. They wanted me to send them a written report within one week – no excuses accepted! This was an impossible deadline but worse, they wanted me to give them my conclusions that night! Against my better judgment – because I wanted to at least have a think about what were, after all, first impressions – I mapped out for them where their problems lay and what they needed to do. Time after time, my suggestions hit a chord with them. They had known instinctively what needed to be done but to have an outsider say it built their own conviction. My task was to confirm how bad things were and what they knew they needed to do to fix them.

The exciting thing was that here was a group of people who were passionate about making a success of this. They were prepared to consider any idea if it would help them and their members win. They clearly had the basic skills. They had the respect of staff and members. They were veteran campaigners – if only in the traditional sense. They were convinced that they could build an organising union and they wanted to start tomorrow.

Creating a vision

They did need to construct a vision of what kind of union had a chance of winning – despite the tough hand that had been dealt to it.

They needed to become an organising union. They were trying to deliver services to their members at a time when what they wanted was a fundamental redressing of the imbalance in their bargaining power. As the report said:

> Unions in the current environment need to be much more than deliverers of an insurance policy of doubtful value. We must construct our unions so that our members experience the power of the collective. Instead of seeing the union official as a hero delivering benefits, members must re-experience the reality of working together and thereby achieving power in relation to their employer.

The thing that the union had going for it was that they had some great officials ready willing and able to do this work. Some of them were Organising Works graduates who had been chafing at the bit for some years waiting for the chance to put their training into practice. Others were some of the best of the old-style union officials who knew that the old ways weren't working and were desperate to be shown how to start winning again. Significantly it was some of the more experienced organisers who had been to an organising course very recently who spoke up most authoritatively about the need for change and for the report to be implemented.

Building consensus among staff and members

With that backing, Mark and his colleagues then spent the next six months running delegate training for every one of the unions' 600 delegates. The key group in this was the 150 delegates in the union's most well-organised sites. He got them to describe what was happening in their workplaces – and their experience was remarkably similar. They saw that the power of their union was ebbing away. He got them to identify what had changed in their environment and the ways in which they were failing to adapt to that environment. He laid out for them the impact on the union. He told them about the scary graph, the declining membership, the fact that they would disappear if the union didn't change the way it worked. He spoke to them movingly, in course after course, about the fact that this would be the first generation of unionists to hand down to their children a set of wages and working conditions worse than those they had inherited. Every time he laid this legacy out for workers, you could see them nod in acceptance as the thought hit home.

His appeal had enormous resonance with them – and many of them were in older age groups. The battle to reform this union was not about just putting an extra buck in their pocket. It was about how future generations of Australians were to be treated. It was about the kind of society that they wanted for their children. They wanted their children, their nieces and nephews to be treated with respect.

That message then became the theme for every interaction with members over the next few years. The union's officers knew that the message had sunk in when workers started to quote the imperative for change back at them in membership meetings.

Implementation of the vision didn't just happen once members were told about it. There were hard realities for the union, its staff and members to face. Before anything else could happen, the union had to stabilise its financial position. The budget had to be balanced. Jobs went, regional offices were closed. Members were asked to take on far more of the work of the union.

Getting help to implement the vision

The union appointed Karen Bartel, one of its industrial officers, as the person who would have prime responsibility for driving the change process through the branch.

Karen completely overhauled the branch's delegate training from the traditional old TUTA (the government-funded Australian Trade Union Training Authority) training modules to an organising focused set of courses.

Staff who had not had organiser training were given it and where necessary the union brought in trainers to take the whole branch through the training.

Throughout the process, the branch called on the resources of its National Office and Louise Tarrant provided a constant sounding board for the leadership. She and the Organising Centre's Jill Biddington helped facilitate the crucial meetings where organisers agreed to restructure fundamentally what they did. Louise created a video that documented the change program so that the rest of the union could tap into what was happening in their South Australian branch.

Ensuring success

The union created a growth team of organisers. These organisers were given much reduced servicing loads of some 200-300 members. But they were not entirely relieved of responsibility for looking after existing members. They chose three areas for growth organising – Adelaide residential hotels, a large disability services provider and aged care facilities.

That meant that the other organisers had to take on larger workloads of around one organiser to every 1500 to 2000 members. They had to do things differently. Some of the smaller workplaces would be de-prioritised – put on a care and maintenance basis and some larger workplaces needed to have their delegate structures re-energised.

It was here that the whole process nearly came unstuck.

Having concentrated the resources in a way never done before, increased membership didn't flow. Yes, delegates were developed and a new member-focused way of doing the work of the union was developed. Members were far happier with the way the union worked. New delegates began to find their way into the union's decision-making bodies.

But density remained static – despite the investment of resources. In each of the designated growth areas, net growth was tiny. The union had planned for short-term wins but they hadn't eventuated.

Why had that happened?

The report had recommended, on the basis of what has worked so well in US unions, that Lead Organisers be appointed who had no other responsibilities. This had been very difficult to implement – in part because the designated lead organisers didn't want to give up their "hands on" connection with organising. The branch had had an unfortunate experience under a previous leadership of a rank of middle management being employed who appeared to make only a limited contribution to the success of the union. The current generation had resolutely turned its back on what were seen as unproductive positions without connection to the real work of the union.

Further, the growth team's lead organiser was not given clear authority over accountability – and certainly the culture among organisers was to be wary of systems of accountability imposed on them. This meant that the organisers responsible for growth had difficulty in staying focused on the entire breadth of the task required of them. They were performing magnificently in building the level of activism. But achieving membership growth was falling off their radar.

Once lead organisers were freed up to do the task required of them, and when lead organisers were appointed to all teams, the level of success achieved was immeasurably improved.

The problem of accountability

The problem of supervision and accountability extended well beyond just the growth organising team.

Right from the start – indeed, from before the report was written – organisers had resisted the whole concept of accountability. Before the change process really began, in the early days of Mark running the union, he had tried to at least get organisers to develop a process of planning one week in advance. That led to enormous resistance. He was accused of introducing the concept of billable hours and of having no trust in the organisers. He was told that it was impossible to plan as unions were essentially reactive organisations – they had to respond to what members wanted on a day-by-day basis.

Once the change process began, the use of leaders and lead organisers to ensure that the union was on track continued to cause friction. The problem was only in part resistance from those being supervised – although that was certainly a problem. The reality was that the lead organisers themselves had no clear idea of what they were supposed to do. After all, they had never worked under lead organisers themselves.

Importantly, they were unsure as to where their responsibilities ended and the role of the elected officers – like Mark – began. Did they have the power to sack? If organisers wouldn't follow the agreed plan, did they have the power to start disciplinary proceedings? If they had such power, was that conducive to building a good day-to-day working relationship with the organisers they were supervising?

This issue was critical. One of the problems that the union had to deal with was a level of poor performance – for whatever reason – from a small number of staff. If the union was to climb out of the morass, these organisers needed to be turned around or they needed to go. If the leadership failed to deal with the issue, a signal would be sent to the rest that high standards of performance were really not necessary. Resources in a branch in decline were so scarce that the union simply could not afford to carry anyone.

The issue was resolved by lead organisers being required – in the case of non-performance of agreed tasks – to report the fact to the Secretary. From that point on the disciplinary process was set in motion. Organisers understood what was happening and that it did not inevitably lead to dismissal. Indeed, a number of those staff dealt with in this way have had access to specific training or have otherwise been persuaded and helped to change their behaviour. Others, however, have left the union. Lead organisers are much more comfortable that the issue is taken out of their hands – once the initial report to the Secretary is made.

The union concentrated on building a different kind of union. Members saw that their power came from acting together. They needed to be organised and they needed to have workplace leaders who knew what they were doing. The organisers have started the process of trying to implement that vision. Of course they have a long way to go but a start has been made and the branch is now renowned for being able to exercise its power through the use of delegates leading members in actions. Far more than ever before that kind of activity has become standard operating procedure.

The organisers too are increasingly focused on growth. The best delegate development program in the world is no good if it doesn't produce a growth in membership and power in the relevant industry. That has happened. A graph of membership (Figure 6.2) is below.

You can see the flattening out in membership decline as the change program took effect – despite the impact in the middle of it of yet another round of government retrenchments and outsourcings. In 2003 the Branch recorded the start of a growth in membership.

Figure 6.2: Membership LHMU (SA) 1997–2004

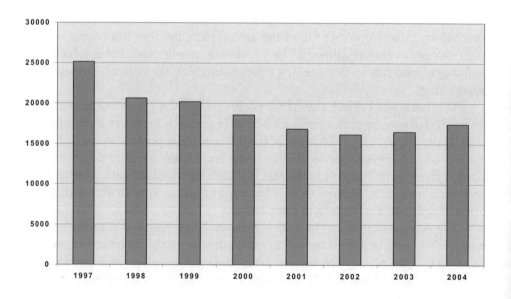

The problem of resources

The problem for the branch was that it just didn't have enough money to hire the organisers that are necessary to get real clout in its chosen industries. The branch could allocate three or four organisers to aged care but the sector had hundreds of facilities and was likely to grow year on year with the ageing of the population. Until the union could allocate the resources to get on top of its lack of density, wages and conditions were always going to be substandard. Certainly, the union had no chance of taking wages out of competition.

It was in that context that Mark and his colleagues decided to go back to the members and ask them to contribute a substantial amount to an Organising Fund. Remember the nature of the LHMU membership. Some of its members earned good levels of income, but a majority earned very little. Many were still dependent on the Award system for minimum wage increases rather than having any hope of getting increases from enterprise bargaining. Until wages could be taken out of competition, enterprise bargaining where employers agreed to increase their wages in comparison to their competitors was nothing less than commercial suicide.

Mark went to his Delegates Convention of 300 delegates in July 2003 with a proposal to lift fees, sufficient to raise an additional $1 million per year. This was to be used solely for organising new members. He asked his convention for two decisions. Should the additional amount be levied on members? If so, how should the new levy apply – a differential rate depending on income or a flat rate applicable to all?

I was at this Convention. He got me to come over to Adelaide to set the picture for delegates on the general situation in South Australia – beyond just the LHMU – and set out for the delegates their responsibility for turning that dismal picture around. It helped too to have someone like me making the point that every union needed to take the kind of radical action that he was proposing.

Let me try to give a flavour of what the Convention was like – because it was a pretty impressive gathering.

The room was packed and the National President, Secretary and Assistant Secretary were present – making the point that this was the most important meeting on the union's calendar. The union's members were there in all their diversity. The blue-collar blokes from Bridgestone were sitting at their table, right next to a table of young female child care workers. Hospitality workers were side by side with hospital cleaners. The union's leadership started with a series of videos featuring the delegates and the videos became a celebration of everything that the people in the room had done. Ordinary people were being featured doing extraordinary things. When members rose to speak, the whole room listened. Ordinary members of the union were respected by all and oozed credibility.

The flow of video material set up a feeling in the room that this was a union that was winning and could win even bigger. Members were happy with their union. It had a sense of purpose. It was clearly growing in power. The benefits were starting to flow through to members. Far more members were involved in the work of the union than ever before. When the union mapped out for members what was possible if more resources were invested, they were able to understand what that might mean.

The delegates saw reports from various delegate organising committees outlining the union's success over the last year in organising new members and defending the rights of existing members. I did my job and finished by using all those un-Australian, evangelical techniques to get the whole room on its feet and chanting support for their union.

It was after all that, that Mark introduced the topic of the Organising Fund. I reflected at the time that his speech showed a union secretary absolutely in control of the agenda. He started by inflaming the passions of half his audience by backing Port Power[1] against "any loser who was stupid enough to support the Adelaide Crows!" This of course got the audience yelling good natured abuse at each other and clearly set Mark up on a high wire with no safety net. He had the absolute attention of every member there. His audience liked him and he liked them. Having got that straight, he spoke strongly in favour of the Organising Fund and the necessary dues increase and the reason why it was necessary. He had prepared comparisons with other comparable unions to use if questioned – as he was. He then put the in principle issue of whether there should be a $1 million fund to a vote. The debate which followed was almost universally in favour. Members spoke movingly about the need for this generation of unionists to provide a better set of conditions for the next – and the wheel set in motion by the union's leadership in those delegate training sessions just four years ago, had come full circle. Only three people of the 300 present voted against.

The debate about how the amount should be raised – a flat or graduated levy – was more divided. I overhead the blokes at the Bridgestone table having their debate among themselves. Some felt that a graduated rate (where they paid more) would be difficult to sell, back in the plant. A majority vetoed that. "For God's sake," they said, "these women from child care earn peanuts. How can we ask them to pay what we pay?" This union had pulled off the difficult task of building solidarity between the most disparate workforces to the benefit of all. A clear majority in the larger meeting came down on the side of a levy which was to be imposed at a higher rate for those benefiting from enterprise bargaining and a lower rate for those only receiving Award wages.

The union followed up with a successful process of educating all delegates – not just those who could get to the Convention – and getting them to vote on

---

1   Port Power and the Adelaide Crows are two Adelaide based football teams in the Australian Football League.

the proposal. Organisers were asked to fill in the blank spots of organisation where delegates didn't exist. The result is that additional funds started to flow to the union from 1 January 2004. An extra million dollars to be spent on organising will mean seven additional organisers devoted to nothing but growth, another lead organiser, a coordinator of member organisers, paid time off for 100 member organisers and a political organiser to be hired to help with maximising the clout the union has with getting organising friendly legislation from the State Labor Government.

What remains to be done?

I interviewed Mark Butler just before writing this case study and his view of the process of change is captured in this quote:

"Change in our branch came through a series of little breakthroughs – and really it's only in the last 18 months that it's all come together.

We now use lead organisers as a matter of course and their role is respected and the individuals are trusted by those they supervise.

We have the structures in place that give effect to our vision of an organising union. An annual convention bringing together 300 delegates from all kinds of workplaces is enormously unifying and builds real enthusiasm for the union as a whole.

We have really good people willing to give every ounce of their energy to make the union strong.

We have been quite ruthless in weeding out those who were either not capable or willing to perform at the necessary high level.

We have a clear plan for each of our industries – and they are not pie in the sky. Each plan has a six or 12 month horizon and they have to be realistic, measurable and time bound.

We have gone a long way to fixing the resource issue. Last week we finalised the hiring of seven new growth organisers – five women and two men. They are enormously enthusiastic and what it means is that where we originally allocated one person to organise Minda (a large disability service provider in Adelaide) we will now have ten organisers doing that job and no other, for the next two months. Once Minda is complete, they will move on to Aged Care and they will really make a huge difference.

The response from members to the fee increase that pays for all this has been tremendous. Every one of our workplaces has been supportive. There is a bit of pride that members of our union – representing some of the most marginalised, poorly paid workers in the economy – are paying more than the well paid blue collar blokes from the big traditional unions.

We still have an enormous amount to do.

We are no good at taking on a really recalcitrant employer on a number of fronts. We can't bring the necessary pressure to bear quickly enough.

Our political organising is almost childish, it's so unsophisticated.

We have a problem in organising pubs and we really need to work out how we crack that area of potential membership.

But the bottom line is that we have 17,200 members and they support 35 officials. Ten of them do nothing but pursue growth in membership.

We think that we have begun to crack the process of getting growth. The key has been to get lead organisers who take charge of the planning process. They make sure that the plans actually get implemented, that we close up the shop as far as we can with employer neutrality agreements and support for delegates structures. Above all, we have really good people in these lead organiser positions capable of doing what is required of them."

He finished by saying:

"The one key constant that has been critical to the level of success that we have enjoyed is that we have managed to keep together a stable united leadership group. Each of them were absolutely convinced of what needed to be done and not one of them wavered from the need to succeed."

You can see from all this that the LHMU South Australia is a work in progress. But the essential factors are there. Their membership is growing and every day their activity turns up new, committed delegates. They understand that the going will be tough and nothing will be given to them by asking for it nicely.

But it is clear that their brand of unionism works.

7

Defining unionism that works

We have seen the dimensions of the crisis afflicting unions and their members and how ill equipped we have been to meet the challenge of an utterly changed environment.

We need to come up with a conception of the kind of union and union movement that is capable of adapting to the new environment. To continue the Darwinian metaphor, after a long time spent swimming in the sea, we have found ourselves washed up on a strange and hostile shore. We have to develop the lungs and legs to be able to make our way on dry land.

Let's pause for just a moment and think through the essence of what a union is.

What it's not

Each year I give a lecture to MBA students at the Macquarie Graduate School of Management. I describe the decline in union density and membership. Their response is invariably to apply a market solution to the problem. Either "You are losing members because you are not providing the services that your members want" or "There is something wrong with your marketing – how much do you spend on advertising?"

They are not on their own. Our enemies provide us with gratuitous advice – mainly to make the point that we are losing density because we no longer provide to workers what they want or need. The *Financial Review* puts it this way:

> No one owes the unions a living. They are not essential to our democratic way of life. They are commercial organisations that should survive only so long as they provide their members with the services that they want.[1]

Market metaphors miss the point. Unions are extraordinary social organisations – quite unlike companies or even many non-profit organisations which form a valued part of our civil society. They inspire quite irrational levels of dedication and commitment from many of their members and from the people who work for them. They have their own culture reflecting the emotional content of their

---

1   Editorial, *Australian Financial Review*, 15 October 1999.

operations – the banners, songs, plays, histories and stories swapped after every union meeting. They have their martyrs – people who were literally prepared to die for the union. Joe Hill is probably better known now in Australia and New Zealand than our own martyrs but we still remember people like Norman Brown killed in the Rothbury miners' strike in 1929 or Tom Edwards on the Fremantle docks in 1919.

Tragically the list of martyrs increased in 1999 when Christine Clarke, a mother of two children, was killed on a waterside workers' picket line in New Zealand by a boat importer, claiming his right of way from behind the wheel of his Landrover.[2]

Union officials see extraordinary dedication constantly. Take Ross Kumeroa at BHP Iron Ore in the Pilbara. He and his colleagues battle BHP's attempt to deunionise their mine on a daily basis. They endure threats and abuse from their supervisors. They know that their union activity makes them marked men when it comes time for promotion or down sizing. They are prepared to forgo an immediate wage increase in order to maintain the integrity of their union.

I think of my brother Mathew, an actor in Melbourne. Unemployed as an actor for six months, desperate for the job he has turned up to do, he found that the cast were being asked to sign an agreement that was not approved by the union. Without a thought he called a meeting of the actors and told them that they couldn't let the union – and themselves – down by signing such a contract. All followed his lead – despite the risk to their hard won jobs.

Then there is Sue Boraston the President of Finsec – the New Zealand finance sector union – who is a bank worker with Westpac in Christchurch. She is battling a life-threatening illness but still goes out at night to knock on the doors of non-members to get them to join the union.

Despite all the inducements from Patrick's, not a single wharfie during the 1998 dispute ratted on the union. They risked their entitlements and future work prospects and backed the leadership of the union – at a time when few believed they had much chance of winning.

I watch each year as a new intake of Organising Works trainees arrives. Some of course, I suppose, may see a union job as a quick and easy way of getting their bum on a seat in parliament. But most are prepared to work for lousy wages just so that they can help build the power of workers.

We look at the generations of union officials – often some of the best and the brightest – who work long hours for a fraction of the wages paid to those with whom they negotiate.

Those same Macquarie University MBA students will often ask me – "Why do these delegates take on the job? What's in it for them?" By and large the answer is "nothing". They do it because they feel a sense of obligation to their workmates to build a strong union in their workplace.

---

2   *Maritime Workers Journal*, Jan/Feb 2000.

These members and officers see something in their union that is far more than just another service provider. They wouldn't do all this to save their mortgage provider, their bank, Qantas or Telstra.

Faced as we are with a determined attempt by both government and many employers to destroy unions, we need to work out what it is in the make-up of the union that inspires this kind of dedication. Because it certainly goes far beyond any estimation of rational self-interest. Bottle that essence of unionism and we have a chance of winning in the end.

My colleagues and I at the Organising Centre have latched on to the concept of an "Organising Union" as the kind of union that can succeed in retaining existing members and grow in its own areas of coverage and into new areas of the economy. We have seen its most current manifestation in the US – but it might just as well have been taken from the ideology of our pioneer unionists with their conception of unionism formed at the start of the 20th century.

Such a union has the potential to meet the traditional benchmarks for successful unionism, higher wages and better working conditions. But the key thing it can do is to inspire many of its members to become an integral part of their organisations so that they will do extraordinary things in its defence. Further, those members can understand the realities of power in the Australian economy. They can be prepared to devote a substantial proportion of the money that their fees raise to fund the exponential growth in organising of new members necessary to turn the density graphs around. The simple fact is that until unions have industry power, they will never be able to take wages out of competition. For as long as union labour is more expensive, employers will always be seeking to destroy the source of worker power – collective organisation.

We may have borrowed the theory of organising unionism in a modern economy from the US but its application may well be easier and more successful in this country than it is there. The values underlying organising mesh closely with the values that have formed the basis of Australian unionism since the 1880s. The values developed by the advocates of "New Unionism" at that time provided the ideological impetus to the organisation of unskilled workers in Australia. They achieved higher levels of density than anywhere else in the world. It may prove to be true once again that Australians will respond more quickly than anywhere else to the demand for respect and dignity for every worker.

Organising unionism is not some strange foreign import. For all our bureaucratised service culture, our institutional dependence, we understand what it is that makes unions strong.

As Karen Bartel of the LHMU in South Australia once said: "We always knew this stuff. Somehow we just forgot about it."

The challenge before us is to find the way to go back to our roots. How can we run unions so that they have the commitment and the enthusiasm that was present at our activist stage?

Getting back to our activist beginnings

One of the problems with getting back in touch with our organising history is that we know only its bare bones. We know that the NSW Labor Council at the end of the 19th century had an Organising Committee – but we don't know what was said at its meetings, we don't know what was said by organisers to workers.

The record is not completely bare. Our more recent history does give us an insight into how organising has worked in Australia and how it might work in the future.

One such story is found in the organising that took place over many years at the Sunshine Harvester Company – the company that was the source of Higgins' Harvester Decision. It was also home to some of the most sophisticated anti-union techniques used against us in our early history. I have written a short analysis of what went on there at <www.actu.asn.au/organising>.

Actors Equity

Yet another example of classic organising is found in the story surrounding the re-formation of Actors Equity in 1939 – now part of the Media Entertainment and Arts Alliance. Hal Alexander has described in some detail how he went about setting up the new union.[3]

Hal was a dancer and the starting point for the whole process was his realisation that he and his colleagues were suffering real and continuing hardship as a result of their lack of power. Far from receiving a decent wage – they often found it difficult to get enough to eat! (He tells the story of catching and killing ducks in the parks of Sydney for his Christmas dinner!) Hal was a brilliant organiser because he could get his colleagues angry at the way they were treated and give them the hope that they could do something about it. Unionism would give them power.

He organised the dancers first by exploiting all his links with them formed over years of working alongside them. He was confident in their preparedness to stick together. Unlike the leading performers, dancers were not under individual contract and so felt free to take direct action without the fear of their contract being cancelled. After building strength with the dancers – and getting a reputation as a successful organiser – he then organised a group of the leading performers – including my grandfather Marshall, a very big vaudeville star.

---

3   Australia Council, archival recording, Hal Alexander, 1980.

They met in secret at "Solly's sly grog joint" at Kings Cross in Sydney to plot their strategy. The stars were important, because they were the leaders – the ones with real credibility with the other potential members. Most importantly, if he could organise them, the theatrical entrepreneurs would find it very difficult to find replacements.

What follows is a story worthy of the Keystone Cops with scenes of Hal dodging security, disappearing backstage through the women's toilet window at the Tivoli to get to talk to the cast. Nothing was going to stop him talking one to one to the performers he was trying to sign up. Step-by-step he started small disputes that gave members confidence that they could win. He got the dancers to stage a sit-down strike one week and a walkout by the chorus the next – just as the orchestra took its seats for the overture! He mobilised the community up and down the north coast of Australia so that no one would attend a touring tent show until a sacked dancer was reinstated. The whole story culminates in 1944 with the Actors' Strike for a closed shop. The legends that came from that strike are still told to each graduating class of young actors. Hal organised the wharfies and other unionists to stack the dress circle of the Theatre Royal. When one of the three scab performers came to the front of the stage and asked "Ah but what shall I do in the springtime?" he was met by a roar of "Join the bloody union!" and a volley of rotten eggs and tomatoes. The strike saw Williamsons' theatres around the country closed – except for the Theatre Royal with its chorus of amateurs. Their touring production in New Zealand wanted to join in – but were dissuaded in case they ended up being stranded over there. In Melbourne, the union organised a huge demonstration of strikers and fans outside the theatres, a cordon of burly wharfies around the comedian Don Nichol (the most prominent and militant of the union's leaders) lest he be served with a summons, and the presentation of the union's own revue – "Stars and Strikes" – so successful that it paid the performers more than they were being paid by their employers!

The stories are colourful but they illustrate a process of organising that we are hell bent on reviving in Australia.

Hal was organising a whole profession. He had enormous credibility because he was one of them – a member organiser. He organised by agitating around the issues that were hottest with performers. He built a committee of workplace leaders. He engaged in limited actions to build his strength and gave the members confidence that they could win. He played one employer against another and got the Tivoli's Wallace Parnell to sign what we would now call a neutrality agreement. He put members in charge of every part of the action and so organised events that the whole process culminated in one key strike aimed at the most strategically important employer. By organising that chain, he organised the industry. He built links with his community and a key part of the leverage he exercised was aimed at making sure he had the support of the public

– the people buying tickets to see Equity members. At every stage, their strikes were fun and minimised the risks to the individual members.

In the 1980s, 40 years after that first formative impulse, I came along as the Federal Secretary of Actors Equity. I didn't think of it in those terms, but I was committed to a more efficient bureaucratisation of the union that he had formed. I – and I think a lot of other union leaders – had a pretty clear idea of what we needed to do to maintain levels of existing membership. Even with the protection of the actors' closed shop, I was conscious of the possibility that it would break down and that we would have to cope with the possibility of actors being able to choose not to be represented by their own union.

With few other exemplars under my nose, I turned to the example of corporate Australia. We started to become conscious of the need for service standards. How do we make sure that every call is answered in a timely fashion? How do we deal with the wave of grievances – the non-payments, late payments, bouncing cheques, cancelled contracts that afflict actors and performers? How do we make sure that members are satisfied with our service?

If only we were able to guarantee a high level of service then surely members would be satisfied and maintain their membership even if compulsory membership ended or was eroded.

What members really want

This way of thinking misjudged the way in which members judged their union. Yes they would be irritated if their message was not answered in a timely fashion – and that needed to be fixed up. Yes, they wanted their back payments chased – and they were much happier and more favourably disposed to the union if their grievance was settled in their favour. But the key motivator for membership was power. Was their union seen as powerful? Could their union mobilise the collective power inherent in the joint allegiance of every performer and get that power to deliver for the collective? Could members be seen to work together and achieve the improvement in what they wanted?

We have to be very clear about what is the essential nature of a union. We are not a business selling a service. We are an entity set up by workers to express and exercise their collective power. We are the means by which our members can stand up to their employers and those with power in the community and say – "Listen to us – we are entitled to, and we demand, the right to be treated with respect. We are not 'human resources'. We demand the right to have our concerns heard not as a matter of grace and favour but rather because you have no alternative but to listen to what we have to say."

In providing a solution based on improving the professional delivery of service to the members, I had completely misunderstood the reason why members were members and often passionately determined that their union win in all the issues facing them. I am quite sure that the majority of members in my old union didn't contact their union office even once in a year of membership. They had no cause to. Only a tiny minority of members had an individual grievance – even in an industry like the entertainment industry which could be expected to generate more grievances given the number of employers and the generally casual or short-term nature of employment. But every member benefited directly from the union's Australian Content campaigns, or its battles to get rehearsal pay, or holiday pay, or repeat fees in television programs. Even the individual issue of the regulation of imported artists, because this was characterised as a fight for employment security for all, became a measure of the union's power – and a campaign in which every member could be involved.

Just as importantly, they were passionate about their union because they were involved in righting wrongs. There are not many members of that union that have not done something to help it. They have marched on Stage Crisis Day, stood up for a member treated unfairly, carried a coffin in the TV Make It Australian procession, defended the union's imported artists policy at dinner parties, written to their local Member of Parliament, gone to general meetings of members, signed petitions, attended cast stop work meetings, turned up at Commission hearings. They own the union's success because they contributed to it.

That is the case for every union. A grievance for the individual member is of overwhelming importance to that member. But that grievance rarely touches the remainder of the union's membership. The issues that touch every member of the union – and each potential member – can generally be covered by the terms of the collective agreement that covers their employment – whether it be an Award, union enterprise agreement or non-union collective agreement. And members can come to understand the fundamental rationale for unionism if they have a direct involvement in the campaigning that surrounds the setting of that agreement. If they have been involved in getting the agreement it becomes theirs. If it is unsatisfactory – and every agreement is a compromise – then blame will be sheeted home where it belongs – either to an employer with more power than the union or the circumstances of the industry that won't support a better outcome.

Organising unionism

What do we mean when we advocate "Organising Unionism"?

Let's go back to the LHMU South Australia case study. At the start of the change process it was pretty clear that it couldn't be described as an organising union. Its membership was plummeting, its delegates and officers were demoralised and members were complaining that the union could no longer deliver what they expected.

The contrast with its position now is stark. I hold it up as an organising union not because of the quality of its bargaining outcomes. Rather what is important is the means by which it gets those outcomes. Members are involved at every level of what the union does. The development of workplace leaders is a prime part of the union's activity. Those delegates are involved in the decision-making that leads to a huge increase in the union's investment in growth. The leadership of the union sees it as their responsibility to give power through union organisation to the whole of their potential coverage – not just those who were organised in some earlier age at a time of strong institutional support for unionism.

And there is a momentum in all this. Because the union is growing, its reputation in the community and among employers builds. It is seen as successful. Good organisers want to work there. Potential members are attracted to a union which is successful. Existing members talk with pride to their friends and colleagues about what they are doing. Employers are less likely to take them on. More money comes in which can in turn be used to fund more and more growth.

Commitment to the building of an organising culture is marked by a series of signposts.[4]

- How many members are involved in doing things for their union?

- How many activists are identified and developed?

- How many workplace leaders are trained and mentored to take on increasing levels of responsibility and at what level?

- By how much is the union growing and how serious is its commitment of resources to growth?

But the way the union thinks about itself is also important. I often look at the union's magazine to see how it writes about itself. Is the magazine full of pictures of full-time union officials or is it filled with members' stories? Do members at meetings ask what "The Union" is going to do about the XYZ problem or do they ask their colleagues about what we can do to fix the problem?

Based on tests like these, it is pretty clear that we have a lot yet to do if we are to build a union movement based on member activism, high levels of workplace leadership and a focus on growth.

---

4   The best article I have come across that seeks to define organising unionism is by my colleague, Louise Tarrant: "Organising Unionism – Back to our Roots." It is available either from the National Office of the LHMU or the ACTU Organising Centre.

Member activism and workplace leadership

If members need to feel the power of their collective, they will do so at the workplace level. If there are no delegates there, it is pretty unlikely that the members can be organised to do anything on a collective basis.

That's what being organised into a union means. Members are placed into a collective structure that they see – every time that they turn up to work – a structure that acts for them when they have a problem; a structure that they can rely on to give them a share of the profits being made by their company.

The problem of the union movement I have described in the previous section is that the vast majority of our members were unionised without being organised. Worse, we taught them to expect nothing more from their union than a transaction – you pay money, "The Union" delivers a service.

At a time of employer aggression, we left most union members to make their own decision, unsupported by any of the structures that might give them confidence in their own collective power.

What we asked workers to do was to take the risky action of joining or staying a member of the union – interpreted by most employers as disloyalty – and all for the sake of taking out an insurance policy. Surely, unless the employee knows that they are certain to be the subject of a grievance, this is not the action of a rational man or woman.

Most workers won't have a grievance and many will be of the view that if they are good at their job, they don't need an insurance policy. If that is the case, it doesn't matter how efficient the union is at dealing with grievances, insurance will not be a sufficient reason to renew membership.

Beyond even these concerns, the insurance model of unionism lost all attraction because of what was happening to the instrumental power of unions over the period of the 1990s. The *Workplace Relations Act* 1996 – to all intents and purposes – stopped the Australian Industrial Relations Commission from settling disputes.

That meant that the union lost a key element of its traditional power – the ability to notify a dispute to the Commission and have the matter arbitrated – irrespective of the union's industrial power on the ground. That is, without a delegate structure capable of taking up and organising around a grievance on the ground – the union lost the ability to force the employer to settle a grievance in favour of their member. It couldn't even deliver on the insurance policy it had sold to members.

Without involving members, unions fail to do the fundamental task that they should be good at – negotiating agreements. Mark Wooden is an academic at Melbourne University and a favourite expert witness for the employers. He tried to debunk our claim that unions can negotiate a substantial differential between union and non-union rates of pay and conditions. To some extent he succeeded. Even in workplaces with high union density (60% on average) he detected no differential. But – and it's a big but – where the workers and their delegates were active, the differential was around 13 per cent![5]

We shouldn't be surprised. What he has picked up is that when unions act like unions and not insurance companies, they work.

Building organising unionism then means that the prime focus of our energy must be to build and resource and support workplace structures. Members must see their union in the workplace every day that they go to work – not just on the off-chance that they may happen to be there the once a quarter that the organiser makes it to their workplace to "fly the flag".

That work and what flows from it is certainly one arm of what we mean in defining a survivable union movement. It needs to be a union movement that allows its members to behave the way their ancestors did when they set up their unions in the first place.

That makes unions survivable, but we need to do much better than that. Workers and their families need unions to grow in power so that they can demand a fair share of society's wealth.

Growth

Central to the idea of organising unionism is a focus on growth. If we are not growing we are dying.

In analysing union membership, ACIRRT[6] has shown just how much more needs to be done before we can say that any sector of the economy can claim to be organised to the extent required to make unionism secure.

Table 7.1: Location of non-unionists by type of employment and industry level of unionisation, 2002[7]

Type of employment	Heartlands	Midlands	Lowlands	Total
Full time	1.1m (19%)	1.1 m (18%)	1.9m (31%)	4.1m (68%)
Part time	.5m (9%)	.3m (5%)	1.1m (19%)	2.0m (32%)
Total	1.7m (28%)	1.4m (22%)	3.0m (50%)	6.1m

5   Wooden, M, *Union Wage Effects in the Presence of Enterprise Bargaining*, Melbourne Institute Working Paper No 7, 2000.

6   ACIRRT, Australian Centre for Industrial Relations Research and Training, Sydney University.

7   Cole, M, Briggs, C and Buchanan, J, "Latent trends become manifest: where were the non-members in 2002?" ACIRRT, December 2003. Figures do not always add up exactly because of rounding. "Heartlands'" is defined as relatively high density in 1994, "Midlands" as medium and "Lowlands" as low density.

There are 1.7 million workers in areas where we already have substantial density. If we could organise those workers – building from our strength – our power to improve the way in which they are treated would improve enormously.

A large proportion of this group is employed in enterprises that already have a union negotiated agreement. They get one of the key benefits of union membership without contributing a dollar and without doing anything to assist the bargaining campaign. Indeed, the fact that they are absent from the collective weakens the credibility of the union's negotiators. (Overall, 1 million non-union workers are employed subject to union negotiated agreements.)[8]

Others are employed in an industry with higher than average union density but in an enterprise that is free of union influence. That means that unless there is a labour shortage, their employer is free to hire the workforce at lower than the union rate for doing the job. That lower cost structure feeds into either a lower selling price for the goods or services produced, with a consequent shrinkage of market share for the unionised enterprises or an immediate boost to the profitability of the non-union company.

It is important that we unionise the million members that benefit from union bargaining and pay nothing for the benefit that they receive. Unions are chronically short of the resources needed to do their work and low density makes their bargaining position weaker. And it is easier to use our existing strength to act as the springboard for that kind of organising.

We must also have the strategies to organise non-union employers competing with unionised employers. In our own self-interest, we have to protect those employers doing the right thing – either by choice or because of the strength of our collective.

We need deeper density in our heartland areas and many unions are currently pursuing that end. But we need to do more than just infill organising.

The ability of Australia's employees to ensure that they receive fair treatment depends not just on unions protecting density in their traditional areas of coverage. Unions must also organise emerging areas of employment.

This is why.

No matter what we do, union workplaces will close, relocate, wind up, go bankrupt or be bought out. Whole industries will disappear. The Felt Hatters' Union was once a force to contend with in the Australian union movement. They are not exactly a force to be reckoned with today! If our strategy for building the collective power of workers depends just on the retention of the union membership first established in the previous century, we are doomed.

If we are to be truly successful, resources must be devoted to those areas of the economy only lightly touched by unions and the values that they espouse. Why should hotel workers not be treated fairly, not earn a decent wage that

---

8   ACTU, *Future Strategies*, May 2003.

allows them to raise their families with a decent standard of living? Why should workers in the communications industry have to take anything their employers care to dish out? Why shouldn't child care workers be paid commensurate to the responsibility of their job? How is it that the insurance industry can get away with disempowering its workforce by forcing the union out?

8

Organising and leadership

Some officials and commentators have interpreted the push to an organising culture as a push for grass roots control of union activity. The members are always right and left to themselves they will get it right. Develop activism and workplace leaders and leave it to them. Indeed, the ACTU's push to organising is questioned on the basis that it is another example of "top down" control of unions – at odds with a philosophy founded on control from the bottom.

But a fourth arm seems to be always present in the shift to organising. Yes, member activism, workplace leadership and growth are key signs of an organising culture. But equally strongly, leadership – from the top down – always appears to be present as well – if the change in the operation of the union is to take place and if the power inherent in an active, growing union is to be realised.

Let me start by giving an example of the importance of leadership in the construction of a union that has the concerns of members at the centre of a union program of action.

Paul Goulter, the former Secretary of the New Zealand Finance Sector Union (Finsec) and later of the New Zealand Council of Trade Unions, tells a marvellous story of the difference between the union as a third party and a union that is seen as an organised group of members.

During his period at Finsec, employers in the finance sector started to use a common range of consultants who saw their mission as ridding the industry of union influence. They started very successfully with the major insurance companies. One of the largest employers, NZI, announced that they wanted to negotiate terms and conditions of employment with their employees directly rather than go through a third party in the form of Finsec. Indeed, NZI went so far as to form an in-house union so that employees would have a homegrown replacement for Finsec.

Paul, as the leader of the union, correctly identified this approach as an attempt to deunionise these employees. He let loose the entire resources of the union to try to defeat the effort. He commissioned leaflets that were delivered to every member. He portrayed the employer action as an attempt to divide workers from their union. He pointed out that while the employer's offer on wages and conditions might well be generous at first, it would only get worse as the collective power of the employees was eroded.

The result was that within a week of the employer's campaign starting, he received over 600 resignations in the mail from members working at NZI.

Union membership had been wiped out and the union utterly defeated.

That process was then followed very soon after by the Bank of New Zealand (BNZ). Again, the employers started a process of "information sessions" for employees at the bank. It had decided that it didn't need to speak to its own employees through a third party – the union. It wanted to be able to speak directly to them and determine what were the issues of prime concern to its employees. It set up in each bank branch what were termed BITs – Bank Information Teams. These were to be units of employees who would be involved in detailed consultation with the bank on the issues that were of concern to employees. Together, employees and the bank would work out how the issues could be addressed.

Finsec – and Paul in particular – now had a big decision to make. Its leading activists saw this for what it was – an attempt to destroy union organisation at the bank. The union's organisers were under no misapprehension either. If the bank succeeded, their ability to exercise power within that bank – and indeed within the whole of the banking industry – was at risk. They urged Paul to unleash a major campaign against the BITs – just as they had done at NZI.

This he refused to do. He had learned from the earlier fight. Fighting for the survival of a third party union – as Paul puts it, the ""Big 'U' Union" – just didn't work.

Instead he decided to make absolutely no attack on the BITs or the Bank's new processes of employee consultation. The union would only act as a resource to members about the new process for getting a collective agreement at the bank. If members rang the union, the union's organisers would talk to them about the pros and cons of the employer's offer. They would help members make up their own minds about the bona fides of what the bank was offering.

Members did in fact go to the meetings of the BITs and started to participate in the bank's preferred process for dealing with its workforce. They started to ring the union and ask for advice. And the advice they were given invariably turned out to be right. When the member was warned that they might need to check whether the bank was giving them the whole picture about an issue – and they did check – sure enough – the bank was revealed to have its own barely-hidden agenda.

Gradually members worked out for themselves what was going on. The bank wasn't serious about wanting to share power with its workforce. It was keen to ensure instead that employees had as small a say as possible as to how their work was organised and paid. It wanted to see the cost of their labour reduced.

More and more members started to demand that the union be brought back into the picture. More and more of them began to drift away from involvement in the BITs. Union activists too, started to take a more prominent role on the BITs – asking the bank to involve the union in an assessment of the changes to employment conditions that were being proposed.

At the end of the day, Finsec's Union Council for BNZ took over the negotiation of a new collective agreement. True to his earliest determination, Paul refused to allow the paid officers of the union to become involved in the negotiation of the agreement. The bank wanted to talk to its employees and that's what they would have to do. The difference was, of course, that he trained the members of the union council to do the work. Instead of a divided workforce, the bank was then faced with a united workforce – united behind an organisation that it owned and controlled – the BNZ Council of Finsec.

Why did the union lose the first attack and win the second so handsomely? The difference – as Paul puts it – is between big "U" unionism and small "u" unionism. At NZI, Finsec was defending a third party – something that was seen as quite external to the workforce. It was put in the position of opposing something that looked and felt like an organisation that the workers themselves owned – the Staff Association.

At BNZ, the union refused to set itself up as a target. Rather, it was the members who realised that in fact the bank was targeting them and their exercise of power as a collective. They decided how they would be represented. If they decided to go along with what the bank wanted – that was their choice. As it happened, the Union Council was forced to accept roll backs that most members didn't like at the end of the day – but that was their choice and they knew who to blame – the employer.

The story tells us something about a new kind of unionism – but it also says a great deal about the role of leadership. If Paul had asked his activist members – the members of the BNZ Council – what should be done, almost certainly they would have told him that they needed to fight the bank's new strategy tooth and nail. But as leader, his job was to reflect carefully on what worked and hadn't worked and devise a winning strategy based on that experience. The solution he came up with revolved around empowering those same activists and more widely the members they represented. But at no time could he absolve himself from the responsibility of directing how the workers could win the power to be represented collectively.

That story mirrors our experience in Australia. The idea that employers want to deal directly with their employees is a very common catch cry among human resources managers. Bosses don't like third parties – and that is why unions should be kept out of the equation. They much prefer to deal with individual workers – deprived as they are of the power of the collective.

In hostile environments, where we have successfully organised unions, it has invariably been on the basis of setting up small "u" unions. We have created functioning unions at a workplace right from the word go. Employees understand from the very beginning of an organising campaign that they are the union. If the union is attacked – that is synonymous with the employer attacking its own workers.

But it appears that some see a dilemma in all this. By making members the centre of the union's activity, doesn't that mean that workers must determine what happens at every level of union activity? If workers are to be the key decision-makers then shouldn't organisers and union leaders step back and become mere facilitators for workers as they determine for themselves what issues are important and how the imbalance in rewards between capital and labor should be redressed. If small "u" unionism is the aim, how can leaders impose their will on workers?

Indeed, at a fundamental level, if this philosophy of organising has at its core the empowerment of workers, then who are we as self-appointed union reformers to come in and change every facet of union organisation? Maybe the members like the kind of union that they have had and given a choice, would much prefer for things to continue as they are? Rather than "taking out a debate to members" shouldn't leaders just measure union satisfaction rates and keep delivering what they have delivered in the past?

I suspect that this debate about how genuine we are in wanting to give workers power over how they are treated arises in part as a reaction to the traditional way in which Australian union leaders related to the workers they led. In an environment where strong workplace organisation was unusual, leaders could get away with a model of union organisation that was highly directive.

Those of us trying to invent a new and better way of working – like Paul Goulter with his small "u" union model – have really tried hard to make sure that leaders develop their skills of listening and assessment to make sure that the union is doing the work the members want done. If we believe that strong unions are those where members have a sense of ownership, we do everything we can to involve them in the decision-making process. We put them at the centre of the bargaining process – rather than as interested bystanders. We keep them informed at every stage of the campaign as to what progress is being made. We try to get them to have a say in which issues are deal breakers and which will have to wait for another day. We get them to discuss and decide on what action will be taken in support of the claim and we get them to get involved on as broad a level as possible in the escalating pressure tactics that will show the employer how serious and united we are.

But does this mean member control at every level?

Let's take a few examples.

What about the case where an employer makes an offer that goes a fair way to satisfying members' demand for improvement in their collective agreement? The members don't like it – they have worked hard to build their power, they have gone a long way down the path of building pressure through escalating pressure tactics and their demands are reasonable. But trying to press on and get everything means that members will be exposed to the risk of failure.

And if we say that members get to determine the issues around which bargaining takes place, what about those issues that are obviously important but are not of immediate concern to particular groups of workers?

A workforce dominated by young workers would rarely put superannuation at the top of the list of bargaining priorities. The result of improving super-annuation will only have an impact in 40 years time – and they have mortgages to pay right now!

Can we expect that male-dominated industries will put paid maternity leave at the top of their list of priorities? Can we expect such members to take a reduction in wage outcome in order to get a benefit for a minority of the workforce?

What about social issues around which many unions will seek to campaign? Many union members fall for John Howard's line that oppressing refugees is an essential part of being strong on "Homeland Security". If workers are truly in control of their unions, doesn't that mean that their views on refugees should become the policy of the union?

David Weil[1] teaches a marvellous American case study that has real reso-nance with Australian union officials – the case of the Professional Air Traffic Controllers (PATCO). In 1984 they took on their employer – and the newly-elected Ronald Reagan – and lost catastrophically. Their union was destroyed and every one of the 15,000 air traffic controllers lost their job – and were only able to seek employment anywhere in the US federal public service when Bill Clinton pardoned them 15 years later. PATCO is the strike from which many American unionists date their decline.

The PATCO case study throws into perspective the issue of the balance between leadership and rank-and-file involvement. Robert Poli was the leader of the union and he was recently elected to office on a ticket of militancy. The members chose him over the incumbent because Poli promised to do what they wanted and take on the administration – no matter what. He delivered on his election promises.

Despite the fact that the employer actually made an offer that went a long way to satisfying the most obvious demands of members, he took his union out

---

1   Professor at Harvard's Kennedy School of Government. For the PATCO case study see Weil, D, *Turning the Tide, Strategic Planning for Labor Unions*. Lexington Books, 1994, pp 12-21.

on strike. They wanted a strike, he had promised it, and he gave it to them. He failed to read the signals that were available to him.

With the benefit of hindsight it is easy to say that the members were mad and doomed to defeat. But can we criticise Poli? PATCO was truly a member-centred organisation – on the face of it, what this book is all about. Poli was doing nothing more than delivering on his electoral promises.

But no one is elected to lead the union to defeat. We don't use the words "union leader" by accident. If members wanted a facilitator – they would call them union facilitators. Leaders have a responsibility to involve members at every step of the decision-making process. That's absolutely true. But it also means that leaders have to lay out for members the consequences of their actions. They have to educate members about what is really going on in the minds of employers. They have to give members the benefit of their experience in dealing with similar situations. If a deal needs to be done – even if members don't get everything they want – then the leader has to be the one to give the members the bad news and help them to understand why it has to be done. He or she has to make a recommendation and argue the case.

We do members no favours at all if we lead them to believe that unions achieve everything they want, the first time bargaining takes place. The purpose of union organisation is to set up an institution that will deliver benefits to union members for every year it exists – not to achieve everything that workers could want in the first year of its operation.

The maritime dispute of 1998 is a perfect example of the role of leadership in the context of a major and well-understood industrial dispute. John Coombs, National Secretary of the MUA, and Greg Combet, then ACTU Assistant Secretary, coordinated one of the world's best fightbacks by a union facing utter and catastrophic defeat. The federal government aimed to make Patrick's its very own PATCO. If they could destroy the MUA, they could destroy any union in the country.

The union movement had a hard fight but with a combined legal, industrial and community strategy the employers were defeated and the architect of the war on the wharves, the federal Minister for Employment, Workplace Relations and Small Business, Peter Reith, was discredited.

But think for a moment about the deal that was done by the union. To this day, the *Australian Financial Review* marks the anniversary as a victory for the forces of capital. The collective agreement that John Coombs signed gave the employers much of what they had sought. Casual labour was introduced onto the wharves. The wharfies lost a great deal of their control over their work. John Coombes suffered heavy internal criticism from his rank-and-file over the agreement. Many muttered that it was a sell out. And yet the wharfies marched back through the gates as a united force to take back the jobs that had been taken from them.

John Coombes acted like a union leader – and took the criticism.

His view was that a deal had to be done. While the union was winning the battle, it could not be certain that the public, other unions and the union's community allies would tolerate a continuation of the dispute. The danger was that it would shift from a defence of the wharfies' right to organise to just another fight about wages and working conditions. Remember that the one part of Reith's propaganda barrage that the public bought was the idea that wharfies enjoyed excessively good conditions of employment. Victory meant getting the members back to work with their collective organisation intact.

That was the deal he took to his members and the deal that they endorsed.

That he was right has been proved in the years since the dispute. The agreement gave away much but it allowed collective organisation to be retained as the foundation of the power relationship between employer and workforce. That meant that at each of the collective agreements entered into since the dispute, more and more of the claims sacrificed in 1998 have been regained. If we believe in the power of the collective then for as long as the union exists as a united, determined organisation, the treatment of its members will advance.

This balance between creating on-going organisational capacity and the terms of the immediate industrial agreement is constantly misunderstood.

Most members have never been involved in a full-on industrial struggle. They can have difficulty in recognising when they have won. Victory rarely comes in the form of utter surrender from the employer. Instead, the employer will make a judgment – occasionally even on a rational basis – about the commercial consequences of continuing to resist union demands. A deal will be offered. It may involve bringing in a third party. "I will never agree to what you are demanding but in order to secure a settlement, what about we have the claims assessed by an arbitrator?" It may be that the union only gets half of what it has demanded – or that the benefits are phased in over a period. It may be that the offer is made at the end of the most insulting diatribe the members are ever likely to hear from their employer. In almost every case, the employer, in seeking to settle, will want the settlement to be capable of being portrayed as a win for the employer. Face-saving is just as important to the employer as it is to the union.

In all these cases it is critical that the union leader understands what is going on and does his or her job – that is, he or she provides leadership, explains to members what is going on, makes clear the nature of their victory and helps members to understand that winning part of their claim sets them up to bargain for the rest at the expiration of the agreement.

I fervently believe that leaders must not be dictators and members must control their union. But there will even be cases where the union leader is obligated one way or another to override the wishes of members. Imagine that a union takes a strike vote that leads to just 51 per cent of members agreeing to strike action. The first question that needs to be asked in such a situation is why the leader ever allowed such a vote to be taken. If the organising has been done properly, if communication trees are in place, if the leader is listening to the whole of the membership rather than just a militant few – the leader should have known that the membership was split. The vote should never have been put until something approaching a consensus was achieved.

But if that hasn't happened – and a vote has gone ahead – what must be done? The union leader must do whatever it takes to avoid implementing that strike vote! What has happened is that the members have signalled to their employer that they are split and that if the employer continues to push hard, there is a real possibility of the union fracturing. Of course union solidarity means that all should follow the decisions of a majority – but close votes like this are a recipe for disaster.

One of the most critical responsibilities of the union leader is to get members – including the most militant – to make a realistic assessment of their strength. We need to ask, "How long will we need to stay on strike to get what we want?" and "Can we realistically stay out for that long?" If the employer is trying to provoke a strike, then the leader needs to educate members about what will happen if they take that bait. Many of the best leaders will talk about their greatest achievements being the time they got the members to stay at work – no matter what the employer's provocation.

What of the issues I have raised earlier in relation to issues that are not obviously of prime concern to members in particular workplaces? Are the wishes of women in male-dominated workplaces always to be ignored because they will never command a majority? Should superannuation be exclusively the concern of an ageing workforce – despite the fact that superannuation only really works when it starts right at the beginning of each worker's working life? What about worker attitudes when they are founded on ignorance? Does having a union that is member focused mean that unions are no longer a voice for the oppressed and the less privileged?

Again, these issues were of little concern when member involvement was not critical to union success. The union executive took a position and that was that.

Something more is required now.

Most unions have always sought to act as the voice of working people on a wide range of issues beyond the immediate concerns of the workplace. Rarely has that voice been informed by any detailed assessment of what members actually think about the positions being taken. Rather, union leaders speak out, based on what they think will have the support of members or because to speak out is the correct thing to do.

That will continue to happen. Union leaders are elected and arguably, members will depose leaders who continually adopt positions with which members disagree.

Our power to intervene effectively over political issues increasingly comes not from our institutional power but from our ability to demonstrate that we are able to shift the attitudes of our members on either issues or political preference. For example, despite a great deal of activity at a leadership level from all sections of the labour movement, Prime Minister Howard has been able to ignore completely anything we might have to say on the subject of refugees. They only have to look at the opinion polls and they can be confident that our members' views do not differ markedly from those of the rest of the community.

The challenge for leadership now must be to go to our members and talk to them about why we have taken the view that we have. Imagine the impact if we could shift the attitudes of a substantial number of our 1.8 million members on a wedge issue like this. There are occasions when we have managed to do this.

The NSW Transport Workers Union for many years has been very reluctant to get involved in taking positions on anything except bread and butter issues of immediate concern to their members. Indeed, they have made themselves unpopular by criticising unions that have taken such positions.

Yet that union was at the forefront of the fight to isolate Fiji after the coup that deposed its democratically-elected Labor Prime Minister. More importantly, its actions were not confined to the public release of statements from its leaders. Its members, aircraft refuellers, baggage handlers and ground staff at airports around the country, voted to place a ban on servicing any plane destined to stop in Fiji.

This of course was a body blow to the island's economy. Fiji's economic mainstay is tourism and it's difficult to get there if you can't fly there. The union risked an enormous amount in taking the action it did with the threat of secondary boycott injunctions and intervention by the federal government – not to mention the airline companies themselves.

How did it happen?

The leadership made the decision to educate these members over a period of time about the importance of supporting workers in Fiji. To begin with, aircraft support staff in Fiji had already demonstrated their sophisticated understanding of international solidarity. In a strike by the Australian Transport Workers Union in 1978, Fijian refuellers, baggage handlers and operational staff had refused to deal with planes bound for Australia. For their trouble they were then imprisoned. The strike in Australia wasn't settled until the then Australian government was pressured to intervene with the Fijian government and had the workers released from gaol.

All that was ancient history but the TWU leadership knew that they had a debt of honour to repay to these Fijian workers. How could they communicate that to their members 14 years later?

The leadership of the TWU was prepared to talk to their members around the country about their shared history. What was happening in Fiji was not just another coup in an out-of-the-way place but was something that had real consequences for workers with whom the union had a close relationship. Most importantly, the union leadership made sure that the Fijian workers were given a human face. They asked Felix Anthony, Secretary of the Fijian Trade Union Congress, to come to meetings of refuellers around the country to talk to them about what was happening to unions and workers in Fiji after the coup. His message fell on receptive ears. Many of the workers were first or second generation Australians and their parents and grandparents had come to the country as a result of oppression elsewhere. Support for Fiji moved from being a theoretical issue to a struggle by real people whose rights were being infringed.

It was on that basis that refuelling of Fijian flights stopped.

The same can be said about bargaining issues that are not of immediate concern to the workers in a particular industry.

A good example of what is required is provided by the Electrical Trades Union's[2] (ETU) 36-hour-week campaign in the Victorian construction industry in 1992. Dean Mighell, the Secretary of the union, conducted meetings of members all over Melbourne – educating his members about the need for a limit on the number of hours worked. The members agreed with the union's claim for a limit on hours – but they presumed that this would become a back-door means of increasing their wages – additional hours would be worked at overtime rates. When Mighell made it clear that he was talking about an absolute cap on overtime, he met strong resistance. Workers stood up and spoke in favour of the ability to work overtime. They needed that additional money to pay off the mortgage or to fund a holiday.

Mighell's response was to ask them how many of their sons or nephews were looking for work in the building industry and couldn't get a start. He put to them the position that the building industry needed to invest in the training of the next generation of builders and they had a part to play in that. If their sons and nephews and the sons and nephews of friends were to have a chance, jobs had to be created and that wasn't going to happen while the building companies could meet the labour shortfall by making the existing workforce work longer hours with additional pay.

That position won through. The workers had achieved good rates of pay. They could accept that while they didn't want their pay to decrease – they had commitments to meet – the additional restrictions on hours should be real so

---

2   A Division of the Communications, Electrical and Plumbing Union.

that additional labour had to be trained and places made available for the next generation.

Equally, workers in male-dominated workplaces can understand that it is unjust that women in their workforce get such a raw deal when they are pregnant. They know that is what their wives and daughters have gone through and will go through unless something changes. If we talk to them about what is at stake for the whole society, quite often they will have little difficulty in understanding why issues like paid maternity leave are worth fighting for. If we don't talk them through the issue, then we can hardly blame them for not wanting to fight for the rights of a minority.

Superannuation is a similar case – for younger workers, it is not an intrinsically hot issue. But it does require that the union's leadership go to the trouble of educating its members about the need for something better than 9 per cent employer contributions. Just issuing an edict won't work any longer.

Leadership at every level becomes more and more important the further down the path of organising unionism we go. The more power we give members, the more skilled leaders must become.

Members want their union to be a force for good. They want it to be successful and they want their lives and the lives of their families to improve. They rely on their union to preserve the gains made in the past and to set out the foundation for a better life in the future.

They demand that their union and its officers provide them with the guidance, support, information and inspiration that they need. They don't have the luxury of being able to withstand defeat by aggressive employers. They don't have the time to indulge in a process of trial and error until they work out for themselves which strategies and tactics work. They elect their leaders to do that for them.

Work intensification and the pressures of modern family life also mean that workers tend to be closely focused on their immediate concerns. That doesn't mean that they are unable to see the importance of building a society founded on principles of justice for all. After all, union members tend to be the people who care for their workmates – the people who are predisposed to acting fairly and treating others justly. They are open to being given an understanding of what is the right thing to do in relation to issues beyond the workplace that impact on society as a whole.

The whole point of a philosophy of unionism built around organising principles is that it is a philosophy that demands the empowerment of the individual member. Such a member won't be told what to think. But someone has to take the time to open members' eyes to what needs to be done – to what is going on in the society around them.

That is the role of union leadership.

Conclusion

All this is simple, isn't it? If all I am suggesting is that unions get more delegates, get them active, demand that organisers get out there and organise, allocate resources to growth – well that's no big ask.

Any of the union leaders who have had a go at this project – and you will meet a few of them as you read on – will laugh at the idea that this is easy.

In rethinking unionism, what we have proposed requires a fundamental reconception of the way in which our unions work. It means that every part of our unions has to do things differently. In particular, it means a very high order of leadership skill from those in charge of each union. The rest of the book aims to spell out just exactly what kind of different behaviour is necessary.

But first, before we go on, can I take a moment to refocus on the point at which we started.

We are in crisis. Every single union. Even the ones not under direct attack and with high levels of membership. We know that no union can afford to be the last union left standing.

Only one industry has 50 per cent membership. In every industry we have less power than we had in 1993.

Working people are failing to receive what they are owed: jobs that pay them enough to live on: hours of work that they need to support themselves and their families: freedom from the petty exercise of authority by their employers and supervisors; access to the training that they need to achieve career progression; decent retirement incomes. All this at a time when our economy is booming, profits are sky high, the rich are getting so rich that we can dust off those 19th century cartoons of cigar-smoking capitalists getting fat on the backs of workers and start using them all over again.

All that is happening because we are in crisis and because we have lost power.

Power has to be rebuilt. That is why the difficult process of change that I outline here needs to be undertaken.

9

Strategic choice

Since his early work on strategic planning,[1] David Weil of Harvard University has refined his thinking and has come up with a very useful framework he calls "Strategic Choice".[2] I want to use that framework to guide the analysis of how our unions need to change to once again restore the power of working people within our society.

The key problem for unions is power and how to build it and Weil believes that it is possible to divide the power-building task into two facets – strategic leverage and organisational capacity. It's the interaction between these two elements that gives us an estimation of power. To get real power, we have to work out ways of improving both. He set up the following diagram.

Figure 9.1

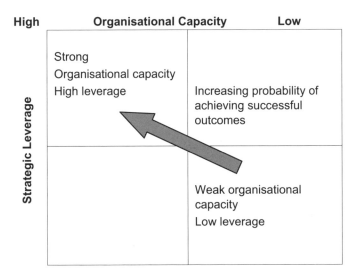

---

1 See Weil, D, *Turning the Tide, Strategic Planning for Labor Unions,* Lexington Books, 1994.
2 Weil, D, "A Strategic Choice Framework for Union Decision-making" in *Working USA: The Journal of Labor and Society,* Vol 8, March 2005.

If both organisational capacity and strategic leverage are high, then the union can plot its power as sitting in the top left hand corner of the rectangle. If both are low, the plot point sits at the bottom right corner of the diagram. Power equates to the top left hand quadrant of the diagram.

For example, the Maritime Union of Australia just prior to the Patricks' dispute would probably have put their organisational capacity pretty far along the horizontal axis. There was room for improvement but it had a very good tradition of internal solidarity, was relatively financially viable and had good leadership.

Its leverage, however, would not be recorded very high on the vertical axis. The federal government hated it, Patrick's CEO Christopher Corrigan was a determined, cashed-up enemy, replacement workers could be trained relatively quickly, recently-changed regulation severely limited the ability of the union to take aggressive action in its own defence.

We would therefore put its power over to the left hand side – but not very high on the vertical axis. As the union started to win public support for its position during the dispute, perhaps its leverage started to rise. When international solidarity started to bite, it started to rise even further. Then when the run of legal cases started to go in the union's favour, its power moved even further northwards.

Let's apply the framework to the situation of the Australian union movement as a whole.

When we had an arbitration commission, closed shops, relatively friendly governments, high levels of full-time employment, little change in the location of employment, 50 per cent density –the union movement was powerful. We can account for our power by redrawing the diagram. With favourable legislation and strong institutional support, we had real leverage. So we would have scored ourselves highly on the vertical axis. With closed shops, 50 per cent density and an efficient working model of union performance, organisational capacity was in a good state.

However, our organisational capacity was interconnected with our strategic leverage. Once the power of an institution like the Industrial Relations Commission was curbed, the ability of our organisations to deliver benefits to members was reduced. Once closed shops were ended, the fact that we had no organisers (in the American sense of the term) left us incapable of maintaining membership – let alone an increasing membership.

Since 1994 we have been working on organisational capacity. When Chris Walton[3] came back from the 1993 US study tour and was given the job of setting up and running Organising Works, he was filling one of our most obvious gaps – the lack of organisers. When he and I re-established TUTA after its abolition by the conservative government, we used that new institution to reconceptualise

---

[3]   Chris Walton is now an ACTU Assistant Secretary.

unionism so that they could survive in their new environment. When Greg Combet published *unions@work*, he gave the imprimatur of a new, energetic ACTU leadership to these ideas. That publication became a landmark in building consensus within the movement about what might work – despite the fact that it was in no way prescriptive.

Throughout that period, more and more unions – like the LHMU in South Australia – have tried to build organising unions.

Weil's diagram shows us that the implementation of all these organisational capacity changes alone is unlikely to be enough to build the power of workers. Strategic leverage needs to be increased if we are to get the full benefit of building our organisational capacity. And, just as the two axes of strategic leverage and organisational capacity were linked at the dissolution of the old way of doing things, so are they linked in the process of our revival. As we shift further along the horizontal axis of organisational development, so does our ability to impact on the axis of strategic leverage.

Our history provides us with a good exemplar of what needs to be done in this regard.

Faced with the aggression of the employers and the failures of the Great Strikes, unions in the 1890s and 1900s adopted a three-pronged strategy of revival. The central element of that strategy was the need to rebuild union structures and organise. Deficiencies in this area were recognised even while the Great Strikes were in progress. Unions had to become far more inclusive so that they were seen to represent the whole of the working class.

At the same time they decided to pursue two strategies that were aimed at improving their strategic leverage – the formation of a Labor Party and the pursuit of arbitration. But the timing is important. Unions organised, grew strongly, had the capacity to wield influence and that gave teeth to the demand for structural change in society.

So it is with us now.

We have to do the work of building organisational capacity. Those who have done some of the work that is required must continue and deepen the process of reform. But increasingly, we need to use the capacity that we have developed to impact on our current lack of strategic leverage. Only in that way can we really hope to give workers the power that they need.

We need to have a core of unions that have motivated their membership as never before to be active in their own defence and the defence of workers generally. We need to give the community in which we operate a sense that the union movement is once again a living, breathing, vibrant force for good. We need to seek allies within the community so that people of good will, once again, will be prepared to come out and defend the rights of workers to stick up for themselves. We need our allies to be prepared to condemn the worst of employer behaviour.

Part 3

REBUILDING
ORGANISATIONAL CAPACITY

10

Doing the union's work differently

If our aim is to build a series of unions that have at their heart a concentration on activist development, member activity and growth, what needs to be done structurally and operationally to bring that about? Clearly, unions as they have existed in Australia and New Zealand are not adapted to such a purpose. Rather, they are designed to manipulate an institutional structure to the benefit of workers – but the structure no longer exists.

Our environment is now far more elemental. Our survival and growth depends on us building unions that workers want to be part of and participate in. We need to educate non-members about the potential inherent in union organisation. And we need to be able to operate in such a way that employers remain neutral while workers make up their own minds about whether they will organise or not. Workers who have had the chance to understand the difference between their power as individuals and as members of a collective will almost always choose to be represented by the collective. The problem they face is that employers will do everything they can to prevent them from making that decision freely. Our key strategic aims then are threefold. First, we have to construct unions that can organise in such a way that members identify with their union and want to remain as members. Secondly, we have to find the time to talk to non-members and educate them about the advantages of participating in the union's work. Thirdly, we must have the capacity to demonstrate to the employer that it is commercially irrational for them to resist the wishes of emp-loyees for collective representation.

The purpose of this section is to think through what practical steps we need to take to develop the internal organisational processes that will lead to the construction of a union that meets our tests for an organising culture – because it is that kind of organisation that will be capable of meeting these strategic aims.

The key problem facing unions as they are currently structured is the management of organisers and other full-time staff. Organisers are the people who will get members to be active. These will be the people to identify and mentor workplace leaders and these will be the people who will drive our growth. If we can't free them up to do this work, if we can't ensure that they do what is required of them, we can't build an organising union.

Quick solutions are not possible.

Too often, we hear that leaders will react to the crisis of falling membership by calling all the organisers together and telling them that they are the problem – "you are just not working hard enough", "you have to get out and start to recruit." We have then calculated how many members have to be recruited each day to get us out of trouble. We add insult to injury by implicitly pointing out how easy it is to reverse the trend.

Starting off a change process by demoralising the people who will be a key to its success is not a good way to begin!

The problem of grievances

If we analyse what organisers do with their time, we will invariably find that they spend a lot of time handling individual grievances from members. Indeed, the most common line used by organisers visiting workplaces has been, "Do you have any problems?" Most organisers are emotionally hot-wired to respond to a member who is in trouble with their employer. They are good people who have a passion for ensuring that people are treated fairly. The instant a member rings they want to rush to the rescue.

If the key task before us is to campaign for growth and power – and that means that the organiser has to spend most time building new networks of members, mentoring and training activists and delegates and negotiating collective agreements, the organiser just can't be allowed to rush off to fix problems. The key union activity is collective union activity. It is not fixing individual claims against an employer. After all, the vast bulk of members in a given year won't have a grievance – indeed, if the union has done its job, it is far more likely that the employer won't dare treat a union member unfairly and if it occurs, there will be delegate structures in place to handle it. The union's resources have to be spent on the bulk of membership, not just a few.

If the ultimate aim is to empower members and build the level of organisation, then collective actions are a lot more important than the legal case that delivers a big benefit to a single member. That means that organisers need to spend more time on campaigns about important issues for members – superannuation or health and safety or on collections of issues that are important to a wide range of members – like enterprise bargaining.

There are cases where grievances move up the hierarchy of importance. If an individual issue has wide ramifications for a larger group of members, then it can be pursued collectively and the union's strength built in consequence. Dick Shearman of the NSW Independent Education Union (IEU) first made me think carefully about this. I was giving a session to a national meeting of IEU organisers. I suggested that some grievances were individual issues and couldn't be organised around – like unfair dismissals. He pulled me up straight away.

"Why the hell," he pointed out, "is the union defending a member if that member can't get the support of his or her colleagues!"

So it is possible to imagine a world where we can have our cake and eat it too. We can build union activism – get members used to exercising collective power – by getting them to campaign around an issue with widespread ramifications that at present only affects one member.

But let's be real about it. Each union will have a large number of grievances each year and members expect that these will be dealt with. There is no way that any union has the time or resources or capability to organise around every one. It takes time to have a meeting of members, petition, organise the delegation, produce buttons. We don't always have that time. The vast majority of grievances need to be dealt with in the quickest and most efficient manner possible. We need to ring fence the organisers from the flow of grievances so that they have time to do their most important job – organising members collectively.

There are a range of tactics that can be used. I want to sketch out a few of them and some I will deal with in greater detail later as we have a look at how they work in practice.

Being selective about which issues to take up

Unions have to be selective about which grievances they take up. Some union officials – and members – are under the mistaken impression that each union has a contract with members to take up any grievance they wish raised. No such open-ended contract exists. Unions are perfectly entitled to set up a process for evaluating the merits of each grievance to see whether it is worthwhile to pursue the claim. Unions have the option of saying no and they need to have a process to ensure that a rational decision is made as to whether to proceed or not. It is a good idea to make the union's policy on pursuing grievances explicit and print it in the material sent out to each new member.

One union I have dealt with decided to clean up its grievance files. They found nearly a quarter of their grievances were over a year old. When they investigated further, they found that most of them had little chance of a successful resolution. The officials just couldn't face up to telling the member that their grievance had no chance of success! That's crazy. The members lived in hope and then thought worse of the union when it couldn't deliver a result.

Although we need to be biased in favour of our members, unions find themselves defending the indefensible far too often. If employers want to sack our members they should have a damned good cast iron case or we will want to take the issue on. They need to be able to show that they have followed a fair procedure. They need to know that if they don't act fairly, we will defend our members. But if workers are late 20 times, then maybe they should start to turn up on time. If they are incompetent in doing their job then maybe they do need to retrain or seek an alternative career. If they are caught stealing from their employer, they should surely have known the inevitable outcome if they are caught. Very often, far from winning the approval of other members for defending members no matter what, the union gets other members seriously off side by going down this path. An incompetent worker will often mean that his or her colleagues have to work harder to take up the slack. Late attendance means that someone else has to work later. Theft means that every worker becomes subject to heightened surveillance and intrusive security measures. Above all, incompetence means that the public suffers and in many areas of unionised employment, this is a very important issue for union members.

From an organisational point of view, defending the indefensible often proves to be the most difficult and time-consuming of jobs for the union's officers. Resources are wasted when they could have been used to really build union power elsewhere – or even in that particular workplace.

One caveat needs to be placed on this. We are entitled to be suspicious about disciplinary procedures when they are used against a delegate. Too often, the most obvious way to attack a union's workplace organisation is to attack the delegates. Disciplinary procedures are set in train purely to show the workforce that the employer is all powerful and no one is safe. Workplace leaders will be targeted and destroyed. There is too, often a personal element to this. Delegates get up the noses of employers and supervisors because they say "No". They are the human face of the union's ability to interfere in the management's ability to do anything they damned well like – and managers often don't like that.

Delegates need to be inoculated against the possibility that this will happen and warned that their behaviour must be squeaky clean. If delegates abuse the system, it makes it almost impossible for the union to protect them.

Where there is little substance to an employer's attack, they need to be shown that nothing will stand in the way of the union's willingness to defend the local representative. If it takes a legal challenge then the union funds that challenge. If the issue is one that can be organised around then the union will do that. Indeed, so important is this issue that it involves not just the individual union. Attacks on delegates should become an issue for the whole of the union movement. Unions should be willing to call meetings of local Trades and Labor Councils to mobilise action against employers who feel free to interfere with the rights of workplace leaders to do their job of representing workers. If employers do manage to get away with this kind of attack, unions will lose power in organised workplaces. Workers lose the hope that they can have a say in how they are treated at work.

No better example of the kind of defence of delegates that is required was found in the battle by the Service and Food Workers in New Zealand in 2004 to get their colleague Andrew Bolesworth reinstated at the Dunedin Casino. The union mobilised not just its own members, it went to the worldwide union movement and inundated the casino with a flood of messages of support from thousands of unionists around the world. They understood that nothing could be allowed to get in the way of the defence of their workplace leadership. His reinstatement sent a signal to the rest of the workforce that they could organise because here was a union with power capable of defending them from arbitrary employer action.

Taking up grievances for non-members

Unions have to examine their policy in relation to the demands of non-members for help. It is too easy to say we won't speak to non-members. Hanging up on such a person may well sour them against unions for the rest of their life. We may also be hanging up on an issue in a workplace that is a high priority for the union to organise.

Yet, if the non-member with a grievance has a claim that will cost the union thousands to pursue, and their workplace is not an organising priority, then the union can hardly be blamed for not taking it up.

Someone has to be nominated within the union to make a judgment about such a claim. Unions cannot afford to find themselves spending time on a non-member without careful thought about whether time and energy is to be spent on it.

Clear guidelines have to exist to help the official make a decision. If the grievance is in an area being actively organised, then it seems pretty clear something needs to be done about it. If the issue raised is something that affects a large number of workers then again, it may be sensible to decide to pursue the claim. If the issue represents an outrageous abuse of employer prerogative, then as a matter of principle the union may well decide to take up the claim. If there is a good reason for the non-member not joining the union, then that might be taken into account.

If it is decided that the grievance is not to be taken up, the worker needs to have the position explained to them in as sympathetic a fashion as possible. This worker is a potential member.

Some unions with high levels of membership and an active presence in their industry will decide to publicise the fact that non-members will not have their issues dealt with. They take the view that non-members have been app-roached and asked to join. In making a conscious decision not to join, the worker has rejected the union and can then hardly complain if the union is unable to help him or her at a later time. Even here though, the best practice followed by unions like the Queensland Public Sector Union (QPSU) is to provide for an appeal mechanism so that special circumstances can be taken into account.

The important thing is that there is a policy in place that ensures that people are treated fairly and that organising opportunities are not missed.

Getting members to follow a disputes' procedure

Members will often come to us about a grievance. What they are really asking for is advice. Do I have a reasonable claim? Am I entitled to this, that or the other? We hear the facts of the case, make a judgment and rush to take the claim over. "Yes, you are entitled to that – why don't I take that up with your employer?" The union official who does that is falling into the trap of treating union membership as a transaction. You've paid your money so now I am going to rush to deliver a service. Worse, he or she has educated the member to think that all our rhetoric about empowering members is just that – rhetoric. They now know that if they just leave it to the organiser – all problems will be solved.

We also have to remember that the aim of the game is to build a constructive relationship with unionised employers. We don't want them to be fighting us morning, noon and night. We want them to work with us to ensure that our members are treated well and to allow us to pull back resources from the unionised companies and divert them to their non-union competitors.

We also know that that is what our members want. Peetz found that "employees seek a generally 'cooperative' – but not acquiescent – relationship between their representatives and their employer".[1]

So why is it that an organiser intervening quickly and raising an issue with the employer, raises the temperature and damages the cooperative relationship between employee and employer?

Of all people, union leaders ought to know how irritating it is when a union representative jumps in and inserts herself between the employer and the worker right from the very beginning. Because it happens to union leaders! It irritates the hell out of them, when the various unions representing their own staff rush in and raise an issue – before it has been raised with them by staff.

The lesson is that having someone act as a third party instantly raises the stakes in any dispute. The third party is in effect saying that the employer has stuffed up – before the employer even knew that there was an issue to be addressed. Raise the temperature in this way and we then have to get over the employer's loss of face if we want to get the member what he or she wants. That means the member and the union now have two jobs to do: we have to get the member's issue fixed and we have to fix up our relationship with the employer.

The first step then must always be to ask the member, "Have you raised this issue with your employer or supervisor?" If they haven't there can be no grievance because the employer hasn't yet had the chance to say "No!"

---

1   Peetz, D, *Unions in a Contrary World, The future of the Australian trade union movement*, Cambridge University Press, 1998, p 53.

We can help to explain to the member what their rights are. We can role play their interview with the employer because it will often be an intimidating thing for a member to do. We can suggest that they take a friend or the union delegate along. But we do members no help at all if we wrap them in cotton wool. If they are not prepared to even raise the issue themselves, what chance will they have of holding firm when the union official arrives at the site and starts to stir the pot?

The union is entitled to test the degree to which this is an important issue with the member. If they are not willing to take the first step, why should we waste valuable and scarce union resources pursuing the issue?

Batching of grievances

Large employers will have a range of grievances each month. One American union local[2] has started a process of getting their employers to nominate one day each month when the human resources department and the relevant union officials can get together to deal with the cases at the one time. This obviously saves a lot of time. Certainly, issues that are urgent – like dismissals – can't be dealt with in this way but a good proportion of grievances are not urgent and members are prepared to wait.

Batching also allows the individual member to be less exposed to the ire of their management. They are just one among many grievances.

The other advantage to this procedure is that it allows the union and the human resources department to identify issues that keep recurring. If members continually complain that a provision of their enterprise bargain is not being adhered to, then something systemic needs to be done about it.

It strikes me that this may well be worth experimenting with in Australia.

Getting outside help with grievances

Members can ruin an organiser's day just by bringing them a huge backpay claim. If they have raised it with the boss and the boss has rejected it, they may have a cast iron claim for recompense. If the Award has been breached, the member has a right to the difference between what he or she was paid and the amount to which he or she was entitled. The problem is that calculating the claim can take an amazing amount of time – which the organiser just doesn't have. It is a job that needs to be controlled at all costs.

LHMU in Western Australia has come up with a creative solution which is worth thinking about.

2　A local is roughly equivalent to a branch of an Australian union.

They know that their members – many of whom are low waged – are often underpaid. Most underpayments come from small workplaces and the member often waits until they have left that workplace before lodging a complaint.

The Department of Consumer and Employment Protection has a statutory obligation to pursue complaints from workers who believe they have been underpaid. Yet the practice has been for the department to refer a union member to the union rather than deal with their complaint.

Following negotiations with the new Labor Government, the union has been successful in persuading them to pursue any complaints referred to the department on behalf of its members. The union is still the conduit between worker and department, it is still defending its members – and gets the credit for that – but the bulk of the work is done by the department.

Another alternative that has been used by at least one of the SEIU's Building Services Division (Local 1877) in the US is to require that their emp-loyers contribute to a contract administration fund. They reason that employers are the source of most grievances and should therefore pay to make sure that the contract is enforced. The money raised from this levy is used to hire and train delegates to be released from the job and come in on a rostered basis to meet with members and talk through their grievances. The result is that it doesn't have to spend its own money fixing up problems caused by inefficient management, delegates are trained in dealing with quite high level grievances and members' problems get dealt with efficiently.

We have to be careful applying this in Australia. If we seek such a provision it needs to be the subject of an agreement which is circulated to members so that there can be no suggestion of a secret commission being paid. It needs to be separately accounted for in the union's accounts so that anyone can see where the money has been spent – and that it has been spent on contract enforcement.

Yet another possibility is to encourage the involvement of labour law firms in the conduct of grievances – at least once the possibility of a conciliated settlement has been exhausted. They may well be willing to take on cases that they determine have a reasonable chance of success – and in the case of success, they recover their costs from the other side where the proceedings are not in one of the Industrial Relations Commissions. If they lose, they bear the cost of the loss.

If they don't think that there is a reasonable chance of success then the union may decide that the principle is important and the outcome is of signi-ficance to a wider group of members. The union is prepared to bear the risk of losing. In that case, an argument can be made that the members generally should subsidise a case being brought on behalf of an individual member.

Using call centres

Call centres have become popular with business precisely because they are such an efficient way of interacting with customers. The cost of talking to someone over the phone from a call centre is a few cents while face-to-face interaction, when we include all the costs of travel, setting up the meeting at a time and place suitable to both member and organiser and provision of a meeting place, costs real dollars.

A number of unions have set up their version of such a facility – and I deal with this issue in talking about the Member Service Centres of the Queensland Public Sector Union (QPSU) and Community and Public Sector Union (CPSU) in Chapter 11.

For the purpose of completeness in this section, dealing as it does with freeing up the load on organisers, let me just give this summary.

Experience in a range of unions has shown that call centres are enormously useful in streamlining the way in which interactions with the union of every kind are handled. Members get the chance to have the bulk of their questions and concerns handled immediately. Unions are able to track the efficiency with which member concerns – whatever their nature – are handled. Unions have a capability to use out-bound calling to support organising campaigns.

Above all, a huge range of queries is diverted from internal organisers. More importantly, the temptation to try to help members with all their grievances is diminished enormously. These calls have been handled by someone else in the organisation.

There are problems with call centres. Unions should be organising around some grievances and call centres can become so efficient that these organising opportunities can be lost. Centres are expensive to set up properly and unions need to maintain a heavy level of IT investment if they are to remain efficient. The work of a call centre can be both stressful and repetitive.

The biggest problem is where organisers are freed from the grievance load – and yet still fail to spend their time organising delegates and activists. We deal with this problem at length later.

Unions have started to use their call centre as an entry point to employment as an organiser. Again this can be a problem. Call centre organisers do get a very wide knowledge of all of a union's industrial Awards and instruments. They get to know at least a sample of membership. But they may become imbued with a culture of servicing members when what they need as organisers is the ability to develop activists and lead workers in organising collective action. Some unions are using their call centres for out-bound organising calls and this gets over this problem to some extent. I suspect, however, that we need to provide careful training and mentoring for call centre organisers who move over to field organising.

We need to develop our out-bound call centre capacity more widely. It is notable in the US that the most common form of union call centre is a purely out-bound facility. These are enormously powerful operations used in industrial and political campaigns.

Some unions have indicated to me that they think that call centres are inappropriate for them because of the breadth of their coverage. The mix of members, workplaces, geography and industrial instruments is just so great that no one call centre could possibly cover their field.

I disagree. The technology supporting call centres is so sophisticated that it can support an almost unlimited number of industrial instruments. By questioning the member about their place of employment and the particular problem they have, a call centre search engine – if the database is correctly set up – should be able to provide the appropriate place to search for the answer very quickly indeed. Certainly, I am much more confident about the consistency of advice being offered by the call centres in operation than I am about the advice being given by individual organisers around the country who are already snowed under with the weight of their union's expectations.

Of all the techniques for diverting the grievance load from organisers, the use of a call centre is the most powerful. Where they have been set up and resourced, the difference in the daily workload of organisers has been startling for organisers. Members show that they appreciate the fact that their union is capable of increasing its responsiveness while at the same time endeavouring to build its power.

Should organisers spend their time on routine visits to workplaces?

One of the great things about a lot of unions that enjoyed unchallengeable closed shops is that they were conscientious about representing the members – conscripts or not. A very few may have sat on their hands and done nothing other than sit in the office and answer the phone – but these were pretty rare.

Instead, most unions set up quite complex systems for their organisers, requiring them to visit every workplace in their geographic area of coverage. Thus the Finance Sector Union could tell me that in such and such a State, every one of the bank branches would be visited twice per year. The Health Services Union would say that every hospital would be visited once per quarter at least – and some of the big ones, every month.

Our problem is that we are chronically short of resources. Organiser time is both expensive and scarce. We have to organise simultaneously our existing members so that they can withstand employer attack and organise new members so that we get more powerful. Every action of an organiser has to be put under the microscope to see whether it is sufficiently valuable to be retained.

Routine workplace visits generally fail the test. The job of an organiser is to develop delegates so that they can be confident about doing the work of the union. We will never have enough organisers to permit them to organise new members one by one or to get them to be active members one by one. We have to get organisers to work through delegates and activists who can then do the work of talking to members and non-members face-to-face. An organiser flying into a workplace – particularly if it is a large workplace – rushing around, handing out business cards, shaking hands, asking how things are going – the exercise is known as 'flying the flag' – is not identifying or developing delegates.

If the workplace is a large one, the organiser is not even making her presence felt among a significant number of workers. Even if she stays for an hour, how many sensible conversations can be had? Ten? Twenty? A hospital employs thousands of people; a bank processing centre, hundreds. How can such a visiting schedule touch all the people working night shift? Or the people not rostered on? Or the people who are so busy that they don't get the chance to have a conversation.

This last problem is particularly serious. In most workplaces, the most respected people are the ones who are good at their job. That will also mean that they are among the most committed to their job. If we schedule our organiser-to-worker interactions at a time that is not convenient for this group of people, we make it hard for ourselves to talk to the people who are most likely to be workplace leaders.

Randomly-scheduled visits leave these interactions to chance and the time of organisers is far too precious to build our power by relying on luck.

We are not saying the organisers don't talk to members. We are saying that the contact has to be systematic. The aim of the conversation is to build power by building activism.

There may be one exception to all this. If the union decides that it is strategically important to organise a series of small workplaces where it is impractical to create a delegate structure, then a visiting program will have to be developed.

Finally, I am highly suspicious of workplace visits where the employer is in any way hostile to the union. The quality of the organiser conversation with activist or potential activist is absolutely critical. But workers are rarely stupid. They know that to be seen talking to the union organiser on work time – whatever the right to access that the organiser might have – is career suicide. It is going to be very difficult indeed to get much that is useful from such a conversation.

This doesn't mean that the organiser stays locked in his or her office. What it does mean is that randomly-scheduled visiting programs that are not linked to a thought-through program of activist identification, development, lead gathering or organising are going to be of limited use and should not be allowed to tie up the time of organiser.

11

Member service centres

Queensland Public Sector Union's Centre

It is impossible to get a complete understanding of the QPSU's Member Service Centre, without appreciating that it came into existence in the context of the election campaign that saw Alex Scott[1] and his team of officials take over the union in 2001.

The previous and long-serving Secretary, Gordon Rennie, had announced immediately prior to the election being called that he would not be seeking re-election for reasons of ill health. Alex, his Assistant Secretary, decided to run and he was opposed by one of the union's senior industrial officers. A third candidate appeared, running for the vacated Assistant Secretary position, who echoed the electoral direction of the industrial officer.

The election quickly developed into a battle between a proponent of organising – Alex – and two proponents of increased levels of servicing.

The industrial officer put out a 20-page campaign platform which had the title – "Balanced Servicing". This proposed that the union actually reduce the number of organisers and increase the numbers of industrial advocates. Both she and the other candidate attacked the organising platform of Alex Scott on the basis that its organising focus would inevitably mean that service to members would be reduced.

For Alex, this was a very difficult argument to counter. The membership, remember, had not been involved in debating a shift to organising. He was placed in the position of getting their support for a new way of working – at a time when the membership appeared to be deeply unhappy with the recent performance of the union. They were unhappy for two reasons. The union had performed badly in enterprise bargaining with the government – at least in comparison with the Queensland Teachers Union. And there was a strongly held perception at every level of the union that it was incapable of responding to individual member concerns. The specific complaint was that members could not even get their phone calls returned.

---

1   Alex Scott, General Secretary, Queensland Public Sector Union, 2000–.

Trying to sell an organising agenda that involved, for example, an appeal for members to be more self-reliant, and a cut in the number of organisers looking after existing members so that they could concentrate on organising new members, would have been electoral suicide. These concepts are saleable – but not in an environment where opponents aim to seize on any possible weakness for electoral advantage.

Instead, the Scott team sought to deal with member concerns head on. Their aim would be to show members how to build their bargaining strength by organising and building activism, while at the same time guaranteeing better responses to individual member problems. Something new was needed. They suggested that members should turn to the ACTU for advice – and that advice was set out in *unions@work*.[2]

Members were to be involved in the work of the union as never before, in that the union would become an organising union. The Scott team would guarantee that service standards to members – far from being diminished as a result of the shift to organising – would be created and adhered to. The union would set up a Member Service Centre (MSC).

With some irony, one of the protagonists within the Scott team commented: "Alex stood on an organising platform and then spent the whole election talking about how he was going to service members better!"

The whole credibility of the new administration depended on making sure that the new service centre worked and that it also freed up the organisers to do the work that needed to be done – rebuild the power and performance of the union as a whole. Density needed to be dramatically increased and a whole new level of membership activism needed to be achieved.

The MSC – how it operates

The centre is staffed by seven industrial officers and the MSC Manager – Darren Hooper. It has two functions:

- Acting as the union's "telephone front door";

- Being the industrial servicing centre for members.

Every call coming in to the union is answered by one of the industrial officers who are rostered on to the MSC to answer the phone. In that role, they have three tasks. First, they need to block calls going to organisers directly.

Secondly, every effort is made to give the member the help they need at their first contact with the union. If they want information, it is provided. If they

---

2   *unions@work* was a report by the new Secretary of the ACTU, Greg Combet, and a group of senior national officials on the way forward for unions. It had four main areas of concern – strength in the workplace, growth in new areas, technology for the times, a strong union voice.

want advice on how to handle a matter, then that is given. Every call that is dealt with at first instance means one less game of telephone tag – timewasting and frustrating for all concerned.

Finally, the industrial officers are constantly alert to emerging trends in grievances so that organising opportunities can be identified.

The second function revolves around the handling of individual grievances. Some of these can be used as organising issues where the organisers get the help of other members in the workplace to ensure that the member gets a fair deal from the employer. The vast majority are dealt with by the MSC as efficiently and quickly as possible. Grievance handling is done by one of the seven industrial officers – advised by the MSC manager where necessary. All these officers are rostered on to the phones. They are guaranteed ten-hours free of phone duty each week when they can follow up their outstanding cases. They also have time while rostered on to the phone to do some case work – calls come to each officer at the rate of one every five minutes on average and each call lasts approximately one-and-a-half minutes. Time not on the phone allows the officer a chance to return e-mails and phone calls that are outstanding. Detailed work that needs concentration is done within the allocated ten hours.

To give you an idea of the scale of the work, the union currently has 28,000 members and they have approximately 330 grievances at any one time. The grievances are supported by one major Award[3] that covers about half the members. Six significant other Awards cover another 5 to 10 per cent of members and then there are approximately 40 minor agreements and Awards. The position is complicated significantly however, by the public service's practice of issuing a large number of ministerial directives and departmental policies pursuant to the Queensland *Public Service Act* 1996 which can regulate industrial issues like travel allowance and overtime. The Industrial Relations Minister issues up to 50 directives and many of these are uniquely refined by departmental policy.

Let's than have a look at how a grievance might work its way through the system.

A mythical member rings the MSC at 9am to find out whether he is entitled to overtime payment for work he has done over the last two years in the Department of Natural Resources. The industrial officer questions him about his claim and discovers that no time sheets exist that show that the additional work has been done and his immediate supervisor has refused to recognise that the member has a claim.

While the member is talking to the industrial officer, she checks the membership record to make sure that he is in fact a financial member. The membership needs to predate the commencement of the events that give rise to

---

3   An Award is a decision of one of the Industrial Relations Commissions which regulates the minimum terms and conditions of employees.

the claim. If there is no membership or the member has joined just so that the union will do the work of processing the claim, the policy of the union is not to handle the grievance. This policy has been very well advertised to members and receives strong support. A let-out does exist – if the person making the complaint doesn't qualify for assistance it will be submitted to the lead organiser for the area. If a benefit to the union exists from assisting the individual – despite the union's policy – then it can be taken up.

The member is, in fact, financial and is a long-standing member.

What does the industrial officer do?

The claim is a classic. It's a stuff up. There is an entitlement to overtime if the work had been done, but the regulations say that overtime can only be done where it is approved and where there is a record of it having been done.

The facts surrounding the claim will be critical to working out whether the member has a case that can be pursued.

The first step is to get the member to fill out a form outlining the grievance and send it in to the union. The form gives the member space to describe what has happened, and to allow the member to identify who the union delegate is in his workplace.

Our member does this and sends it back in to the union where it goes to the MSC manager. Darren looks at it, checks the details against the policy on membership and also uses his knowledge of all the grievances coming in to see whether it might not be part of a trend that means that it could become an organising issue. He decides that in this case, it is quite an isolated case and so should be dealt with as an individual claim. He also notes that the member is not able to identify a workplace delegate – so notifies the organiser handling the Department of Natural Resources that there might be a problem there. If the member doesn't know the delegate it may mean that there isn't one or that the delegate is inactive.

Darren then allocates the grievance on the basis of who has the lowest workload among all the industrial officers – bearing in mind any impending leave. The only other consideration he uses is whether it is a workers compensation matter – in which case it goes to the one industrial officer who specialises in this area. Information on leave and workload is available to him as part of the IT system that supports the centre.

The allocation of this work is then logged onto the computer. The industrial officer is required to make contact with the member within two days of it being allocated so that the member knows that he hasn't been forgotten by the union. The manager will run a report on initial activity every two or three days to make sure that the case doesn't remain unopened.

Industrial officers are free to handle the case as they see fit – although a significant proportion will discuss cases regularly with Darren on how it should be run. (At any one time, due to turnover, a significant proportion of the staff is likely to be relatively inexperienced.)

The MSC's aim is to do a file review of every grievance once a week but realistically this only takes place every fortnight. Again, the IT system – Microsoft Outlook and the union's own electronic filing system – forms the basis of this review. Files move between suspended or active. Suspended means that someone else – the member or the employer – is due to do work on the case so that the industrial officer can't do much about it. Active means that it is the officer's responsibility to advance the case.

As a rule, the basic means of dealing with cases is to get the employer to do most of the work. If calculations on back payment are necessary – why shouldn't the employer do the grunt work? The job of the officer then becomes to make sure that prompt replies to information requests are received.

Let's go back and apply this to our member from Natural Resources. Once his form is returned, Darren has allocated it to one of the industrial officers. She discusses with him some of the inherent problems in the case. Did his employer authorise the overtime? Why isn't there an official record of the overtime?

The problems now begin to resolve to some extent. The member says that his supervisor actually did authorise the overtime. Indeed, the supervisor asked him to do the overtime knowing that it meant him working long hours. The problem was that right from the start, when he submitted overtime forms, they were returned to him unsigned. This had been going on for nearly six months and no money had been forthcoming.

The first question that the officer asks of this member is "What did your boss say?" The member has to have at least raised the issue with the employer. In this case, it is clear that the member has tried to get the issue resolved himself. The officer therefore progresses the matter to a formal grievance addressed to the department's Director General. The officer will help the member write it and it can be in quite simple terms. Alternatively, if the member wants to put his side of the story then that is encouraged. The union will accompany the letter with a statement of claim, that is, the union writes a comprehensive summary of the claim to the employer in the form of:

"The union understands that our member has been asked to work overtime over the last six months. We further understand that he has submitted time sheets but that they have been returned unsigned with the result that no money has been paid to the member. We ask that you investigate this matter and make payment to our member for the time worked."

In the letter, the union or the member will ask that if the claim is not granted that reasons be supplied. If calculations on the overtime are needed or evidence that the time has been worked will add to the force of the case, the officer will ask the member to supply the relevant information. The aim is to get the member to be as self-reliant in this process as possible. The MSC doesn't want members to become dependent on the work of the industrial officer. Rather, the officer will coach and support the member, not do the work for him.

The letter is then sent to the employer. On the officer's computer screen it becomes suspended until a date two weeks later. If no response is received then the officer is reminded by the system to chase a response.

The department will then investigate the claim.

Once the result of the investigation is received, and if it is unfavourable, the industrial officer will have to decide whether there is a reasonable chance of success in appealing it. If there is, that will be the job of the industrial officer and an appeal will be taken either to the Public Service's own review body or to the Queensland Industrial Relations Commission.

This pattern is followed with most grievances. That is, members and employers are encouraged early on to do as much of the grunt work as possible. They are asked to research the claim, provide evidentiary detail, write the letter and in the case of the employer, respond in detail. The union directs all grievance resolution through correspondence for reasons of transparency and efficiency.

A majority of grievances are resolved without a union officer ever meeting the member, an even greater percentage of grievances are resolved without either the member or the union officer meeting with management. If meetings are necessary then wherever possible this is done over the phone. Delegates are used to ensure no member has to meet with management without physical support. With just ten hours of work time free for handling grievances, industrial officers don't have the time to be travelling to attend face-to-face meetings.

The intensive part of their work really comes when they need to access the tribunal system. The key skill of the industrial officers is they know the system and they are well skilled in the fundamentals of natural justice. This is invaluable for members trying get justice for themselves. They can give advice to members that will maximise their chances of success.

Where a delegate is identified on the form, the member is asked would he or she mind if the delegate was notified that a grievance existed. If the member doesn't mind then a report on progress will be sent to the delegate and the delegate will be contacted and asked if they could assist the member if any meetings with the employer are necessary. In this case the question has little relevance, because the member indicated on his form that he didn't know who the delegate was.

What though of the mechanics of the system? The union has invested heavily in IT support for the MSC, it works very well and is continually being enhanced. A new membership system has been developed – and after early teething problems it does the job in a highly efficient manner. The case management part of the system is state-of-the-art. Darren can tell anyone who asks, the average time it takes to deal with a case, how many are allocated to each officer, which cases are slow to resolve, whether the officer is responsive to the time-tabling of actions required by the system.

Recently, the system has been upgraded to allow the manager to check everyone's voicemail messages. If a call hasn't been returned within a day, the matter can be raised with the officer. The return of phone calls – despite the electoral history – has been the last frontier of complaints but this new enhancement has cut the problem of slowly returned calls dramatically.

The next step in IT enhancement is to replicate the intranet database of the Community and Public Sector Union's MSC and the first version of this is now starting to operate. This allows the officer to search on a key word to find the relevant part of the industrial instrument, be it directive, Award or enterprise bargain, so quick advice to members can be given while they are on the phone. Up until now, officers have had to scrabble through a pile of paper to get to the right answer and this is obviously inefficient.

Darren reported to me that the staff of the centre is of a generally very high standard. Some he describes as lifetime over-achievers – and that requires some managing! The payoff is that their work output is fantastic and everywhere I have been in the union, everyone acknowledges how happy members are with the service. The organisers are incredibly relieved. The piles of phone messages waiting for their return to the office have largely disappeared and they no longer have to worry about the burden of unresolved grievances hanging over them. They have time to organise.

SEIU Local I, Chicago

Some variations on the QPSU's MSC exist. One is found at the SEIU's Local 1 in Chicago. Here the union has developed an MSC that mirrors almost exactly what the QPSU has done – despite the fact that both were developed quite independently of each other. The one key difference is that Local 1 has separated the call centre function from the grievance handling area. This has enabled the union to use members with appropriate language skills at the point of first contact, who might not necessarily be comfortable handling the grievance.

CPSU's MSC, Sydney

The CPSU's MSC in Sydney was the first in the country to construct such a comprehensive, technologically-based centre. It is grander in scale than QPSU's. They have to cope with a larger number of members and industrial instruments, as well as with the demands of a relatively small but significant private sector group of members.

The union provides a centre that takes calls from every State and has to cope with different time zones. The staff operate in two shifts between 8 am and

8 pm (EST). The payoff is that members from around the country are able to access authoritative union advice when it is convenient to them – and that will often be outside work hours.

Their MSC administers the updating of the membership record – which at QPSU is handled by administrative staff separate from the industrial officers.

Again, the quality of the service has been driven by the internal political imperatives of the union. Not everyone on the council of the union agreed to the centralisation of grievance handling. Some divisions saw this as an attempt to undermine the power of divisions and take power to the union's national body. It meant that when a majority of the union agreed to go down this path, it was vital to the political survival of the leadership that it worked very well indeed. The result was that the union invested heavily in the IT resourcing of the centre, the training and recruitment of staff, and an appropriate level of staffing.

Again, similar levels of success have been reported and it is now difficult to imagine how organisers did their job before this technique of diverting grievances from organisers was adopted.

The CPSU has experimented with some out-bound organising capacity. Once a member joins they are rung, the details are checked, they are welcomed to the union and they pass on the name of the local delegate and his or her phone number is passed on. The centre then takes responsibility for sending out a new members' kit of materials.

They have also experimented with out-bound calling as a support to the organisers' contact with non-members. They have reported low levels of success in getting non-members to join over the phone but have experienced good results in educating non-members about issues around which the union is organising.

The CPSU reports that there is a relatively high level of turnover at the centre with many telephone organisers moving on to take up positions as organisers with the union. They begin their new jobs with a superb understanding both of how to talk to members and the content of the unions' many industrial instruments.

Conclusion

The key with each of these MSCs has been the level of investment in setting them up on an entirely professional basis. In each case one capable person was given the job of leading the development process. The way in which it was to work to suit the needs of the union was clearly thought through. Strong investment in state-of-the-art IT was provided and the staff were given the skills to do the work. As time has gone on, the operations have been continually reviewed and where necessary, improvements made.

The payoff has been obvious to anyone dealing with these unions. Members report very high levels of satisfaction with the professionalism of the service. Calls are returned and cases are handled in a highly efficient manner. No one has their case lost and if officers are not capable of doing their job, their deficiencies quickly become apparent.

The union can track issues in the various industries and workplaces. Developing trends are identified. By polling information on the one database, organising opportunities – issues that affect a range of workers – become self-evident. The possession of accurate data on the behaviour of individual employers forms an inherent part of the pressure that can be placed on them.

Internal organisers suddenly have the time to do the work they must do if the union is to build its power. They develop activists, ensure that density in their workplaces rises, plan action during enterprise bargaining campaigns, organise around issues of widespread concern to members.

Union leaders are able to go to members certain in the knowledge that the basics are being done. They can turn their attention to how the resources of the union can be used to increase the power of the union across the whole of their potential coverage.

12

Splitting the organiser workforce

If organisers are freed of many of the responsibilities that weighed them down in the past, what should they do?

Louise Tarrant – after a visit to the US to look closely at two Service Employees International Union (SEIU) locals – developed the following chart (Figure 12.1) which later appeared in *unions@work*. It sets out the relationship between the two parts – internal and external – of an organising union.

Notice that the organising union builds its growth from its strength – the depth of member activism. Members are used in the new member organising process both as member organisers and at times, when pressure needs to be brought to bear on a hostile employer, through the pressure of numbers on the street. The growth program builds the strength of existing members and vice versa.

It is implicit in the diagram that the role of the organiser is not simply to recruit new members. Rather, members have to be organised. Yes, we want them to join, but more importantly we want them to be active so that they can play their part in organising within and beyond their own workplace. The organiser's role not that of a sales person with a book of union tickets to sell. It is to identify activists and get them to do the recruitment.

This use of member activism, the constant development and empowerment of members, is really the core of what has been called "An Organising Model of Unionism".[1]

Organiser time needs to be spent at both these ends of activity – building growth among potential members – the Americans refer to this as external organising – and building activism among existing members – they call this internal organising.

If our planning and accountability processes were good enough, it should be possible for us to get our organisers to do both. In practice it doesn't work that way.

---

1   The best book I have come across about this is still Metzgar, J (ed), *An Organising Model of Unionism*: *Labor Research Review 17*, Midwest Center for Labor Research, 1991.

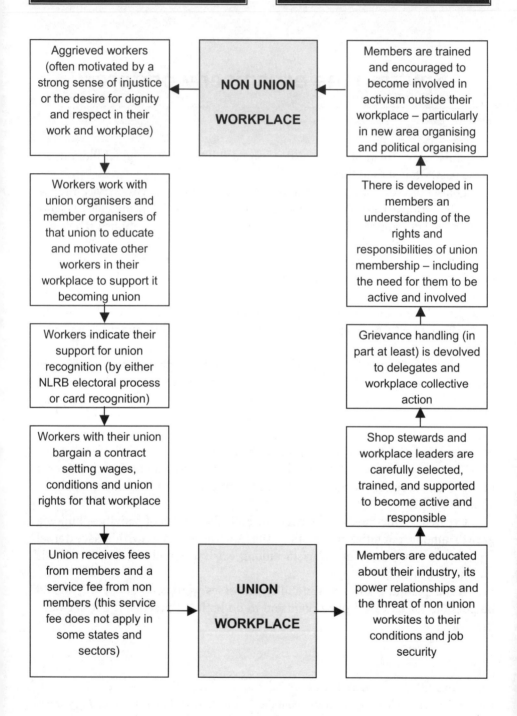

The first time I really was confronted with this issue was at a seminar we organised in 1999 during the FIET[2] (International Federation of Commercial, Clerical, Professional and Technical Employees) Congress in Sydney. The SEIU had sent a delegation of some of their top officials so we put them to work one night talking about organising to a group of Sydney officials. I asked Eliseo Medina – their Executive Vice President – why it was that they put such emphasis on dividing the work of their organisers so rigidly between external and internal tasks. He put the point very clearly and forcefully:

> The answer is simple. We want our organisers to think about nothing else other than building the union's power in non-member workplaces. We want them to get up in the morning thinking about nothing other than organising new members and going to bed at night reflecting on just one thing – how successful have I been in organising new members?

Just think of the dilemma facing just about every organiser in the country. Even if they have been freed of the grievance load, they are expected to do both jobs – sign up new members and get existing members active. What happens when one of the existing members rings up and says they need the organiser's help? Even if it isn't an individual grievance which has been sent off elsewhere, how can the organiser possibly say – "Sorry, I have to spend time today looking after a group of people who haven't even joined the union yet." That is not going to happen. Faced with a challenge from the employer – it doesn't matter how well educated the membership is about the union's need to grow – they expect to get the organiser's undivided attention. They are going to be very unsympathetic to a bunch of non-unionists taking the time of an organiser that they haven't contributed one dollar to support.

And that is what happens.

Faced with a choice between helping a group of members and organising a group of non-members, organisers always find their time devoted to the members. Of course, most workplaces in Australia are open shops – that is, no one can be compelled to join. It is likely that no matter how well organised the workplace, there will always be at least a few non-members or maybe there will be members who are not financial. The organiser should spend time in getting those workers joined up and part of the collective. When the member rings up with a problem that affects a range of people at a workplace, that is the organiser's opportunity to bring in the people who have previously stood apart from the union. When enterprise bargaining comes around, the union will have two aims: get a good agreement and increase density in the workforce. But that kind of 'infill organising' is a long way from the kind of program that is necessary that converts low-density workplaces of 5 or 10 per cent membership, to high-density hives of union strength.

---

2 FIET has now become the Global Union Federation, UNI, the Union Network International.

The two functions need to be split. Just as I have suggested that organisers need to be freed up from the grievance load, so must organising functions become more specialised. Internal organisers need to be freed to do the collective work currently being done by organisers and some industrial officers for existing members. External organisers have to be freed to do nothing but grow the size and power of the union.

There is of course a problem with using these two terms – internal and external – because they are North American in origin. In their context they have a quite specific meaning and in Australia we have to give them a slightly different meaning. Where a union shop is possible in Canada and the US, the split between internal and external can be quite clear. The workplace is either organised or it is not. If the union has been granted bargaining rights by an employer or has won it through an election, it is an internal site. Workers either belong to the union or they pay a contribution to the costs of bargaining and enforcing the contract.[3]

External sites in North America are those workplaces that have no union representation and the union starts from scratch.

In Australia, of course, the closed shop is illegal. No one can be required by an enterprise agreement to join the union.

That means that there are a lot of workplaces where there are no members, some will have a few and then in the areas of union strength, there will be workplaces with better than 50 per cent membership.

When we describe someone as an internal organiser then, their area of operation needs to be spelled out. Do they concentrate on the high-density worksites? Do they have responsibility for those worksites with just a few members that may nevertheless have a union negotiated agreement?

The same dilemma faces us when we describe someone as an external organiser. Does that mean someone who only organises greenfield[4] sites – that is, places with no union membership at all? Or do they go to "unionised" sites that have low density? Or do we deploy them in sites where bargaining is about to take place and we need to beef up our power?

For the purposes of this book, therefore, external organisers are growth organisers. They are given workplaces, indeed industries, that the union leadership determines are a priority for organising effort. They can therefore be sites that have quite high levels of density but the union wants to do even better. Or they can be places where the union doesn't have a member and are entirely greenfield.

---

3   In the US, as we might expect, union shop is under attack. Many States have passed "Right to Work" laws and the public sector generally forbids union shop.

4   "Greenfield" originally referred to a site where the factory was built entirely from scratch – on a green field. Australian organisers now use it to refer to any workplace where there are no members or a negligible number.

13

Organising existing members

Most internal organisers are going to be given a sizeable 'patch' to look after – whether it is a geographical group of workplaces in the case of a fairly homogenous union or a set of workplaces within the one industry in the case of a union with varied coverage.

They need to have a look at the whole of their area of responsibility to work out how they should approach the task of organising these workers. The techniques used to do that are very largely the same as should be used to organise non-union workers.

Typically such an organiser will be given between 1000 and 2000 members to look after. Some will be scattered in small workplaces – others concentrated in larger workplaces. All workers are important but we have to be realistic. It is crucial that organisers be helped to prioritise those workers that are essential to the union maintaining its power in an industry or geographical area.

For example, in the retail sector power depends on making sure that the major employers are organised. That means that organisers at the Shop Distributive and Allied Employees Association (SDA) need to concentrate hard on organising the major retailers rather than making a priority of the many small players in their patch.

Once that decision is taken, what should that set of high priority workplaces look like if they have been well organised? Let's suppose they contain around 1000 members in a typical organising patch.

I use the following tests to assess the degree to which the organiser can put her feet up and have a rest:

What is the density of membership? If it is 90 per cent then the unionisation rate is great and the union has a high degree of credibility in negotiating with the employers in the patch.

How many delegates and activists are there? This is important because 90 per cent density on its own can hide some degree of member conscription which can disappear overnight. It can also set the union up for very rapid deunionisation in the case of sudden employer attack. Remember what David Peetz found?

> The impact of union delegates and union activism in preventing deunionisation is startling. Among workplaces without a delegate in 1989-90, 21 per cent had

deunionised by 1995-6. Among those with a union delegate in 1989-90, just 2 per cent had deunionised by 1995-6. [1]

High density denotes good unionisation – but that is different from being organised.

The third measure is the quality of the delegates that exist in the workplace. A pile of contacts – people who will stick a leaflet on a noticeboard is great. But a committee of 20 people who have been trained and proved that they enjoy the support of their colleagues and will lead widespread action within a workplace – that's what will give the union real power.

To get to that position – high levels of density, activism and a well-balanced mix of experienced and new activists – takes concentrated effort. However, a lot of the organising going on at present is reactive in nature. The organiser waits for a hot issue to come up or for the delegate from heaven to volunteer. That just isn't strategic enough. Unions need their core workplaces organised now.

The union needs to spend time identifying their core workplaces. Which employers have to be organised in order to achieve strategic power within an industry? The answer to that question gives the internal organisers their priority targets.

The key to organising is to plan how to achieve power in the selected workplaces. Organisers have to envision what the workplace will look like once fully organised and what the steps are to achieve that end. Those steps can then be roughly timetabled so that the organiser has a sense of how long the process should take and, at any stage in the process, whether the campaign is on track.

Enterprise bargaining

The big free kick that internal organisers have is the opportunity in most areas to organise around the enterprise bargaining or Award variation process. Remember what this gives us. A log of claims is simply a group of issues that members want fixed. They know that fixing the issues through an enterprise bargain makes the result enforceable. And if we are careful about the tech-nicalities, we have the opportunity of taking protected industrial action in support of our claim.

Again, the trick is to fit the bargaining process in a single workplace into our plan of organising activity. Organisers who try to run a range of bargaining campaigns simultaneously, always skimp on the time allocated to building member involvement and activity. Timetabling is critical. We need the prepara-tory work to begin months before the agreement expiry date – the identification

---

1   Peetz, D, *Unions in a Contrary World, The future of the Australian trade union movement*, Cambridge University Press, 1998, p 121.

of activists, the building of workplace structures, the development and testing of communication networks, the issue development, the agitation in the workplace, the building of a consensus around the key issues.

Many unions have attempted industry-wide campaigning through either the alignment of bargaining expiry dates or the negotiation of a master agreement. This is obviously the best way to build bargaining power. It has the potential to take wages out of competition across a whole industry. Ultimately, our success will depend on the degree to which we can move away from negotiating workplace by workplace. But it takes huge resources and the existence of a very solid core of well-organised workplaces. Organisers should be able to spend their time working intensively in the less well-organised workplaces, while the solid core of workplaces is largely self-sufficient. If that situation doesn't exist, the more fundamental work of building up the number of self-sufficient workplaces will have to be completed so we can address industry-wide activity.

Planning

I don't trust long-winded written plans. I have a simple test as to whether planning is being used to keep campaigns on track. If I can't walk into the organiser's office or work space and be shown the charts on the wall mapping the achievement of set tasks, I am prepared to bet that there is no implementation of the plan going on – even if the planning was done in the first place.

Setting tasks in a plan has to be about focusing on things that can be measured. We may not like the setting of numerical targets but they sure concentrate the mind!

If escalating pressure tactics are important in building the confidence of the workers, show me how many have been done, what was the result, how many people were involved? By the end of the first month, is it reasonable to expect that at least half the workers will have participated in a low level action? If that is too soon, then by when do we expect this to be possible? If we are waiting for six months before anything happens, I suspect that we are not succeeding.

If we agree that density is important, we have to set a target for the number of new members and timetable it.

Once we start this kind of counting, we have to be honest with ourselves. I don't want to see how many members the organisers or delegates say have been signed up. I want to see the completed membership forms entered into the membership system.

If we are serious about building an organising union, you can see why I have carried on earlier about freeing up the organiser to be able to do this job. This is a monumental task. They have to have the time to do it.

Identifying and developing workplace leaders

How do we identify the real workplace leaders who can then be persuaded to help us get the contacts and communicators that we need in every section of the workplace?

There may be existing delegates, but they may be completely unprepared for a more hostile environment. They may have volunteered when the employer accepted the role of the union, when being a delegate was about distributing literature for the union office. In some workplaces, being a delegate may even have been part of the promotion process! These delegates need to be prepared to change and if they can't or won't, they will need to be replaced. The organiser needs to test the degree to which existing delegates are prepared to be active.

Organisers make mistakes about this. Too often we get the delegate from hell – the person always in trouble with management who figures that the safest place to be is sitting in a delegate's seat. These are precisely the people who are unlikely to have the respect of their colleagues.

We also have a tendency to pick the loudest of our members. Courage to speak up is a valuable commodity but the key is someone respected by their peers.

I was reminded recently of how damaging a poor delegate can be. I gave a lecture at Sydney University to a group which contained a couple of unionists and a large number of human resource managers. Many gave me stories of delegates in their workplaces behaving badly, table thumping, unreasonable demands, a refusal to be constructive in sorting out workplace problems. These human resource managers were not anti-union but even allowing for some measure of exaggeration, it was clear that problem delegates were educating the employer to turn against the principle of union organisation.

Research done by the LHMU reveals how damaging poor delegates can be for the union itself. Members of the union reported, as expected, that their satisfaction levels were very high when they were happy with the performance of their delegate. But crucially, having no delegate at all was better than having a delegate who was not up to the job.

So what are we looking for?

When talking to a group, look for that person to whom the other members defer. The deference shown may not be verbal. It may just be a flick of the eyes to make sure that what has been said meets with the approval of the real leader standing off to one side of the group.

Asking members directly who everyone respects or looks up to will often reveal the person who needs to be persuaded to become the key delegate. Another method is to ask a member, "If you needed help with a problem, who would you go to?", or ask the workers – "If you were the boss, who would you appoint as the supervisor?"

Check the gender and ethnic balance. Our aim is to have our committee truly representative of the workplace. Some feminised workplaces will elect a man to do the talking on their behalf. But the real leader, when action needs to be taken, will be a woman whom the others respect. She may not be prepared to do the talking but she needs to be on the committee.

Similarly, non-English-speaking-background (NESB) workers may elect a native English speaker to do the talking. But the key decision-maker will be the community leader who has the workers' respect on a day-to-day basis.

The people we have identified have to then be tested. Give them a job to do. It's one thing for them to say – "Yes I will help" – but it's another to actually help. If they won't do the work of the union at some level at least, they may be a union sympathiser, but not an activist. Remember that we want a very high level of self-sufficiency so that the organiser can go elsewhere and build up another set of workplaces.

Tasks have to be real. Members will resent the waste of their time if tasks have no real point. The organiser has to explain to the worker how the chosen task fits into the overall campaign to organise the workplace or improve the lives of workers.

It is also crucial that the task fits with the worker's own skills and level of confidence. The task has to be appropriate and the organiser needs to walk it through with the worker so that the potential activist is clear about what has to be done and how.

The organiser then needs to find the issue to organise around. The mantra taught in organiser training is right – we are looking for issues that are widely felt, deeply felt and winnable. When an organiser comes across a rostering issue they should generally fall to their knees and give thanks to the great god of organising! We can fix it, rostering affects everyone covered by the roster and it impinges on every part of the worker's life – his or her ability to get a decent night's sleep, look after the children, get home to a spouse, go out with friends.

But enterprise bargaining has the same effect. Even if every worker doesn't feel equally angry about every issue, your delegates' committee should have surveyed their members so well that you can be absolutely confident that there is something in the proposed agreement for every single member.

Make sure that we don't have preconceptions about the issue. Wages may well not be the problem. The workers may even know that a wage increase is out of the question because the boss is not doing too well competitively. But they may be really annoyed that the pie warmer is broken or that it's difficult to get a car park or that the supervisor gets to go home early to look after her kids but the workers are shown no flexibility at all.

It is important that the workers are given a structure within which to work. They want to know that the organiser knows what he or she is doing. I like the title "Workplace Organising Committee" or "WOC". The title makes clear what is going on. This is not a social club. Its members are not getting together to fix grievances. It's not even a bargaining committee – although it may do that, as part of its organising activity. These workers are getting together to get their workplace organised. That's the agenda and the organiser needs to make clear that he or she is very serious about it. Its meetings have to be businesslike. They are not gossiping sessions, nor should they be taken up with long rants about how bad the boss is. Instead, tasks are reviewed, the next steps are identified, the members get the chance to role play how they will act on decisions and a date for completion and report is set. The key here is that the organiser is not doing the work. With such a committee set up, it is the WOC members who are identifying more and more activists, deciding issues to organise around, and gaining the confidence to start putting pressure on the employer.

The intelligence set out in a workplace map[2] drives the systematic contact programs of the organisers and workplace leaders. It tells them which potential members in which sections of the workplace are a priority. It says that women are weakly organised or that the Vietnamese workers must be approached. It shows them where effort must be concentrated to build density. Some sections are strategically more important than others. But we shouldn't be too cute about this. Our job is to build a majority – to build unity across the widest group possible. Just organising strategically important sections is not enough.

Again, mapping is not an end in itself. We don't just want the information, we want the delegates and activists to be involved in gathering it. We want them to understand the nature of the power dynamic in their own workplace. We want them to think through why it is so important that we have a contact in the dispatch room or the cafeteria or wherever. Above all, they need to do it because they know the workers in each area far better than we do. Remember what we are getting them to do is to build their own union in their own workplace. They have to own it at every level. The last thing we can afford is for the union to be the organiser's union. When the pressure comes on, workers will walk away from someone else's union very quickly. Attack the union that they have built with their own bare hands and you are attacking the workers themselves.

Throughout the process, the organiser should be evaluating each of the activists. Her job is to develop them from just a union contact person to some-one willing to spend time in another workplace as an organiser, to make a housecall at night and to negotiate the next enterprise bargain with the employer.

Evaluating means that records need to be kept. With a patch of 2000 members, an organiser can have to keep track of up to 300 to 400 activists. They need a database. Generally, unions that are serious about delegate development will grade their activists 1 to 4. Each progression will be determined not by gut

---

2   A representation of a workplace so that the union's strengths and weaknesses are revealed in every one of its sections, social groupings, gender divisions and so on.

instinct but rather on the basis of what the activist has actually done for the union. If they contact five other people they are indeed an activist – at level 1. If they come out housecalling with the organiser, they are a 4.

Organisers in Australia tend to be a bit worried about evaluating the people that they work with. Get over it. This is a tough game. Most employers would love the chance to destroy our workplace organisation. What members need is a completely efficient, professional process that gets them to win – gives them the opportunity to demand and get, respect from their employer. Keeping track of the development of each activist is just a part of that process. The more organised and professional we are, the more confidence the members have in us. The job is too important to be left to gut instinct or chance.

Two-way communication with members

Generally, we have the advantage in any battle with the boss because we have credibility. The members are the union and they trust their colleagues at work. They work with them every day, they share the same experiences, they rely on each other's support. Employers are remote, with their own agenda of either making higher levels of profit or securing their own jobs through demanding higher and higher levels of productivity.

Employers may try to split workers from their union but they will be defeated if the union leaders have a clear line of communication with workers. That is, in a single day, can a union leader speak face to face with every worker and get their feedback on what has been proposed?

Why is that important?

If the employer manages to communicate better with our members than we can, we don't have the chance to build unity. If members can't talk to us, we can't know what they think.

That's why employers put so much energy into communicating with their staff. They may have video addresses by the CEO, train supervisors in communication techniques, produce glossy staff bulletins.

We have to be better than them.

Organisers alone can never match that effort. Apart from not having the time, organisers as individuals don't have the required credibility. Employers and supervisors are in the workplace every day. They have a relationship with our members that is far more direct than any organiser can ever expect to have. That's why, to be better, our communication structure must depend on members in the workplace – who have the most credibility of all.

To make contact with every member in a day and communicate a message and get feedback requires a very large number of activists. The way I find out how many are needed is to ask the members or delegates. "Given the work intensification in your workplace, how many people can you have a serious face to face conversation with in a single day?" Most will say around five – some will say a few more. Whatever the number, that is the ratio we need to develop.

I first saw this kind of exercise used by Chris Walton with great effect in helping the SDA organise David Jones in Melbourne. Again, the delegate structure was vestigial with just one delegate for the whole store. Density was low. The workers could scarcely be described as militant!

But by developing a communications tree and then showing every member how well organised their store was, people understood that the union had its act together. It could do things to improve the position of workers. It had power. Their leaflet (opposite) shows you how confidence can be built.

Every person in that store knew someone on that leaflet.

Density in the workplace grew and the union started to win benefits for members.

I again saw these techniques used by Troy Burton at BHP Iron Ore in the Pilbara.[3] The company had done its level best to destroy the union at that mine. It had offered generous individual contracts to the workforce, just under half had accepted and the union loyalists were placed under the most severe pressure to either leave the mine or accept the contract. By the time Troy turned up in the Pilbara, the conveners or delegates were demoralised and unwilling to take the boss on in any way at all. Power had entirely shifted to BHP and the workers who had stuck with the union looked and acted like a defeated group. They had no hope at all that they could win. Their only motivation in sticking with the union was that they couldn't bear to scab on their mates.

The organisers decided to try to set up a communication tree within the mine so that every member of the union could be identified and the organiser who was going to work with the miners – Will Tracey – could know from day to day what members were thinking.

The conveners sat down with the inevitable butcher's paper and wrote down the name of every single member in each of their areas. Contacts were then nominated who they thought might be prepared to talk to five specified miners. Delegates who would be prepared to talk to those contacts were identified and so the tree was constructed.

The next step was to test the tree. A very simple question about something relatively innocuous was proposed and the conveners agreed to send it out the next day. Within 24 hours, an 80 per cent response was returned and the conveners were enormously heartened. But the organisers – Will and Troy – refused to accept that that was good enough. As they pointed out to the conveners, if that represented our support among the members, we had just lost majority support (45% of workers were not members and had individual contracts).

---

3   The story of this struggle has been told by Bradon Ellem in *Hard Ground, Unions in the Pilbara*, PMU, 2004.

My SDA contact is:

Huw Giles
Cookware

Liz Flicker
Ladies' Co-ordinates

Bronwyn Vincent
Accessories

Helen Dylan
Children's Wear

Meg Casey
Gift Wrap

Ted Bloch
Security

Wendy Weiner
Men's Fragrances

Jenny Evans
Australian Designers

Leslie Adams
Lingerie

Alana Boston
Union Delegate
Ladies Shoes

Marshall Blau
Business Shirts

Sam Redgrave
Men's Suits

Kate Nina
Furniture

Josh Beckham
Men's Jeanery

Matt Goodwin
Food Hall

Nadine Flood
Cosmetics

Kevin Doyle
Men's Underwear

Debbie Schneider
Cosmetics

Louise Burwood
Home Entertainment

Rachel Kennedy
Men's Designer

Ben Braniac
Docks

Emily Stewart
Food Hall

Amy Gladstein
Small Electrical

Mathew Narita
Travel Goods

John Ramsay
Visual Merchandising

Dalinda Fermin
Manchester

Kate Coleman
Men's Knitwear

Jennifer Ackland
Stationery

Maria Robalino
Cosmetics

SDA — supporting each other for a stronger voice

Authorised by Michael Donovan State Secretary (Names have been changed for reasons of privacy)

They went back to the tree and worked out where the connections had failed. Who hadn't responded and why not? Each of the contacts who hadn't done their job was then followed up and either replaced, given some support in how to approach the workers for whom they were responsible or their excuse accepted for not participating on that particular day.

Each time the tree was used, everyone involved had their confidence boosted. Once more, despite everything that the company was throwing at them, the members were improving their level of organisation. As confidence grew, so did their preparedness to do more and more for their union. While the battle at BHP is far from over, it will now be a surprise if BHP manages to prevail.

Can the organiser devote all her time to such a campaign? Generally not. Remember that if we are prioritising workplaces amounting to a relatively small proportion of the patch, there will be some reactive work to be done in the non-priority sites. The union's own organisation will require time – staff meetings, help with other actions and so on. The key is that if the priority targets are not made the central focus, the union as a whole can't advance. Success in these campaigns is the make or break of union success as far as the union's internal organising is concerned.

Existing members are the core of any union's strength. They give it its character – its reputation for activism, its renown as a defender of the rights of its members. Failure to organise them means that we are forced to accept whatever the boss offers us in enterprise bargaining. De-unionisation is always possible and growth is impossible. Growth can only come from a firm base with a reputation for strong, self-confident action. In short, potential members want to belong to a union that looks powerful. That's what internal organisers deliver.

14

Organising new members – the role of external or growth organisers

Rather than talking at a theoretical level I want to tell the story about organising a very difficult target and draw from that some of the lessons that are more widely applicable.

Organising Coppabella

Coppabella is about a thousand kilometres west of Brisbane and run by Roche Mining. It's an open cut mine producing 5 million tonnes of coking coal each year. Central Queensland open cut mines are huge, ugly things dominated by heavy machinery, drag lines, dust and heat. They work around the clock to get the most out of the investment in machinery and they are among the most productive mines in the world. It was a relatively new mine – opening in 1999 – and it was covered from February 2001 by a greenfields agreement that the union had entered into to ensure that there was some safety net protection for whoever was employed there once it opened. There was at least one union member employed but he kept his membership secret for fear of being victimised. The attitude of the company was anti-union – as was the case at most of their other mining operations.

Most of the workers were 'clean skins' – non-union members with little or no experience of working in the coal industry.

Bernie Farrelly, a newly-minted Organising Works graduate, was asked to take on the campaign. Bernie, a young man of about 40, had a long history of experience as a delegate with the MUA – notably as the Cairns delegate during the unsuccessful attempt to deunionise that port immediately prior to the Patrick's dispute. As an Organising Works' trainee, Bernie had been part of the team organising coal mines in the Hunter Valley in NSW. Coppabella was to be the first mine he took on single-handedly.

He landed in Coppabella, suitcase, laptop and mobile phone in hand and set up house. He had a reasonably good briefing from the union about the mine's history, a copy of the greenfields agreement and a basic idea of the nature of the workforce. He had two names – a miner who was a friend of

someone else working for the union and the name of the mine's one member –
who had lost his job at his last workplace as a result of being a union delegate.
The night he arrived he started by knocking on their doors to get the ball rolling.

These two characters then gave him pure organising gold – a copy of the
rosters. They provided a complete list of workers and how they were arranged in
working groups within the mine. The two of them told him that a few of the
miners lived in single men's quarters at Nebo 50 kms down the road, so off he
went. He had no idea which caravans held the miners so he cold-called the first
caravan he came to. Really, he was just hoping to find out which doors to knock
on. The great god of organising smiled on him because this person became the
very first person that Bernie signed up. He then took Bernie to two more
caravans. By the end of his first night on the job at Coppabella he could report to
Troy Burton, his lead organiser back in Sydney, that he had signed up three new
members, had his first two contacts prepared to help and a complete list of
names and work locations!

The next night found him at Coppabella railway siding where he had heard
other miners lived in some caravans. Sure enough he found one more willing to
sign up. More importantly though, with six workers now signed up, he was able
to start going through with them the lists of names he had and start the process
of identifying the people likely to be leaders.

The process of filling in the database then began. The whole roster was
entered. Each shift and each section of a shift needed a workplace leader
prepared to talk to the people he or she worked with about what was going on.
Bernie visited house after house, caravan after caravan, pub after pub trying to
make contact with the people that had been pointed out to him as leadership
material. He needed to have on his side the people the other workers respected
if he was going to be able to take the company on. The conversation he had with
these workers was designed to get their involvement but he also needed their
help in finding the organising issue that had the potential to unite the
workforce. The first time that the new union came out on show it needed to be
able to demonstrate that a majority of workers were united behind it. There
were a lot of issues that irritated the people he spoke to but the key problem was
which one to pick.

Each night that Bernie returned to his digs, he debriefed the day's events
with Troy.

The decision was taken to run on two issues: Roche were short paying the
workers on holiday pay; and failing to provide a second shift break of 30
minutes (they were only getting 15 minutes). The first issue was a matter of
respect. Why was it that Roche could think it could get away with short
changing their miners when the rest of the industry got full payment and the
workers had a legal entitlement? The second issue was about safety. As the shift

went on, concentration levels tended to drop and the miners needed the full break to make it through to the end of their shift in one piece.

They organised around these issues in the most low-profile way possible. A letter was drafted and workers were asked to sign it – although they were told that their names would not be revealed to the management until a significant group had signed. Delegates' names would not be revealed at all at this stage. Remember, at this time, there was no union presence on the site, little experience of unionism and certainly no conviction that by sticking together, change could be made.

In the end, Bernie fell just short of getting his majority – but he went close. Eighty workers signed the letter and the identity of the delegates was not revealed to the company until they had given a written undertaking that the union's members would be protected from victimisation.

The union demanded that the company set up a consultative forum between delegates and company representatives to consider these two issues and any others that might arise.

The company responded that they would not meet with the workers' delegates unless they had the opportunity of vetoing the people that the workers appointed!

The result was that the two sides became locked into an argument about how these issues were to be settled. The more the delegates saw of the company's attitude to negotiations with their workforce, the more irritated they became at their lack of respect for their own workers.

At about this time, the Mining and Energy Division – the union sponsoring the organising campaign – began a nationwide campaign against all Roche operations. The CFMEU will never be accused of subtlety and their publicity was intense. Large signs appeared outside all Roche operations depicting a large cockroach, above the slogan "Roche Busters".

Bernie quickly realised that this campaign needed to be carefully handled as the workers, so far, certainly did not identify with the CFMEU. They scarcely knew who they were. Their only contact with a union officer was the contact they had with Bernie. They were setting up their own union to deal with their own issues. They hadn't asked for the help of any third party. The anti-Roche campaign had the potential to be turned into a weapon against the new union. The propaganda could sound as if it was aimed at the workers as much as Roche and that by choosing to work for Roche they were somehow demeaning themselves.

The local CFMEU lodge responded to this problem very well. Their leadership met with the newly developed workplace leaders and assured them that they were absolutely behind them. Their campaign was aimed at the management practices of their employer – not at the workers in any way at all. More importantly they backed up these assurances with a prominently displayed half-page advertisement in the local newspaper, welcoming the new members from Roche at Coppabella and assuring them of the local lodges' support in organising their employer.[1]

This sent two signals. The CFMEU was a cashed-up powerful union that had the money for these kinds of ads and the message itself got through. These guys really were on the side of the Roche workers.

The first crack in the company's image of invincibility came when they were forced to accept the workers' chosen delegates and bargain with them. They had to get the issues that had been raised settled and it seemed clear that the workers and their representatives were not going away. By just getting in the door of the company's office, the workers were shown that getting together and sticking together at least had some hope of budging the company. Nevertheless, the talks came to nothing and the delegates reported this fact back to meetings held at the start of each shift. Again, the fact that the workers felt strong enough to hold these meetings in company time were important signals to both company and workers that they had rights and could exercise them. No work began on a shift until the meeting was over and members and non-members were welcome to attend.

The delegates then decided it was time to increase the pressure on management. They expanded the issues around which they were negotiating on the back of a survey of all the workers to see which issues were of concern to them. What emerged was that workers were extremely agitated at the shift system in operation at the mine. They had to work six days on and three days off when the industry standard was an equal number of days off and on. When the workplace leaders raised this with the company, they offered the workers equal time off and on – but on reduced pay. Significantly, the company made the offer by ignoring the leaders and going directly to each worker.

This did no good at all.

The workers had asked their delegates to act on their behalf. They took the company's actions as an insult to their clearly expressed wishes for representation. And to add insult to injury, the company's offer was "crap".

Bernie and the delegates now had a letter with 120 names on it demanding that the company negotiate properly.

The company responded that the workers had no choice. They had four days to vote on their offer or it would be withdrawn.

The workers refused to vote until all the other outstanding issues were resolved. They knew that they had the power and that productivity at the mine – with report back meetings being held regularly and a ban on overtime in force – was at an all time low.

---

1   The Lodges were Peak Downs, Goonyella Riverside and Mooranbah North. They provided enormous support to Bernie throughout the campaign and to the workers after he left.

Something had to give and it did. The company head office agreed to meet with the leaders of the CFMEU in Sydney to hammer out an agreement with the union on the issue of neutrality. The company agreed to issue a letter at all its workplaces that guaranteed the rights of its employees to join and be active in trade unions and made it a dismissible offence for any supervisor to breach the company's code of conduct on this matter. In return, the CFMEU agreed to call off its campaign against Roche.

The specific Coppabella issues also had to be settled if productivity was to be maintained and some semblance of a harmonious relationship between workers and the local management re-established. The various issues in dispute were taken by the company to the Commission in Brisbane. The union was represented by a Brisbane-based industrial officer, Bernie and one of the mine's delegates. After a range of meetings, and continuing campaigning by the workers back at the mine, a resolution was found. The company agreed to a million dollar payout to workers to compensate them for the shortfall in their holiday pay. The workers voted to accept that offer and then agreed to renegotiate their enterprise agreement.

Had we won what we set out to do?

Our aim in these campaigns is to leave behind a self-sustaining workplace structure – a lodge – with elected office bearers, a culture of workers standing up for their rights and a high level of density. Ideally, we wanted a good working relationship with the company where union organisation is taken as a given and the two sides work out how the mine can be operated productively while giving the workers the respect and reward that they deserve for the difficult job that they do.

All this was achieved. Their lodge was established as part of the CFMEU and elections – hotly contested – were held.

Bernie could go to his next organising target satisfied that he had left behind a self-sustaining union structure which, without his involvement, went on to negotiate a new enterprise agreement which provided for a four days on/ four days off roster, ten hours less work per week and an increase in pay.

The employer was neutral with regard to the representation of its employees and could get on with managing a highly productive workplace.

The miners at Coppabella were without doubt a self-reliant, fully functioning part of the unionised coal mining industry. They had power and they weren't going to be pushed around by anyone.

What are the elements of success?

The problem with telling a particular story like this is that we immediately think up all the ways in which it is easier to organise a coal mine in a regional area than it is to organise one of our own sites. After all, you would think after all their history, coal miners are pretty open to being organised. That may be true of traditional coal miners but remember that the company had – probably deliberately – recruited its workforce from the non-union WA metal mines and local farms. These workers were anything but your usual suspects. When you really think about it, this was a pretty difficult site. If it worked in these circumstances I suspect that these techniques will work just about anywhere.

So what did the union do right?

Well organisers reading this will be tempted to say that it was Bernie's brilliance that got us through. And all of us at the Organising Centre will tell you that he was good raw talent but it was really his Organising Works training that did the trick. And the CFMEU will remind us that it was their money and support that enabled it all to take place. And don't get me wrong, Bernie is a bloody good organiser. And the training turned him into that organiser. And nothing would have happened without the money and support from both the local lodges and the union as a whole. But it's a lot more than that.

The union could concentrate its resources on the target. Each organiser generally took on responsibility for no more than 100 workers. Where Bernie's organising experience over the eight months of the campaign differs from that of most other organisers is that he had just 200 workers (more than we think is ideal) to organise and that was the sum total of his responsibility. He could really focus on the outcome he wanted and there was a very clear win or lose about the whole project. To paraphrase Eliseo Medina's words, "he got up in the morning thinking about Coppabella and went to bed that night thinking about how he had gone that day at Coppabella."

Secondly, we put an experienced lead organiser in charge of the project – Troy Burton. Troy was responsible for working through with Bernie what approach was likely to work. He kept him on track with regular – and usually daily – de-briefings. He took the time to go on the road with Bernie – despite the cost involved in supervising the project from a thousand kilometres away. Clear numerical targets were set and success was tracked through the Organising Centre database. We didn't count just members signed up – although that was important. We wanted to track how many were leaders, how many had done something to build their union, how many were prepared to reveal themselves to the company as a union supporter. If there hadn't been sufficient success in a relatively short period of time, it would have been Troy's call to pull out the resources and put them elsewhere.

Bernie started with his list work and that formed the basis for talking to the workers about getting themselves organised. He knew the mine and its place in its market. He worked through the activists and he talked to the activists and developed them through house-calling. The very fact that we were smart enough to house-call rather than go anywhere near the workplace gave the workers confidence. They knew that anti-union hostility would reach fever pitch if an organiser showed up at work and the union would suffer enormous loss of face if the organiser was thrown out by security. The workers organised in secret until the point at which they were confident that they had the strength to exercise power and start a low risk action. Bernie got members to sign up other members – indeed, after the initial burst of recruitment he rarely signed up a single member. At every stage, the campaign proceeded at a pace and comfort level set by workers. The union as a whole moved in and persuaded Roche to sign a neutrality pact so that the workers didn't have to keep themselves in a state of permanent revolution. The mine was left with high density, and a comprehensive lodge structure. Two of the delegates made the front page of the Union's magazine (one of them later addressed ACTU Congress) and the workers got to see their story plastered over the centre pages – along with the other successful organising victories the unit delivered. Coppabella was fully organised. Bernie could be re-deployed to another mine.

This story of success has now been repeated in a range of different environments across the country. They tend to have the same elements of success. The LHMU in West Australia recently organised 1300 education assistants into the union. They did so by making sure that they had sufficient resources to pursue the systematic contact that is required. As with Coppabella, they provided for a 1:200 ratio of organisers to potential members. In this case they paid to book members off the job, trained them as member organisers and set them loose to talk to the previously identified non-union education assistants. Because there were so many of them, that was an expensive operation. They spent $300,000 on the exercise. But they signed up so many members that they gained an increased annual income stream of $500,000. They started with one member organiser and only once she started to be successful did they gain the confidence to put on another five member organisers. In future, they will back their judgment and start with a team of six.

What works

Let's set out what we have learned over the last few years about organising workplaces.

Consider what is going through the minds of a group of non-union workers before an organiser goes anywhere near them.

They are probably generally fairly happy with their job. They have a job, which is a lot better than the alternative, their pay comes in and they may even be working in a job that they have trained for. They may see themselves on a career ladder – albeit on various rungs of the ladder.

The exception to this will be among low paid or casual workers – less than half of these will be satisfied with their level of pay nor are they satisfied with the quality of their jobs.[2] Many casual workers will "live in fear" – aware that the slightest complaint about the way they are treated will lead to no further shifts being offered.[3]

Permanent workers may not be afraid of the employer and his supervisors but they are likely to be at least very respectful of them. The workers know that these people have real power. The power to sack them, give them lousy shifts, the worst jobs, the withdrawal of flexibility – crucial in order to balance work and family responsibilities. They determine whether a pay increase is offered or whether the worker moves up the career ladder. Even if the worker leaves the job, the employer can do serious damage to his or her ability to get the next job.

A third of the employees are likely not to trust their employer and another third don't know whether they can trust him or not.[4]

The worker may in fact be being treated quite badly. It's just that they don't know what fair treatment is. They could be being paid less than the going rate in the industry for this kind of work or even less than the Award rate. If they are young, they may accept harsh treatment as the norm. That's the way the world of work is – as far as they have experienced it. Because we deal with these issues every day of the week, we must never presume that workers understand the degree to which they are being ripped off.

And even when obviously wrong things happen – like the bastardisation of apprentices or the sexual harassment of young women – the worker may feel that they have no power to seek redress. They haven't got the money to get advice, they don't know where to get it, they feel that the system is rigged against them and it's "my word against his".

There may be a few union members in the group, there will be supporters of the ALP or the Greens. Some will have been in unions before – but these will have had both good and bad experiences of unionism. Some will be pathologically opposed to unionism because of their family background or because of some real or perceived bad experience of unionism. Most will see some place for unions in society but few will automatically think that unions can do anything for them in their workplace.

All will have quite a keen understanding of the demand for labour in their industry or sector. They know that we have a relatively high effective unemployment rate, they will have some relative or friend who has suffered long periods of unemployment, many will have spent considerable time looking for a job.[5]

---

2   Watson et al, *Fragmented Futures*, Federation Press, 2003, p 26.

3   Pocock, B, Prosser, R and Bridge, K, "Only a Casual ... How Casual Work Affects Employees, Households and Communities in Australia" paper delivered to conference *Work Interrupted,* Melbourne, 2 August 2004.

4   Moorehead, A et al (eds), *Changes at Work. The 1995 Australian Workplace Industrial Relations Survey,* Longman, 1997, Table 12.14, p 255.

5   Watson et al, op cit, p 33.

They will understand that a large proportion of the workforce is casual and they will not be keen on anything that puts at jeopardy their job security.

The job of the organiser is to let workers understand how their treatment stacks up. Are they getting a fair share of the employer's profits? Should they have a say in how they are treated? What should reasonable treatment be – what does it look like? When things go wrong in the workplace who can the worker turn to? Even if the employer is treating them well by industry standards, do they have a say in how the workplace operates? Could their situation be better? Should the industry standard be better? After all, the standard for annual leave used be two weeks per year. If unions hadn't started to campaign for first three, and then four weeks leave, we would still be taking two weeks off a year.

The fundamental task is one of education. The workers need to have the opportunity of having their eyes opened to how they are being treated. What could be possible if only workers had a say, and had some power. If they are being poorly treated, there is something that they can do about it. They need to form a union. But before that can happen they need to have the hope that this will be possible. Building hope is the most difficult element of the process.

In many ways the job of organising such a group of workers in Australia is tougher than in America. There the employer can be forced by law – however difficult that may be – to grant recognition to his employees' wish to be represented by a union. In Australia, recognition comes only by the power exerted by the workers. There have been cases where the vast majority of workers have become union members and demanded that the employer bargain with them. The employer's response has been to do anything but bargain. The only persuasion possible has been a fairly crude battle over who was the more powerful.

Saul Alinsky – one of the great American community organisers – analysed the work of a union organiser in this way:

> He has taken a group of apathetic workers; he has fanned their resentments and hostilities by a number of means, including challenging contrasts of better conditions of other workers in similar industries. Most important, he has demonstrated that something can be done, and that there is a concrete way of doing it that has already proven its effectiveness and success: that by organising together as a trade union they will have the power and the instrument with which to make these changes. He now has the workers participating in a trade union and supporting its program. We must never forget that so long as there is no opportunity or method to make changes, it is senseless to get people agitated or angry, leaving them no course of action except to blow their tops.
>
> And so the labor organiser simultaneously breeds conflict and builds a power structure. The war between the trade union and management is resolved either through a strike or negotiation. Either method involves the use of power; the economic power of the strike or the threat of it which results in successful negotiations. No one can negotiate without the power to compel negotiation.[6]

---

6   Alinsky, Saul D, *Rules For Radicals*, Vintage Books, 1989, pp 118-119.

For all that to happen will rarely be easy. Fifty-two per cent of working Australians would like to be a member of a union.[7] Just 23 per cent are.[8] Why the discrepancy? My guess is that they are too scared to be a union member or they lack sufficient hope to think that a union could survive at their workplace. Most work in workplaces where there is no union presence. They know that making a move towards the union will not be approved of by the employer and may even end with them missing out on a long-coveted promotion or getting the sack. Alternatively, because there is no union there now, they can't imagine that a union could get itself organised in the future.

If it is not easy, we have to do the job properly. We have to work hard to make sure that we give workers every opportunity of working out for themselves whether they are being treated fairly. They have to be given the chance of overcoming their understandable fear of taking action in their own defence.

Let me have a guess about the way in which most unions at present go about this task of getting a workplace organised.

Most unions still have rights of access – although the federal government is trying to take these away. The organiser from a union with Award coverage will pay the site a visit and will try to meet as many people as possible and engage them in conversation. With a bit of luck she will have been to training and will use our standard frameworks. She will be trying to build rapport, ask questions, look for issues, and listen hard to build up a picture of the workplace and any likely activists. If she can't get access, she will stand outside – the site has been identified as a target by the Secretary of the union – and rain or shine there she is at the gate, handing out a leaflet, smile on face, trying to engage people in conversation.

Any information she gains may be written down when she gets back to the office – names of people prepared to speak to her, possible activists, issues she has identified, around which organising might take place.

The next day, the process will be repeated at another workplace and the next, at yet another worksite. The best time will be when someone rings in with a problem. The organiser will then hit the road, get out to the workplace and talk to the worker. Again, the training will kick in. Is the issue deeply felt, widely felt, winnable? Is this the way in to the rest of the workforce? Do you have any friends who feel the same way? Can I talk to a few of them at the coffee shop after work?

This is the process we are using to organise 7 million potential members?

Let's be honest about this. If that is the sum total of our organising approach – no matter what resources are thrown at the problem, we are never going to win. Too much of our current organising practice is amateur hour. We rush in

---

7   ACIRRT, Survey of community attitudes, 2001.

8   ABS, 6310.0, March 2004.

as if joining the union and standing up to the employer is as simple and obvious as buying milk for your cereal in the morning.

Think about the people I have described in a non-union workplace. Even if their employer is not particularly aggressive, the workers know the score. Employers are not happy about having to deal with a union. If workers think we are fat, loud-mouthed, aggressive blokes – and yes, they still think we wear cardigans[9] – bosses think we are devils complete with horns and a tail. We are the people who send businesses broke with crazy demands that can never be met. We are the ones who take away their power to manage! And even if they have more realistic preconceptions than this, they will still see their employees unionising as an implicit criticism, an indication of disloyalty.

It is one thing to have the organising techniques perfected – the listening skills, the ability to build rapport, the anger, hope, action framework – but they need to be located in a wider strategic framework that makes the decision to be unionised far safer for workers.

Walking in cold to a workplace is as much use as a used car salesman going door-to-door trying to flog a clapped out Holden. Given that scenario, we would instantly ask ourselves "Who are you? What are you trying to sell me? What are the costs going to be? What's the hidden agenda? Why are you wasting my time – I don't need what you have to sell."

Preparing the campaign

If a group of workers is going to be organised, they need to understand as soon as we talk to them that we know what we are doing. We need to know about their employer. What is his profitability? How many workers does he employ? What other sites are there? How important is this site to the whole operation? Can the site be relocated overseas or to another State? Can the work be outsourced? What are the skill levels of the employees and are their skills in short supply? Can the workers be replaced? What do we know about the employer? Does he have form in other worksites as a person treating workers badly or opposing unionisation? Who is his lawyer? If it is one of the usual suspects when it comes to aggressive anti-union campaigns, we need to be very professional about the conduct of the campaign or we are risking these workers' jobs. Are there any other parts of the firm that are unionised?

We also need to think through a way of finding out about the workers before we start to talk to them. Have we searched our membership records to see whether there are any of our members working there? Have we asked around among the union's delegates to see if there is a friend or relative that they know who is working there? Is there any way we can get a list of

---

9   Labor Council focus groups, 1996.

employees? Have we checked to see whether there have been any unfair dismissal proceedings involving workers at this site? Is there another union with members there? Are there maintenance workers going in there as labour hire workers who are in the union? Can they tell us about what it's like to work there?

Once we are confident that we know the basics, we need to start to build up a list of who is working there. The best way of doing that is by asking workers to help us. If you've seen the film *Norma Rae* you will have seen that process in action. The organiser there does stand outside the gates looking stupid and handing out a leaflet. But he has a purpose. He is looking for just one person who will take the leaflet and respond. Norma Rae takes it repeatedly and ridicules it every time. The leaflet's too long, then it's got too many big words. But he knows he has her. She's responded and he follows her up as the one that will crack the whole site for him. What's the first thing he asks for? He wants a list of names. That is his tool for organising the whole plant.

Again, if we keep our lists on a pad of paper in our bag then we need to rethink whether we are really serious about those 7 million workers out there without any power at all. If the organiser gets sick – what happens – the whole organising campaign stops and the activists are left high and dry? Does that look professional? Is that reassuring them that the union knows what it is doing?

The Organising Centre has prepared a database based on Troy Burton's work that is available to any union who wants it. Other unions, like the LHMU, have modified their membership database to contain the information. The Queensland Independent Education Union is investing in an American database to be used by their growth team of organisers. The virtue of these databases is that they act as a tool not just for creating a list of names but for controlling and guiding the whole organising campaign. What are we aiming to do as the campaign goes on? We want to have a broad based organising committee consisting of activists in every section of the targeted employer. We want to know how many of the workers are with us or against us. We want to know who are our leaders and who are our most committed opponents.

I saw just how valuable a database like this can be in the campaign to organise the workers at Rio Tinto's Iron Ore operations. The organiser there – Stewart Edward – used a database that gave him a clear record of how he was going. By colour coding each of the various categories of member – contact, activist, leader – he was able to show that in virtually every section and occupational grouping at the site, he had started to make progress and that some 10 per cent of the workers were prepared to be active. He could map where he had no contacts and would spend his time building activism there. By showing his organising committee where they were making progress, they would work even harder to get the database in shape.

House-calling

The work described above needs as far as possible to be done in secret. The walk through the workplace I have described on day one of the typical organising campaign is as good as a letter to the management's lawyers warning them to get their injunctions printed! What's more, we make the announcement that we are going to organise the site, without any strength on the ground and knowing nothing about whether there are issues to be organised around or what those issues might be.

No matter how skilled we are as organisers in communicating with non-members, they are not going to want to talk to us openly in front of the employer. Even if they do, it is not going to be a useful conversation. There may be exceptions, if we start with a position of power or in an isolated workplace.

We may even get a few sympathetic people to both speak to us and sign on but if we talk to them in front of the employer, all that has happened is that we have identified our supporters to the employer. All the workers who are sitting on the fence – and that will be most of the rest – are likely to be educated that joining the union is a very bad thing indeed. Our supporters will start to get intense management supervision, the "more in sorrow than in anger" chats, the lousy shifts, the performance management interviews, the warnings about breaches of long ignored protocols.

What we want is to get the obvious sympathisers signed up – of course. But we want to do it in secret and then ask them to talk to the people sitting on the fence about why we need to get their workplace organised. We need them to get our lists developed. We need them to find out what issues are liable to unite the workplace. Organising a workplace depends not on our rusted on supporters. The people who make the difference to success or failure are the people who know nothing about unions or about whether the deal they are getting is fair or not.

The key to getting the people in the middle supporting the setting up of a union in their workplace is the conversation that we have with them. At present, the most common of our conversations happens in the workplace – for all the reasons I have outlined above, probably the worst place that conversation could happen. At best, organisers have shifted the location on occasion to the pub or the coffee shop around the corner from work.

I want to make the case that the best place to have the conversation is at the worker's home. Most organisers instinctively come up with the 20 reasons why that won't work. Workers will hate the idea of the union organiser becoming like a door-to-door salesperson. They will think it is intrusive if we knock on their door at night. It isn't safe for organisers to be wandering the streets at night. We will be interrupting the workers' precious family life. House-calling may be okay in the US or Canada but it is not culturally appropriate to Australia or New Zealand.

If we are honest, there will be other reasons at the back of our minds. Organisers don't want to spend their nights tramping the streets knocking on doors. Working nights means that any social life goes out the window. We don't like the idea of people rejecting us and slamming the door in our face.

In the face of all this, why do I persist in trying to get Australian and New Zealand organisers to use this method of face-to-face contact? The reason is simple. *There is no better place to have a quality conversation with a prospective member.* Remember what we are doing when we talk to a worker about joining the struggle to organise a workplace. We are talking to someone we have probably never met before and seeking to gain their trust. We have to build rapport. They have to see that we have a similar outlook on life to them. We are asking someone to think deeply about the way they are treated at work. We are trying to overcome their very real and accurate perception that doing something about this will place them at odds with their employer. By the end of our meeting we will 'call the question' and ask them to do something concrete – sign a card, help us talk to other workers, give us information about their employer – but we will get them to do something. That's a big ask.

The first constraint on us achieving all this is time. This is not a ten-minute conversation. Unless they are for some reason absolutely dying to join the union and help with the struggle – and that can happen – the conversation is going to take time. That instantly knocks out quite a few venues. Few people can stand around at their workplace and have a lengthy conversation. Not many can do it in a coffee shop during a break.

More important than time, however, is the mental attitude of the worker. Do they feel comfortable and unpressured talking to us? Are they worried that someone will see them talking to the union organiser?

The benefit of talking to a worker in their home is that is where they are most comfortable. If at any time they decide that they don't want to talk to you anymore, they can ask you to leave and you will. They know that knocking on doors at night is difficult – you have demonstrated your credentials. You are serious about organising their workplace.

In a worker's home it is easy to build rapport. If the kids come out to meet you, you can talk to them. You can establish contact on the worker's terms. That is the foundation on which you can talk through the issues. Because it is in their own controlled environment they will feel far more ready to open up to you about how they really feel about work. In their own home they will talk about what action they are prepared to take.

Organising house by house allows the organiser to have a far better chance of controlling the speed at which the union announces its presence. We want to let the boss know we are organising when we have a clear majority on our side. We risk everything if he can act against us when we are weak.

How do I know that house-calling is successful? It's true that I was first convinced by American and Canadian officials telling me of their success. Their perception is backed up by the academic work of people like Kate Bronfenbrenner and her colleagues.[10] House-calling with its opportunity for one-to-one contact is one of the factors which give far higher chances of organising victory.

But the clincher for me is that just about every time in Australia or New Zealand we have tried this kind of contact, provided we have done the preparation, the experience has been positive. Workers have even said, "Gee, it's good that you are going door-to-door. It's the only way that you have a chance to get the jump on the boss." Others are touched that we are so serious about organising that we will actually take the time to come to their house. Far more workers understand what we are doing and agree to help at the end of one of these conversations than we expect. At the end of 30 minutes in a worker's home we are much more confident that he or she has quite a deep understanding of what is going on and what will be necessary. We are far more confident than we would be at the end of any number of mass meetings or snatched conversations in a pub or coffee shop.

Are there problems with house-calling? Absolutely.

It depends on having good lists of names and addresses. That's why I have earlier described the importance of creating good lists before organising. However we get them, we must have lists that are accurate and up-to-date. House-calling is hugely labour intensive. It works only where the union allocates sufficient resources to the campaign. We waste those resources and destroy the self-confidence of our organisers if most of the addresses we give them are wrong.

We have enormous problems finding the best time to call on people. I have spent an entire Sunday with a list of names, getting one hit – and that person turned out to be the management stooge! House-calling requires that we spend a lot of time driving around in cars – all time wasted. The payoff always is that when we do make contact we have a much better chance of achieving success.

We need to do the work in identifying the issues that might be a starting point for our conversation. Given its labour-intensive nature, we don't want to spend our precious time in a worker's home fishing for the right issue with no prior knowledge of what the workplace problems are likely to be.

Does it muck up our social life?

I'm afraid so. We have to be there when workers are home available to talk to us. That means that our private lives suffer. It's one of the reasons why being an organiser is not an easy job. And union leaders have to be conscious that working nights means that organisers will be late in the next day. It means that

---

10 Bronfenbrenner, K and Hickey R, "Changing to Organize, A National Assessment of Union Strategies" in R Milkman and K Voss (eds) *Rebuilding Labor, Organizing and Organizers in the New Union Movement,* ILR Press, 2004.

organisers will be given days off during slack times. I don't believe that dedication means that organisers have to live in the union office or on the job.

What about safety?

Bill Granfield is the President of HERE Local 100 in New York City. This is the union that organises workers in restaurants and catering firms.

I asked him how his organisers went house-calling workers in their homes in the suburbs and inner city of New York. It sounded pretty dangerous to me.

His answer was that that was where workers lived every day. If organisers were the representatives of workers, why should they be afraid to go to the homes of workers? Provided that they were clearly not the police, welfare or immigration, people in these neighbourhoods tended to be pretty welcoming.

That is true of us I am sure. At the same time it is also true that we have to be sensible about security and take basic precautions. But we have to be prepared to do whatever will help us succeed in giving power to workers.

Remember why we are making the shift to organising in the first place. Workers need power if they are to have a decent life and we have to be prepared to do whatever it takes to bring that about. Let's face it, we will be taking workers way outside their comfort zone and we have to be prepared to get outside our own.

Educating workers

The key activity is educating workers about the situation they are in. They may not be able to recognise bad behaviour when they see it, thinking it's what every employer does.

I remember a young Organising Works trainee organiser Catherine Palaszczuk (now Savage) from the SDA in Queensland telling me about trying to organise one of her Red Rooster outlets. She kept asking the workers whether they had any complaints about the way management was treating them. All replied no, the boss was very fair. The meeting with the workers she had organised started to break up when one of the young women came up to her and quietly asked, "Is it OK for the boss to make us clean the restaurant at night after we have clocked off?" You can guess the rest. She is a good organiser.

Educating workers is primarily about communication. It is often difficult for the organiser to reach every section of the workforce but the workers themselves can be given the tools to get messages across to their co-workers.

Management at one of Sydney's biggest hotels doubled the price of meals in the staff canteen without explanation. The workers were relatively lowly paid and this increase made a difference. It was also doubly galling because they saw their senior management regularly eating in the hotel restaurant, apparently for free. They decided to have a lunch in the foyer of the hotel in front of the registration desk. Not every worker participated but every worker got the message that the change was unfair and that something could be done about it.

Escalating pressure tactics

If we want workers to be involved in the union, we have to take things at their pace, rather than at the pace of the most radical of our supporters. If we do that, we educate workers about the way a union works: they decide on the action; they are comfortable about what they do; they see that acting together works. That's why escalating pressure tactics are so important. We will scare off fence sitters if the first thing we do is propose a course of action that is too intimidating.

I am a repeat offender in this regard. I went on the road a few years ago with a young organiser from the Municipal Employees Union[11] Rebecca Zinghini. I suspect she thought it was pretty good having such an expert with her! She was organising sports centres and she brought me along to a meeting with a potential member. Her aim was to find out what issues he had and whether we could do anything about them. He described a situation where a council's management was treating the staff in an outrageous manner. We certainly could put a stop to it. So yours truly jumped in, took over from Rebecca who was doing a perfectly good job and suggested that he might like to get a group of his colleagues together and we would go and get an appointment to see the Labor Mayor of the Council.

You couldn't see him for dust!

You get the point. I did. What we might consider to be minimally risky may be very intimidating for others.

We have to start with small united steps that build the confidence of those involved. We may pick actions that are not directed at the employer at all. We may ask workers to take action in support of increased funding for the industry or respect for workers delivering a service to the public. Even with the big step of taking industrial action, we can build worker confidence in the power of the collective with preliminary steps.

For example, the workers at Star City Casino in Sydney wanted to test whether they could trust each other to actually stop work. Prior to their strike, they decided to do something small: if you were going to strike, you wore a blue band aid on your left little finger. They all did and the strike went ahead.

When Star City Casino tried to make wearing white socks the cause of a formal warning to one young worker, the entire staff on his shift came to work the next day wearing white socks.

---

11   Now called the United Services Union.

Workers in local government have flown balloons from their desk that said "The boss's wage offer is hot air." The BHP Iron Ore workers once queued up one Monday morning to insist they have a drug test in case they were over the limit. A long delay in starting work ensued and of course the company was stuck with the cost of the test. On another occasion they plastered signs on the notice board "Remember, it's on at noon tomorrow!" The company thought that a strike was being planned. They flew in security officers from Perth – over 1000 kms away – to protect their property. At the appointed time, when a cake appeared to celebrate a birthday, BHP looked pretty silly.

Very often the point of these actions is to test whether they can act together, but they are primarily to have a laugh at the boss's expense. It instantly reminds the workers that they are in charge of their union and that they can have a bit of fun in the process.

The aim of the campaign

Every time an action is taken, the workplace should be moving closer and closer to high density and developed activists. We are not really taking these actions to cause economic harm to the employer– their point is to show the workers that they are capable of organising collective action when they need to. The long term message is that to keep doing that, they need to do more. They need to be activists themselves – and at the minimum volunteer to speak to five other people in their workplace.

Most good organisers get this point about building activism. They can get members to identify themselves as union supporters and take a lead in full view of the boss. They can get workers to exercise real power by embarking on their campaign around stunts and short stoppages.

But I am amazed how often organisers are shy about getting members to sign the union card. There is something in us that makes us embarrassed about putting the question to the worker. Are you with us or not? Are you going to join us? Or are you supporting the employer and the way he treats you and your colleagues?

I can understand that people are reluctant to do this. I'm not in love with selling raffle tickets for APHEDA[12] either. But we have to ask ourselves do we believe in what we are doing? Do we think that joining the union does make a difference? Do we need them to sign up so that we can start rebuilding the power of workers and their families? Because without that card being signed, the whole process of organising the workplace stops. You can't be a union

---

12   Australian People for Health Education and Development Abroad (APHEDA) is the
      ACTU's Union Aid organisation.

member in theory. We either have your signature – your written pledge of allegiance to the people you work with – or we don't.

Lead organisers

Success depends on more than just the skills or techniques of the individual organiser.

Lead organisers are critical if we are serious about deploying a team against a particular target. We need someone to track the progress of the team as a whole. We need assessments to be made of our power and whether it is growing. Where tactics fail, what is to replace them.

Above all, the job of an organiser is a complex one and no matter how good the individual is, they need help from a lead organiser to keep them on track. They need to have someone who helps them with the preparation, the gathering of lists, the construction of a plan that has a good chance of winning. They need to report on a daily basis to their lead so that the union is certain that every day that goes by, the union is getting closer to another organising victory. They need to talk through each contact with a worker so that the organiser can constantly learn how to handle the interaction better.

This is a strange constraint for many Australian unions. The system has been that we hired good organisers and then left them to get on with it. Organisers don't like the idea of having to report to someone about every conversation they have had.

But the conversations we have with members are golden opportunities. We have to give ourselves the best chance that we possibly can for it to be productive.

Tiffanie Reid – an organiser on exchange from the SEIU who we used as a lead organiser in a range of campaigns – taught me the necessity for a new way of working. She was absolutely appalled that one of the organisers that she was mentoring could have proposed going in to a meeting with members without preparing a clear agenda, without planning out in detail the desired outcome of the meeting and without role playing how he would deal with some of the expected objections from workers to the course of action being suggested. I didn't want to look like an idiot so I wholeheartedly agreed. "Yes, yes, Tiffanie – shocking!"

But while I was saving face in front of Tiffanie, I had to admit to myself that I had never planned a single members' meeting at that level of detail in my whole union career! I got away with it because all the people I was talking to were rusted-on members of the union and were never going to be sacked for taking a union stand. The union was sufficiently powerful that employers would generally not dream of really trying to discriminate against a member on the basis of union activity.

Those days are long gone.

In external organising, the people in a meeting are not necessarily members, they haven't established their power in a workplace and they are utterly vulnerable to employer attack. Even in internal organising, the days of workers being impervious to anything the employer can do to them are generally gone. In both cases, we can't afford mistakes. We have to get it right every time and that means that organisers need the help of a lead organiser to prepare what is being said and how the strategy will be run.

In every union trying to organise, because organisers are human and skill levels are variable, we know that organisers are mucking up the most basic of interviews with prospective members. They fail to listen. They forget to inoculate against the boss's campaign. They are not very good at describing how the union will make a difference to the life of the worker. They drag workers way beyond their comfort zones in relation to the action they propose. They don't get the worker to commit to a task. Every time one of those mistakes is made, the campaign moves further and further away from success.

Mistakes will happen. But with a lead organiser on the job we are maximising the chances that we will learn from our mistakes and not repeat them.

Organisers need to be prepared to accept quite detailed guidance on how to conduct conversations with workers. If we are using the organising frameworks, then we need to be able to report how they went and the worker's response. If action was proposed, did we get the worker's commitment to do it? Did we "call the question?" Have we got a signed card? What are the names of the other workers that our worker agreed to contact?

The risks to the worker of a botched conversation are too great for us to leave the process to chance. Organisers suffer disappointment, workers can suffer the loss of their job.

Finally, we need to recognise that the number of people with the skills and experience to be a good organiser are limited. We need lead organisers to be constantly developing organisers so that we have more and better organisers. Those good organisers that we have need to be given the chance to work as lead organisers.

Concentrating resources

We have to concentrate our resources on a limited number of targets.

That's not the way we have done it in the past. It is quite common for a union Secretary to allocate one or two thousand prospective members to a single organiser. Indeed, she will be lucky not to have a few hundred existing members thrown in to look after as well!

We shouldn't be surprised that an impossible task will prove to be impossible!

Most American unions will allocate one organiser to every 100 workers if they really want to succeed in a campaign. In some unions this may go as low as one organiser to every 50 workers. The reason is that the organiser needs to talk to every worker at length and that will generally happen away from the workplace and usually in the worker's home.

That takes time over an extended period. Workers may respond to an initial visit but they will then need to be debriefed once they have completed their first action. Their leaders need time to be developed. They need the reassurance of an organiser to build their confidence. When the employer fights back against the organising push, the union needs to have the organiser there helping develop the strategy to defeat that attack. Defeats will happen and the organiser needs to have the time to deal with setbacks – to renew the confidence of the workers and their workplace leaders in their strategy and the strength of their collective.

Establishing a sense of urgency

It is possible for an organiser to spend years organising a single worksite – chipping away week after week, gradually building density. That is not a sustainable strategy for a number of reasons.

It allows workers to put off the day when they have to make up their mind about joining the union. If we don't face them with a deadline – why not put off signing the card until tomorrow?

Taking time to organise a worksite means that we give the employer time to work out what our tactics will be and who our leaders are.

I saw this at the NSW Transport Workers Union (TWU) with their campaign against a large courier company. Bruce Penton, their Organising Director, told me the story. The company was aggressively anti-union and paid substandard wages and conditions to their drivers. Bruce allocated an organiser to the company and let her get on with it. She chipped away, developing one group of leaders, staging some low impact actions, signing up a few members. The employer responded aggressively. No key breakthrough was made with the result that the members became dispirited and high turnover – because the job was so lousy – meant that the organiser was running in order to stand still. No sooner had she got density up than it fell back as a group of new employees started work.

In effect, the union was training the employer in how to respond to the full range of union tactics, without ever securing a breakthrough that would allow the union to exercise power.

Bruce came to the conclusion that the way to beat a company like this was to hit them with all his organisers for ten weeks. An intensive campaign would mean that the employer didn't have time to respond effectively.

Putting ten organisers onto a thousand person workplace for an indefinite period is not achievable. But putting them into the same workplace for a set period of ten weeks may be. Having that level of concentration gives members an understanding that the union is serious about building industry power but they will only have one opportunity to take the risks necessary to play their part. They understand that it is now or never.

Developing a model of organising

Unions tend to approach each new organising challenge completely afresh – as if they have never done it before. We need to develop a model.

Most unions in Australia, even those well developed down the path of shifting to an organising culture, are struggling to develop a model of organising that works for them– a set of standard procedures that adapts organising's basic principles to the particular circumstances of the union, its industries and the workers it seeks to represent.

Troy Burton and CFMEU Mining and Energy Division have managed to create a process which they have used successfully in the mines they have organised.

They are shortly to start organising non-union mine contractors. That may mean that they alter their strategy to take into account the particular circumstances of that workforce. They will have to develop a new model on the basis of what has worked and not worked in this slightly different environment.

One other union seems to have settled a pattern of organising that works well.

The LHMU National Office's Organising Department's Louise Tarrant, Angela Keeffe and Jess Walsh – have started to refine one such standard model that they use when they have a substantial, if minority, level of density in a large workplace.

A model that depends on organising from a group of existing members seems to me to be pretty useful for most Australian and New Zealand unions. Because of the open shop nature of our unionism, many workplaces will have some membership density. They have a core of members who can potentially act on behalf of the union inside the workplace.

The set up phase of the LHMU campaigns consists of the relevant organiser gathering a list of members and as many non-members as possible and trying to identify a unifying issue around which organising can take place.

The union starts their campaign by phoning every one of the members in that workplace. The organisers test the issue with the members and ask them to be involved either as a committee member or as a contact – someone prepared to distribute information to their co-workers.

Volunteers are visited at home by the organiser to assess the commitment of the member and to educate them as to what needs to be done to lift density and increase activity in the workplace.

These activists are then involved in building the power and confidence of the members – to raise the issue in the workplace and demonstrate the ability of the union to achieve small victories . These members are also used to ensure the list of non-members is accurate.

After some weeks of this kind of activity, the union house-calls the non-members. The aim is to sign up new members so that the union moves quickly to representing the vast bulk of workers prior to going into negotiations with the employer.

The union can then negotiate an enterprise agreement with the employer, secure in the knowledge that it has a large majority signed to the union and with a demonstrated ability to exercise power within the workplace.

There are pros and cons to this approach. We obviously need to have activists in every section. The approach will only work where we have a substantial level of density so that the membership is large enough to act as a pool from which we can draw activists in the right places. It would be better to have a higher level of activism that extends beyond existing members.

But the advantage of the model is that it enables the union to move quickly, concentrate resources and get a win for workers. With a win at the bargaining table under its belt, it will presumably be much easier to approach newly-joined members to become active in the process of agreement implementation. The model also allows the union to act so quickly and in such secrecy that the employer doesn't have time to prepare a counter strategy. Delegate networks are built through phone and house-calling and members are signed up in a blitz. The first the employer knows of the union's strength is when they appear at the bargaining table.

Managing organiser performance

The union has to provide organisers with a 'doable' job. They need to be freed of a grievance load, their efforts targeted at either internal or external areas, they need mentoring, a model of organising that works – everything we have discussed in these chapters.

But it is also true that at present, some organisers don't do very much at all. Our accountability systems are weak, we presume that everyone is as dedicated as we are and that left to themselves, organisers will get on and do as good a job as they can for members. But some staff will be sitting back with their feet up. Others have had enough of the crisis afflicting us. They are demoralised and have given up. Others may be quite prepared to work hard, but don't have the ability to do the job.

Union leaders have to manage as well as lead. We have to make hard decisions about who remains employed by the union if we are to have a chance of serving the interests of members. Having said that, we are unions and we have to do what we demand of bosses. We have to treat our own staff fairly.

Notice, though, that we don't – or we shouldn't – demand of bosses that they keep on every employee no matter how hopeless. Our action in defence of sacked workers is to stop arbitrary, unfair attacks on employment security.

That goes for union staff as well.

The hard reality is that this is a much tougher environment than we have faced in 100 years. Some of our existing staff will not make the grade and we have to face that fact. If they lack the required skills, they need to be given training. If they have difficulty in applying the training in the real world of the union, then they need to be given mentoring and support. They need to be shown where their performance is deficient. They need to be given fair warning that their performance needs to improve. But when unionism is fighting for its life, when workers give their time, pay money, risk their livelihoods for their union, members should be able to expect that organisers can and will do the job of leading them, skilfully and diligently.

The most frustrating part of insisting on accountability for union staff occurs in those unions where staff are persuaded, almost irrespective of the facts, that sacking one of their colleagues is bad and must be opposed. Staff need to make certain that a fair procedure has been followed. But if that is done, the union's leadership – and its members – have a right to expect that poor performance is sanctioned. Leaders doing their job should be supported by staff.

15

The role of the industrial officer

In a union movement highly dependent on institutional power, the key role in many unions has been that of the industrial officer. That's what I was and so were many of our most senior union officials. We were the ones who knew the secret rubric of the Commission, had the confidence to go up against the boss's lawyers, do the deals that delivered for members. Our work was not just backroom wheeling and dealing. We had the ability to go down to workplaces and talk with some authority to our members on the ins and outs of their 'case'.

The *Workplace Relations Act* of 1996 damaged our institutional power and in so doing limited the ability of industrial officers to deliver for their members. In many State jurisdictions, industrial officers have continued to do their job with very little change. The State Commissions retained their ability to settle disputes by arbitration and that meant unions needed advocates with a high level of skill and confidence.

John Howard's most recent legislation will put a nail in the coffin of our institutional power. The Award system, if not dead, will gradually decline to irrelevance. Nowhere in Australia – apart from what is left of the State Commissions[1] – will there exist an arbitral tribunal with the power to settle disputes and make awards. What role then is there for the industrial officers currently employed by unions?

It strikes me that five vital roles remain for industrial or legal officers if organisers are to be able to fulfil their function.

First, the legislation that is due to pass through the Senate will contain a minefield of provisions designed to trip up organisers in doing their job. Rules about access to the workplace, notification about bargaining periods and secret ballots before taking protected action will become increasingly complicated. It will take six weeks to get a one-day strike approved and three days for an employer to lock his workers out.

In addition, the government has given a regulatory mandate to various institutions to actively seek out opportunities to prosecute unions and their

---

[1] State Industrial Relations Commissions will only have the power to deal with those parts of the workforce not employed by corporations. This will largely be employees of unincorporated associations and direct employees of the State Governments.

officers and members for breaches of the law. The ACCC can be expected to pounce on any breach of the *Trade Practices Act*. The Office of the Employment Advocate (OEA) has the job of hunting down any officer guilty of inhibiting a worker's right not to associate together. (We don't see a similar enthusiasm for defending their right to associate!) The OEA will also have the chance to vet and delay the approval of any registered agreement it deems is not in accordance with the provisions of the Act. And most extraordinarily, the legislation gives to the Building Industry Taskforce Star Chamber style rights to interrogate any member or official in the building industry as they look for any possible breach of the law. The legislation covers some eight unions with coverage in the industry. Penalties for breach of any section of these complex laws will be lifted.

A minefield has been set for us and we need legally-competent industrial officers who can advise organisers how to navigate their way through it. The law may need to be challenged but it should not be challenged by accident. If we choose to fight it out in the courts, we need to consider carefully which facts will be most beneficial to the case and which cases are of sufficient strategic importance.

Secondly, industrial officers may in some unions – like the QPSU – be asked to shoulder the burden of dealing with individual claims and grievances.

Thirdly, industrial officers have an important role to play in pursuing the union's bargaining agenda. The task of negotiating an important industrial agreement clause by clause is a skilled one – an organiser may not have those skills. Above all, the task is time consuming and organisers should avoid as far as possible becoming bogged down in days spent at the bargaining table. This is particularly the case where the Industrial Relations Commission plays a mediation role. It's difficult to organise locked inside the negotiating room.

Fourthly, industrial officers can be vital in taking the pressure off organisers trying to represent a large number of members all of whom may well have enterprise agreements coming up for renewal within the same 12-month period. Most unions have not yet found ways of bargaining as an industry. That means that a single organiser can be responsible for the maintenance and negotiation of literally hundreds of agreements. In each bargaining cycle some will be prioritised as agreements around which organising needs to take place, for example, large or strategically important worksites. To do that job properly, other agreements will have to be de-prioritised. In such a case, industrial officers can be given the task of getting the industry standard at the bargaining table and then moving on as quickly and efficiently as possible.

Finally, as employers settle down and realise that unions are not going away, some may well seek to build a cooperative relationship with their collectively-organised employees. Disputes will be settled by mutually-agreed arbitration in what remains of the Industrial Relations Commission. Again in such a case, the proceedings should be handled by an industrial officer, instead of removing an organiser away from the work she has been hired to do.

The current hostile environment means that industrial officers will need to be of the highest standard. We cannot afford to carry officers with a low level of skill. Whether bargaining, advising on compliance or advocating the union's position, we need to recognise that any deficiency in capacity will be quickly exposed – to the detriment of the members we represent and the credibility of the union.

16

Union education

Union education is no different from any other category of union expenditure. It has to be justified against the driving need to increase members' power and the reach of the union into the non-union workforce. That means that training for its own sake – and the education of members is a very worthy aim in itself – is very difficult to justify. This, I know, is hard. Workers don't have enough access to education as it is and their access is being increasingly limited as governments increase the cost of education at TAFEs and universities. But we are desperate. We are at 23 per cent density with little sign that we can get above that in the foreseeable future. Governments and employers continue to drive us out of existence. That means that our education programs have to go under the microscope.

What does this mean in practical terms? I doubt that many unions have thought about what they are trying to achieve in training. If you want to assess how important training is to a union, think of how often the union secretary or one of the senior officials drops in to do a session or have any interaction with the participants. If they are never sighted from one course to the next – that says something about how highly it is valued.

Some unions of course, have no training program at all. Others regard training as something that has to be offered to members or it will look bad. They arrange for courses to be scheduled but if the course doesn't run for lack of participants that is not the union's fault.

Most union leaders understand the importance of having good delegates. They presume delegate training will result in better levels of workplace activism.

Some recognise that good delegates can help us with cementing unionism in already organised workplaces and can do the infill organising that is relatively easy in many areas while the full time organisers get on with the really low density sites or with the work of bargaining agreements. That means that unions put lots of delegates through courses that have some organising content. Much of the training that is offered will be generalised courses based on the original TUTA[1] courses developed 20 years ago addressing the structure of the union,

---

1   The Australian Trade Union Training Authority was set up by the Whitlam Labor Government in 1975, had its funding increased by Malcolm Fraser and was abolished by John Howard in 1996. It had the responsibility of training Australia's delegates and union staff. We refer to it as "Old TUTA" in contrast to its replacement, the union funded, "New TUTA".

the nature of the industrial relations system, the history of the union and unionism generally. Increasingly there will be training sessions on organising and communication skills – how we talk to prospective members about building the power of the union. There may even be sessions on mapping the workplace so that members can see how we go about assessing our power in a workplace.

To work out what training we need, think back to what has been said already in this book about internal organising. We are trying to build self-sufficient union workplaces with workplace leaders who are confident in representing members to their employer and handling grievances, who can speak at inductions or approach new employees the day they start work and activists who are confident about talking to members about taking action or to prospective members about joining the union.

We know, don't we, that the way to develop activists is action. We give workers jobs to do – and when they have done them – *then* they are entitled to describe themselves as activists and not just union supporters.

That vision of self-sufficiency, confidence and action needs to inform our training.

The outcome of every training session has to be action – otherwise I suspect that the training is largely wasted. If it is not applied back in the workplace, how can we justify the expenditure of training dollars?

The selection of participants

Almost all unions randomly select course participants through advertisements in the union magazine or on the web site.

If action is what we are after, random selection of participants just won't work. We have to be far more careful about picking the participants. We want to include all those people that the organisers think are on the cusp of shifting from support to actually doing something. We want the people who will benefit most from the confidence and skills that training can provide.

At present, we can get the "usual suspect" participants – people who look for any opportunity of getting off work. Some unions' trainers report to me that the people they get volunteering for training can have attended a large number of training days while most of the other delegates have received little or no training at all.

Most importantly, random selection usually means that participants come from a wide scattering of workplaces. Remember that at the end of training the participants should be prepared to take some form of action – speaking to other workers, doing a workplace map, taking round a petition, doing a survey. That's very difficult to do on your own – no matter how enthusiastic the member or how inspiring the training. But if people from the same workplace get together, they feed off each other, give each other confidence and have the chance to encourage each other to actually deliver.

We need to construct the participants' list in such a way that workers from the same – or related workplaces – go to training together. If a workplace group is trained together it is far easier to get the relevant organiser to be part of the training – even if it is only the action stage in the last session. And we simply have to have the organiser involved. She has to follow up each of the course participants to find out whether they have done what they committed to do, to give encouragement, to support in the event of setback, to provide on-going advice and mentoring.

Just imagine that you are a worker who has volunteered to be an activist. You take time off from work, attend the training, do the role plays, concentrate hard in the classroom for the entire duration of the course and at the end agree that you will take some action. You get back to your workplace and do what you promised to do – at some cost, because action is always scary.

And no one from the union office comes near you. No one turns up to say what a great job you have done.

Can we blame the activist if they get turned off union activity? Can we blame them if they think less of the union's competence? Are activists not entitled to make the judgment that if the organiser can't follow up on this low-profile, low-stress activity, they will go missing when the workers are asked to do something big and confronting?

The evidence that this is the case is overwhelming. David Peetz and two of the educators at the Finance Sector Union, Carol Webb and Meredith Jones, undertook an analysis of training outcomes in their union.[2] Figure 16.1 illustrates their analysis.

Their graph shows that where the organiser follows up the members post-training, more of them are more committed and scarcely any of them are less committed. Where no follow-up occurs, the union's reputation actually goes backwards.

One answer to this is for the organiser to train the members. And a good organiser is essentially an educator. But that takes time and that is a commodity that organisers don't have.

The role of the union educator

The role of trainer must become one of the key support roles in any union. They have to be at the centre of campaign strategy. When the union decides that the time has come to organise around an issue or a forthcoming enterprise bargain,

---

2   Peetz, D, Webb, C and Jones, M, *Activism amongst workplace delegates*, Queensland Council of Unions Biennial Conference of Executive and Provincial Councils, 24 September 2002.

Figure 16.1: Change in commitment to union, post-training

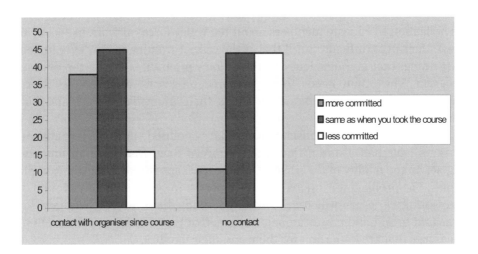

who should have the time to work intensively with the workplace organising committee to get them ready for action? Who has the skills to do it? Who has been freed of the responsibility for looking after everything except supporting the educational development of members?

Why doesn't it happen now? Often because the trainers' time is taken up with running endlessly scheduled courses where participants are randomly selected. They are not given the freedom to involve themselves in the strategy sessions so that they can show lead organisers and organisers what they can do to get a group of members really firing and active. And organisers aren't asking for a trainer's involvement because they have never seen what a good trainer can do for them and the members.

It should also be said that some trainers are not comfortable with such a role. Perhaps they were selected to train because they couldn't organise. Some of our best organisers should become trainers so that they can magnify the union's capability to develop members in a campaign.

Such a structure for union education, located at the centre of campaigning activity, means that union education moves from being a peripheral, expendable activity to being at the heart of union work – the empowerment of members. It fixes the problem of follow up. Organisers will know whether actions planned in a training session are done because those actions form the core of a bargaining strategy that is at the heart of their success or failure.

Education beyond bargaining

Of course, if this is the only training done by the union, then the union fails in its obligation to educate members about the wider forces at work in society that make their lives difficult. But if that is the case, if training is only ever linked to bargaining, that is a deficiency in the *union's* program – not in the education program. The union needs to be prepared to get its members involved in campaigns that lift their horizons above their immediate bread and butter concerns.

As the American organiser Jane McAlavey pointed out to me recently, most workers have half a dozen things that concern them that have an immediate impact on the quality of their lives. Of these, perhaps two or three are workplace issues. The problem for unions is that we persist in organising only around only the workplace issues which are within our immediate control. We have to be prepared to so build power among workers that they can have an impact on all the issues that are important for them and their families.

Unions have always had policies on issues beyond the workplace. A few have actually taken action in support of those policies. They have taken their members en masse to demonstrate outside the head offices of exploitative corporations, organised demonstrations in support of Aboriginal land rights, formed the core of the anti-Vietnam moratorium marches.

If we are to do more than talk about our social responsibility, then we have to campaign around issues like the preservation of Medicare or the rights of workers' children to have access to affordable university or vocational education. Education needs to form a key part of that work. The vast bulk of our 1.8 million members haven't got a clue about what is happening in their society. They may know that something is going wrong with Medicare because they can't get a bulk billing doctor. But they don't know the detail.

The sad fact is that because our campaigning on these issues is limited to the odd leaflet or petition we never give ourselves the opportunity of speaking to our members in depth so that we can move them to action.

Union education is a marvellous opportunity for us to give workplace leaders a clear understanding of what is going on and why they need to get members involved in doing something about it.

Organising around political issues should play a role in building the power of workers (see Chapter 22). If that is to happen, the union education program has to form the core of that activity. If we don't take the time to educate workers about the issues, then we can do nothing more than simply reflect the existing concerns and prejudices of many of our members.

There are two levels of education possible here – one aimed at activists and delegates and the other at members directly. Social issues have the potential to attract different people to the ranks of the activist. Workers may be prepared to leave the bread and butter bargaining issues to the shop steward or delegate.

But issues like Medicare or our involvement in Iraq or Aboriginal land rights or the environment have the ability to appeal to a different kind of member. We should grab that opportunity with both hands and use the education process to inform these members and get them ready to step up to the next level of action.

There is also a role for us to use education as a way of approaching our members generally. Our "issue activists" could be given the ability to run lunchtime training sessions for members on the issues they are passionate about. There is no better way of getting our message across. It also has the potential to bring our members alive with concern for issues wider than simply the usual collective bargaining issues.

Educating to build a movement

The union also needs to have aspirations to organise workers beyond the individual workplaces of each union. Indeed, if Australian unions are to continue to speak for all workers and their families, they need to have the capacity to involve their members in broad movement-wide activity.

One of the strengths of "Old TUTA" was that it brought together delegates and officials from across the movement in common training programs. This also had a lot of disadvantages. It meant that the training was not customised to the particular circumstances facing a single union. It certainly meant that random selection of participants took place. Many would argue that by outsourcing union education to a government-funded authority it marginalised union education and isolated it from mainstream union activity. But delegates from every kind of union spent time with each other and recognised how much they had in common.

We need to recreate that feeling.

Education is about the transmission of skills and information. It is also about the creation of inspiration, motivation and enthusiasm for the struggle in which workers are engaged and works more effectively when workers see with their own eyes the power of a large group.

For most union officials in the current era, the Patrick's dispute was a highpoint in their union careers, partly because they can all tell war stories about being there when a huge number of unionists stood together. It is the fact that we were there in force on the picket lines that provides us with some of our best memories.

Similarly, I have seen the enthusiasm generated among members at delegates' conventions conducted now by a range of unions – the NUW in Victoria, the LHMU in most States, the TWU in New South Wales. We saw that enthusiasm around the country in the week of action against the government's new industrial relation laws. There is something about getting a large number of members together in one place that feeds their understanding of the union as a force to be reckoned with – that reinforces their power as a collective of individuals.

There is a role to play in this area for union education.

Carl Leinonen is the Executive Officer of SEIU Local 1989 in Maine. He worked with us in Australia for ten weeks at the NSW TWU in 2004. He told me of a program that he has run for many years where over 200 members of his own and other unions come together for three days of residential training every year. They start on a Friday and go through the weekend. Participants take in the big presentations at a plenary meeting but then they break into streams for the three days and take elective subjects on issues of every kind from organising to union history. The point is less the content and more the fact that they live together for a Friday and a weekend with a common purpose. They go back to their workplace reenergised for the struggle to come over the next year.

Residential training is of course the most expensive kind of training but the benefits in solidarity, sense of heightened purpose and sheer enthusiasm, may well justify the cost.

Building involvement in union affairs

General education for activists needs to be aimed at those who have demonstrated their commitment to the union as activists. We want to educate more deeply veterans of union activity rather than just members that we think might be prepared to help organise their workplace. (I visited the Las Vegas local of the Hotel and Restaurant Employees Union in 2004 and met their delegates and organisers. The union covers the casinos and hotels in the city. A precondition for being a shop steward was that the member had to have spent time helping organise other casinos. The union was looking for veterans of house-calling campaigns to act as its workplace leaders.)

We want our members to play a part in the union's decision-making process. Yet unions still find it difficult to fill positions on the union's various committees and the task often falls to the people who have done the job for years. Apart from being unfair to them, it means that the union doesn't look like its membership. If we are signing up more young people, people from varying ethnic backgrounds and women, and the union is still run by the same blokes who have done the job for years, we are missing a tremendous opportunity to tap into the concerns of our new members. We don't look and feel like *their* organisation.

The union needs to spend time on building up a cadre of senior activists and shop stewards who receive education in the union's wider operations. This group needs to know what the key policy issues are for the union. They have to have an understanding of the political system in which we operate and why things are the way they are. They should have an understanding of how the union is set up structurally and the important parts of its rules. They need an understanding of the union's history – where we come from – why we are the way we are. We need to refine their organising skills so that they can help us when we need a sudden injection of talent to a campaign.

Again, this is education beyond our bargaining agenda. But we can use it to develop and skill our senior activists so that we have a pool of people ready to step up to the next level of union activity.

Using education to deepen understanding

There needs to be another level of training made available to members. They need to have the opportunity of forming a deep understanding of their union and its place in the industrial relations system and the history of Australia. This won't be for everyone. It may only be for the delegates and activists who have acted in these positions for many years and now want to take their union experience further.

I came across a dozen members of the CFMEU Mining and Energy Division – coal miners – who signed on with Griffith University in Queensland to a course that had been organised by their union. This was an academic course run by the university's teachers and all the participants took it very seriously.

That made me think that the education system has many teachers at every level who are interested in all the disciplines that impact on the work of unions – from industry policy to labour history, from industrial relations to employment law. They are capable of teaching at every level – from adult education to a full university course.

Unions need to explore the demand for these courses and their cost.

The money spent on training has to be justified. But that is easy to do when it becomes an integral part of building the union's power.

The Union Education Foundation

One of the very few free kicks we have in the current environment is the setting up of The Union Education Foundation. This represents the combined investments of various State Labor governments and the ACTU in a fund that can give some limited support each year to resourcing the education of union representatives in the workplace.

It enables unions to have resources that lift the quality of the training that they undertake. It ensures that the educators have the skills to do the job. It means that delegates in regional areas can have access to training. Cross union training across the contributing States can be resourced. But it can never be a substitute for the investment by individual unions in the empowerment of their members. For the foreseeable future that will remain a key role for unions that are serious about getting their members active in building their power.

17

National Offices

National Offices need to fit in with the organising focus of the union we are trying to build. In the past few years they have changed the least but their behaviour and structure must adapt to the threats and opportunities that unions face.

Unions take their structural form from their employers. If the employers are largely nationally organised, then the union will have a powerful national body. If employers are State-based then the union will tend to be a federation of powerful, largely autonomous, State branches.

Let me give some examples.

All the major employers in my old industry were national – the television networks, the theatrical entrepreneurs. Feature film makers could often be State-based but they could make their films anywhere. That meant that the National Office was always going to be the key player either in negotiating nationally or in ensuring that a common set of standards applied to feature film, no matter where the film was located.

The Finance Sector Union is in a similar position. Their membership is concentrated in the big banks, the banks are national employers – so the National Office of the FSU is powerful and negotiates on behalf of all members of the union.

State Public Services have State Public Service unions – the teaching, police and nursing unions all tend to have powerful State Branches that negotiate the conditions which cover their members. Their federal bodies are quite small, provide national representation politically on general issues and protect their coverage nationally.

However, quite a few unions are in a state of transition. They started with State-based employers and they now have to deal with national or even international employers.

The Australian Services Union has local government members in its coverage – and they continue to negotiate locally. But it also covers airlines, which are national, as are many of the private sector employers.

The Transport Workers Union – with its strong State Branches – now deals with a large number of major national employers.

The construction union – again with strong State organisation – deals with national building employers – at least as far as the biggest projects are concerned.

Large sections of the LHMU's coverage are becoming more and more national. Chains of child care centres are springing up, national health care and aged care chains are forming and cleaning contractors are increasingly national. The same can be said for the hotel chains – which are in fact international in their reach.

In all these unions, what is the role of the National Office in a union that seeks to operate according to an organising philosophy?

The first task is to lead the process of change. Whatever the National Office's power, structurally and financially, the national leadership of unions has influence over the rest of their union. They have a role to play in analysing the environment in which they find themselves and proposing the solutions that will give their members more power. Every National Office has to examine where it spends its money and determine to what extent those resources can be used to assist their branches to make the shift to organising.

In most industries or sectors National Offices have an increased role to play in developing and coordinating their union's national strategy.

Remember the prime purpose of organising workers collectively? We want them to have power in relation to their employer – but also in relation to the society as a whole. If employers are organised around the country and we challenge their power in just one State, we will have grave difficulty in delivering what we set out to deliver. Workers who organise collectively in just one part of an enterprise cannot expect to have power – in the normal course of events – across the whole entity. The organising is likely to be done locally. But a fundamental part of a National Office's function is to ensure that collective organisation across all sections of an enterprise is at a uniformly high level.

That is why union form follows employer structure. We must create institutions that have the capacity to do the job required of them – in this case, coordinate national organising strategy. That coordination can be of the internal organising of a national enterprise bargaining agreement or the greenfields organising of a national employer or the push to increase density across an existing national operation.

To organise workplaces, we need to understand the employer's business. For national employers that can best be done on a national basis. By looking at only local operations we can miss strategically important weaknesses or strengths in other States.

Think of the alternative: allowing national employers to fight State unions one by one improves employers' chances of success. The employer can concentrate his resources.

We know that employers are always searching for ways in which they can lower their costs – and the cost of labour is a good place to start. If they are given the opportunity they will seek to bargain first in a State where they judge the organised strength of their workforce to be weakest. Low density or a weak level of workplace leadership means they can exploit weakness to establish a benchmark for all other negotiations around the country.

Similarly, if a State union starts to organise a workplace in one State when the employer has workplaces nationally, the chances of success are reduced. The local manager of the workplace will do anything possible to avoid unionisation. How will it look for him to have an operation which has costs out of whack with the rest of the country? The employer can indulge in lockout action with impunity – a ready-made replacement workforce is available in the neighbouring State.

And even if we are successful in one State we are always exposed to attempts to deunionise. Unionisation will not be accepted by such a company as the natural order of things. They will always be looking for an opportunity to bring their "errant" operation back to the norm of a non-union culture.

Finally, even if for some reason a single State has power over a national company, why wouldn't the workers at that site want to use their power to help workers in other States increase their power by organising. If the best way of increasing power is to organise from strength, then surely States with power have a responsibility to look for ways they can help other States to get ahead?

All this leads to the conclusion that many unions need to re-examine the role of their national bodies.

If employer power exists on a national basis we have to meet that challenge.

We need national researchers who are capable of thoroughly understanding the employer's business.

We need national industry organising coordinators who can bring together organisers from each of the State branches and ensure that a common strategy is followed. They need to ensure that the messaging that is taking place on the ground is cohesive and meets the needs of the campaign as a whole. They need authority. While the concerns of State Secretaries need to be met, if the union is to win in these major national struggles, coordinators must know that they can determine whether a particular State-based organiser is doing the job and make the final call on the strategy to be used.

Where areas of organising weakness in a State are present, the union ideally will have the resources to be able to plug that hole – either by transferring funds to help build capacity or organising the placement of organisers there to do the job.

The National Office, where national bargaining takes place, will need to coordinate industrial strategy and make sure that it fits in with the organising plan. An officer needs to be deputed to work under the industry organiser to make sure that the technicalities of the legislation relating to the taking of protected industrial action is complied with. They need to make sure that bargaining standards for the union are not being undermined and help to educate members as to why these are important. If the campaign is to fit within a Commission strategy then the industrial officer will have to guide that process through the Commission and work out how to integrate the Commission's intervention with the needs of the organising plan.

The workplace leaders need to be linked at various strategic points in the campaign so that they can determine whether offers made by the employer are acceptable. Again, this represents a loss of autonomy for each of the States involved. Even if one State's delegates feel that the deal offered is okay, if a majority disagree, then the campaign needs to continue. This is difficult and requires members and delegates to understand, in advance, how imperative it is to settle a dispute only on a national basis.

If leverage is required, then the union will need to have the resources to examine the whole of the enterprise involved with a view to finding the appropriate pressure points. Can we enlist the support of community allies who are also aggrieved by the behaviour of the company? What information do we have about the company's customer base? Can we get customers to support us in settling the dispute on acceptable terms? Are there political and community allies that will intervene with the company in an effort to get resolution?

These resources – like organisers – may be held at a State level. If that is the case then the National Organising coordinator will have to try to build a coalition among the union's campaigners to ensure that the activities of State officials fits within the overall plan. And again, the coordinator has to have the authority to call the shots in this area. Alternatively, the National Office should have its own capacity to use researchers wherever they are needed.

Of course, all this capacity has to be funded. The fact is that some of the National Offices that face an increasing level of nationally (and internationally) organised companies lack the most basic of resources. If the national body has no money, then it cannot play any significant role in what needs to be done. Sustentation fees of 8 or 10 per cent are woefully inadequate. Such a level of funding means that National Offices can do little more than make sure that the basics of federal registration are looked after and the interests of the union at ACTU, federal government and regulatory authority levels are attended to.

In unions that have a strong State-based tradition I am not so innocent as to think that State Secretaries will wake up one day and hand their power over to a National Office! Instead, the National Office needs to work with their State bodies to work out where these approaches to national organising can be trialled so that everyone can gain confidence with the way they will work. Every union official or member loves to win. The success of these trials will be the best advertisement for a stronger National Office.

Change is difficult. State-based unions value their autonomy. But as with almost every other area of union activity, union officials will have to make the hard decisions necessary to do whatever it takes to win. If we face nationally organised employers then we need national organisation.

18

Financing change[1]

Unionism of any kind is doomed unless the financial future of each union is secure. But organising unionism requires a focus on both a different kind of representation for existing members and a focus on growth in new areas. That growth has to be funded.

No change is possible if the union is bankrupt. That was the point of the scary graph (p 15).

Some might argue that the disappearance of some unions is inevitable as they lose relevance. They will be replaced by new, more vibrant organisations with less baggage. However, there is no evidence that this happens. If we look across the Tasman, we can see that in New Zealand a range of unions went bankrupt or merged immediately prior to their disappearance. In none of these cases has a new union formed. Nor have other unions been able to successfully take over the coverage of the disappeared union.

Any union suffering a decline in membership will have to take aggressive action to ensure that its expenditure decreases as its income decreases. Failure to do this will only mean that assets decline to pay for the deficits incurred until such a point that the union becomes financially unviable.

Controlling expenditure

Unions have been ruthless in scrutinising expenditure in an effort to balance their books.

Approval of travel has been tightened. Business class travel is long gone as a perk of office.

Unions have reviewed the level of affiliations to make sure that they are paying only for the essential affiliations and at the current level of membership.

Cars have been one of the most contentious issues in the management of expenses. Organisers have put up a valiant fight in defence of the essential necessity of the traditional six-cylinder Australian sedan. Many have lost the battle. We are seeing unions buy small, cheap, second-hand cars that do the job

---

1   For a fuller discussion of increasing union fees see my pamphlet, *Running on Empty*, ACTU Organising Centre, 2004.

of getting the organiser from A to B or replacing the provision of cars with the payment of a car allowance.

Mobile phones have been one of the most difficult items of expenditure to control. Organisers now generally get a copy of their own bill so that they know how much workers are paying to give them a mobile phone. Some unions are putting out a "league table" of mobile phone expenditures so that organisers can see how far above the average expenditure they are and adjust their use of the phone accordingly. Those with excessive bills are being asked to explain their high usage of the phone. Some unions are agreeing to pay a set amount per month of a staff member's bill and then any additional payment has to be specifically authorised. Staff are more conscious of the need to use landlines wherever possible. Unions are shopping around for better deals on phones.

Unions seem to be tendering out far more of their major items of expenditure, for example, major items of stationery like paper, and unions are increasingly buying paper by the pallet.

Auditors now have to bid for their contract once every three years and their bills are closely monitored.

Banks are being required to come up with better deals if they are to keep the union's business and the associated credit cards with their associated points systems are being put at the disposal of union travel.

Energy audits of union buildings are being conducted and savings in electricity and water are being made.

Buildings themselves are being re-evaluated. Unions are deciding whether they really need to be in the CBD. Some unions have moved to the suburbs. They have been able to rent or buy much more modest edifices that free up significant resources for organising. Careful reviews of floor space have been conducted. Do we need a training room that is usually empty or can we use a nearby hotel on a rental basis or the local TLC to provide these facilities.

The use of administrative staff has been carefully evaluated. Some unions have been able to co-locate national and State offices so that they can redeploy one receptionist to doing something useful while a single receptionist does the work for both offices.

Most unions have invested in IT to the extent that staff do their own typing and clerical work.

Unions have reviewed their publications, no longer sending a monthly publication full of pictures of the national secretary and organisers, at the top of articles about what a great job the officers are doing for members. We tend to send out targeted publications, less frequently, that have a better than even chance of actually being read.

Most unions have introduced budgeting systems so that income and expenditure can be controlled and so that union managers are not surprised by what happens to their finances on a month-to-month basis.

None of this should be surprising. Union leaders have simply done what had to be done to make sure that their members' money was being expended wisely and so that the union's books could balance.

Program budgeting

Money is a key indicator of the degree to which a union is serious about an organising agenda. If we say that organising new members is important but we don't spend any money on it, we are kidding ourselves.

The problem is that most unions arrange their accounts in such a way that all organising expenses are lumped in together – irrespective of whether they are being spent on organising existing members or getting new members to become active and join the union.

Particularly where unions split their organiser workforces into internal and external it should be possible to introduce program budgeting fairly easily. The money spent on the growth team is the union's investment in its expansion into new areas or into deepening density in its existing areas.

Splitting income in the same way should also be possible. However, here it is important that unions take account of the fact that organising expenses can't generally be expected to be recouped in the year they are expended. Depending on the length of time a group of members stays in membership, the external expenditure can expect to be recouped over a period of years.

Taking the hard decisions –
how the NUW in Victoria found money for organising

Charlie Donnelly is now the National Secretary of the National Union of Workers. When I first knew him, he was their newly-minted Victorian Secretary. I came across him in the management course. He sat in the training room at Currawong – the NSW Labor Council's residential training facility – and took in everything that was being taught – the crisis in unionism, the need for change, financial management techniques, organising, the need for resources.

By the second week of training – some three months later – he came back and reported on what I can only describe as a courageous step forward.

The practice had been for the union to pay each delegate around a 5 per cent commission of all membership income from the delegate's workplace. Not much was required from delegates in return and the vast majority didn't actually collect the income – it came to the union from Direct Debit payments or Payroll Deduction arrangements.

Charlie decided to go to the delegates and point out to them that once the GST was introduced, the union would have to deduct tax from their payments at the top marginal rate.

He asked them to forgo the commission. He suggested that the money saved go to a newly-created organising fund. The fund would be used to resource the union's increasing commitment to organising new members. In addition, it would be used to meet all the reasonable expenses of the delegates in doing their job as a union representative.

The vast majority of delegates agreed.

The policy was quickly put to the test. A full-scale, well-funded election challenge was launched against his leadership and one of the top issues was – of course – the withdrawal of delegates' commissions.

Charlie and his team won over 80 per cent of the vote. It was a huge endorsement of the shift to building the union's power and the determined refocusing of its resources.

Despite the fact that going down this path opened him to electoral challenge, he knew that it was the right thing to do. A lot of the union's resources were being spent in an entirely unaccountable way. The expenditure certainly did nothing to build the union's power. The delegates were committed to their union. They didn't need the 5 per cent to reinforce that commitment.

From 2000-2004, over a million dollars was saved and redirected to organising. The Organising Fund has enabled additional organising resources to be deployed, member organisers have been paid, delegates provided with training, and of course, delegates have been reimbursed for the expenses they incur in representing their union.

Finding resources internally – the Health Services Union, NSW

The HSU in NSW is a relatively large State-based union – in 2004 they had 38,000 members. Its membership is predominantly based in the NSW Public Hospital system and they cover virtually all hospital employees except nurses. Michael Williamson, its State Secretary, took over the position in 1995. He went on to win office at an election by just a handful of votes. He found a union that was back in the dark ages – almost literally. Every second fluorescent tube in their office had been removed to save money!

He had calculated back in 1993 – before taking office – that if current trends continued, the union would cease to exist by 2008. Despite all the advantages of organising workers in very large single site workplaces with relatively benign employers, the union was losing members fast.

He took over the union at a time when Australian unions knew very little about the kind of organising agenda outlined in this book. He simply set out to run the very best kind of union he could and in that way reverse the membership trends he faced on coming to office.

He did everything we would expect of such a union reformer in 1995. He sought to hire good staff willing to work very hard in the interest of members. He increased fees as far as he could. He lifted the industrial performance of the union, using negotiations with the government employer and the power of the NSW Industrial Relations Commission to deliver benefits to members. He set about rebuilding the branch structure[2] in each of the major hospitals and did what he could to resource these honorary officers and get them involved in the work of the union.

He was driven at every stage of this process by the issue of getting the best value he could from the resources of the union. He wanted to do more for members but simply lacked the resources to fund new strategies. Early on, he noticed that the rather lavish boardroom the union had was scarcely used – and the union office was located in the middle of the Sydney CBD where real estate was extremely expensive. By renting a meeting room in the hotel opposite when it was needed and then permanently letting his own board room space, he found that he made small but significant savings. That led him to really concentrate hard on the use the union was making of the whole two floors of its city office.

The bottom floor of his office was taken up with offices for each of the organisers. Yet they were perpetually out on the road, meeting members, doing the work of the union. The office was largely empty.

That realisation started the union down the road of a fundamental reconceptualisation of the way in which organisers were supported. There was no reason for them to be in the office except for staff meetings, training and meetings with senior officials. The union was spread throughout NSW and the organisers worked with the members and branch officials. That was where they should stay, provided that they were provided with the information they needed to do their job.

Information had been held in hard copy in the union's Sydney office. Now, membership forms are scanned into a computerised filing system and all subsequent correspondence relating to that member attached to the file. Every piece of paper coming into the office is now scanned and filed electronically. All original paper records are discarded. Any staff member can enter two key words and search for a file anywhere in the database. What's more they can be found almost immediately. Files relating to particular organisers or work areas are dropped onto a CD and sent to each of the organisers on a fortnightly basis. As well as correspondence files, the CD contains membership and branch committee lists for each hospital.

Every organiser has a laptop that is loaded with all awards and agreements relating to the members she represents. Each of these computers can be linked to a mobile to send and receive information to and from the centre.

---

2   A "branch" in the HSU is the workplace committee based in each of the major worksites. It consists of a President, Secretary and Treasurer and five committee members – at least.

The union has established regional offices across the State and to the west of Sydney. All reports to the head office are electronic so that organisers can work from home one day a week. Every phone call that comes into the union office is handled by a call centre. The caller is identified as a member and the relevant files appear on the screen with his or her name. Where the call cannot be dealt with immediately, it is referred each night to the organiser as an open query. Where the call is dealt with at first instance, a report on the call is nevertheless sent to the organiser so that she knows what's going on.

The next stage of development is to provide every branch of the union with a "Blackberry"[3] capable of sending and receiving files from the union over the Internet. While the blackberry is fundamentally a phone, the phone operation will be disabled. The branch will report each month on a range of key issues – membership density, delegate activity, numbers going through induction, percentage signed up at induction – and so on.

All this has taken immense investment in technology. It's meant the purchase of laptops for every organiser, the creation of a new membership system, the creation of a computerised filing system customised for the particular needs of a union and software to support the call centre. The initial estimate for buying 300 Blackberries and the associated software is around $500,000. Every year sees a hefty allocation to software development. The payoff is that the system works. Organisers and delegates have access to the information they need when they need it. The reports they make possible allow the union to shift the emphasis to the basics of ensuring high levels of financial, active membership.

The union of course, has also reduced the floor area devoted to staff in the CBD by over 50 per cent. That has allowed it to let a very large area to a commercial client at premium rates.

In 2004 the HSU in NSW made a surplus of $800,000 on top of very substantial surpluses for the last few years. It has the money to fund its expansion in those areas of its coverage – particularly private sector health – where density is low.

Securing the delivery of income

Prior to 1996, most unions got the bulk of their income from payroll deduction from their employers. That is, agreement was reached with the employer that where the member had signed the appropriate authority, an amount would be deducted each pay day from the union member's wage. The advantage of the system was that it was a relatively painless way of collecting membership income.

---

3   This looks rather like a rather large mobile phone with a small keyboard at its base. Using an Internet connection, the user can send and receive emails, including attachments.

In a hostile environment, this became a gun held to the head of the union. Jeff Kennett, the notoriously anti-union Premier of Victoria, cancelled payroll deduction agreements with the Victorian teachers' union the day before Christmas. With every teacher on their summer break, that meant that the union had to wait the best part of two months before they could even start the process of signing members over to a direct debit system – where the money came out of the member's bank account or credit card. It took them six months to get a substantial proportion of their membership signed over to alternative payment arrangements and they were forced to sack large numbers of their staff.

There are other problems with payroll deduction. It allows bosses to know exactly how strong the union is in their workplace. Anyone who thinks that they don't check density when going into negotiations for a new collective agreement is dreaming! They understand very well that density is power and they want to know what they are up against.

Payroll deduction also means that the primary financial relationship is between union and employer rather than between union and member. If we are genuinely trying to build an organising union with members at the core of the organisation, it seems to me to be far healthier for the member to pay money directly to his or her union rather than through their employer.

We now have a great deal of experience in shifting members to direct debit – I won't go through it here – but unions need to take advantage of that experience.

Some unions have persisted with payment of fees by half yearly or yearly invoice. Again, I suspect that this is a mistake. We are now starting to charge members significant amounts of money. Paid in one or two lump sums they are a difficult payment for any member to swallow. We need to make it easy for members – direct debit payments each fortnight or month are far more palatable.

Funding renewal and growth

But cutting back and securing the income stream is nowhere near enough.

For most Australian unions, the period of imminent crisis has passed. The worst of membership decline appears to be over. The cuts have been made so that deficits are no longer being incurred. Union budgets are in balance.

We now face a different task. How can we fund the on-going representation of existing members so that members become active and passionate about the fate of their union. How do we fund the growth of the union's membership and power?

All of this takes money.

Just on the basis of what I have proposed already in relation to the representation of existing members – without thinking about teams of external organisers – investment needs to take place.

If we want to free up the grievance load by setting up a call centre, unions need to invest in the technology. If we are going to use these techniques, we must do it properly. If we try to do it on the cheap all that happens is that it doesn't work properly, members become dissatisfied and staff become demoralised. Remember that members are used to corporations that use this kind of technology. They now take for granted a relatively high standard of efficiency – no matter how much call centres drive them up the wall. They will be quick to pass adverse judgment on their own union if it doesn't get it right.

The same can be said for the retraining of organisers. They need training so that they have the confidence to be able to implement some of the suggestions I have made about mobilisation of members. The idea that an organiser gets two weeks training or perhaps a traineeship, over the whole of their working lives is crazy! They need to have the chance to practice rarely used skills, hear about the latest organising and legal developments, assess how they are doing their job. That costs money.

For a membership-based organisation, nothing is more important than an efficient membership system. It requires heavy and ongoing investment in IT. Every union with a decent membership system reports that they need to invest money every year in keeping it up to date.

Unions also need money for education of their members, activists and delegates. This needs to be budgeted for and while there are some means of getting assistance – through the ACTU, getting organisers to deliver training – there is no way of getting this activity on the cheap if it is going to be done well.

And all this is before the union has found any money whatsoever for growth.

Remember what we said in Chapter 7. Infill organising is not enough. We need to lift our density across the industries in which we are organising. Only in that way will we get the power necessary to put wages out of competition. That means that we have to have the capacity to take on the organising of a site where we have very low density or none at all. That requires dedicated resources doing nothing but concentrating on organising that site.

That kind of activity is expensive.

Spending reserves

Some union leaders have said to me that they feel that the only reason that their financial reserves were collected in the first place was to provide for a rainy day. With declining membership, new areas to be organised and continuing government and employer attack, it's certainly raining now!

Unions have incurred deficits in a desperate attempt to halt the slide in income caused by members leaving the union at a rate faster than they can be replaced. They characterise this as an investment in growth.

As Sir Humphrey would say in *Yes Minister*, this is a courageous approach indeed!

It takes unions time to devise a growth program that works. The skills need to be learned by existing staff, new staff need to be recruited and tactics must be refined. We also need to consider the reality that there will be few cases where in one or two years – even if the campaign is successful – the organising expenditure can be recouped.

That means that the leader runs the risk that he or she will drain the coffers without a guarantee that the assets can be replenished any time soon.

Once the organising program is established and the leader can rely on the organising team to deliver fairly certain outcomes in a limited time frame – that is the time to create added impetus to the union's organising effort. At that point, a rational, prudent decision can be made to invest a proportion of the reserves in growth.

In the meantime, unions need to develop a recurrent income stream that will support long-term investment in this area.

So why is it that the recurrent income we get now cannot support the activity that is needed?

The need to increase fees

The dues structure in Australian unions is geared to an environment that no longer exists.

Unions in Australia charge a level of fees that was set on the basis of heavy institutional support for unionism. We used to have Arbitration Commissions that had real power. Lay advocates could take problems there and get them solved cheaply. A single Award would cover a whole industry with thousands of employers. Some unions could do a deal that would last four years and cover huge sections of their membership. The government provided almost full funding for union education for both union staff and delegates.

In such an environment you didn't need to charge high levels of dues.

That level of support now sounds like a fairy tale. Every reasonably-sized union negotiates hundreds of agreements – and often these don't even cover everyone that is represented or entitled to be represented in an industry. Very little money is given to unions to help them cover the cost of delegate or staff education. It takes real effort to sign every single member– whether they benefit from a collective agreement or not.

Despite all this, despite the increased cost of doing the basic work of unionism, despite the cost of increasing density, the increasing resources that

need to go into member retention, the loss of subsidy, the absence of institutional support, the complexity of bargaining workplace by workplace for a
whole economy, *our unions still charge basically the same level of dues.* Some
unions have not even been meticulous about keeping pace with inflation and the
introduction of a GST. The rest have increased fees by only a small percentage
above inflation and GST.

International comparisons between Australian and US unions are
instructive. The following table shows the position of unions in NSW and
Wisconsin, US.

Table 18.1 Current and revised monthly receipts using Wisconsin counterpart dues percentage[4]

Union	Monthly dues	Monthly dues if Wisconsin % used	Percent diff in monthly receipts
CFMEU	27.50	77.88	183.2
NSW Nurses	23.21	33.96	46.3
SDA	23.83	30.41	27.6
TWU	22.92	27.91	21.8
LHMU	20.48	55.81	172.5

The position of unions in the two States – Wisconsin and New South Wales – in
terms of lack of institutional support, level of employer aggression, the difficulty
of organising, is roughly similar. The level of financial resourcing is profoundly
different.

Remember that this comparison is done on the basis of $A1 = $US1. Using
a variable exchange rate only complicates the picture. But certainly, if we did
that, the disparity between the two States would be even greater.

Even in the area of member retention, I fear that unions are ill equipped to
resist a prolonged campaign of deunionisation. We are not even ready to cope
with the far more common preparedness by employers to indulge in lengthy
lock outs or sit out prolonged strikes. Overseas, where institutional support has
always been lower, unions are used to building their financial reserves to provide a cushion against the possibility of major industrial conflict. Very few
unions have that capacity in Australia.

The asset bases of most unions are very low. Even where some of the larger
unions have what look to be sizeable asset bases, when net assets are divided by

---

4   Lund, J, Giving unions their due: a comparison of union dues for selected unions in New
    South Wales (Australia) and Wisconsin (US), July, 2001, ACTU Organising Centre.

the membership to give an asset per member ratio, the result usually is a very small amount. Further, these assets are rarely liquid assets – available to the union in the case of a strike or for an expansion plan. They are usually held in the form of property and are therefore of limited value – except as security against loans. Very few unions have specific purpose strike funds and where these exist, they are insignificant in size, with the exception of possibly the CFMEU Mining and Energy Division

To date, we have relied on workers simply making do in the event of a strike or lock out. This was okay in the days when our strike activity was largely limited to one or two day demonstration strikes. Increasingly, however, while the overall level of industrial action is down, the action that occurs is far more likely to be of a prolonged nature. It is unreasonable to expect workers responsible for the support of their families to stay on strike without some form of financial assistance designed to at least keep body and soul together. We need to remember the lesson of the Patricks' dispute. The financial support provided by most Australian unions to the locked out wharfies was critical to their ultimate success. We won because – at least in part – the wharfies could afford to stay out.

Our limited asset base also means that employers will be encouraged to use any tactic which guarantees a substantial financial cost to the union. Employers have access to our balance sheets. They know our net worth. They can generally work out what it will take to really cause financial harm to a union and will set about exacting the price of the union's submission.

Ken Zin, the American union campaigner, tells the story of briefing 40 British merchant bank coal industry analysts about a strike against one of the most powerful industry players in the US. The first question asked by the analysts was "What is the size of the union's strike fund?" The impact of the answer on his audience was instantaneous. The answer – "$US100 million". Companies are wary of picking fights with well-resourced, determined unions.

Even where employers have not to date taken aggressive action, it would be foolhardy for us to remain unprepared. The reality is that the last ten years of economic reform has shown us that no union, over the long term, is safe from employer aggression.

It is for all these reasons that at its meeting in 2003, the ACTU Congress adopted a new policy setting a target for union fees. It is worth reading the whole resolution:

(a) As a guide and over time, unions should aim to establish base union membership fees at a level equal to 1% of Full-time Adult Weekly Ordinary Time Earnings (AWOTE). This would currently represent a weekly fee of approximately $9 per week. (That is, $468 per annum)

(b) The AWOTE benchmark is based on full-time earnings and unions should consider establishing reduced fees for part-time or casual employees as appropriate.

(c) Increases in union fees or levies should be specifically targeted at funding organising campaigns and strategies for union renewal and membership growth – including union education and activist development.

(d) The democratic involvement of union delegates and members is an important part of any proposal to increase the level of union membership fees.

6. It is recognised that from time to time unions may also need to adjust the level of membership fees to cover increased union operating costs and to fund improved service delivery to union members.

The following table contrasts the rate recommended by the ACTU Congress with the rate that was being paid by a number of the most significant unions in 2002.

Table 18.2: Selected NSW Union dues – 2002[5] and ACTU Congress Recommendation

Union	Annual Fee
SDA (Retail Union)	$286
HSU (Health Union)	$338
NUW (Warehouse Union)	$286
AWU (General and Rural)	$334
AMWU (Manufacturing Union)	$351
NTEU (Tertiary Education)	$328
NSWNA (NSW Nurses)	$352
TWU (Transport Workers)	$283
LHMU (Hospitality and Miscellaneous)	$290
ASU (Private Sector White Collar)	$424
ACTU Congress recommendation	**$468**

The ACTU recommendation is the minimum amount needed to fund the level of activity expected of a modern trade union operating in our hostile environment. It is not a target that the Congress suggests can be met some time in the next millennium, but what we need to charge now. We need to shift the broad range of unions to that new plateau. Some few unions now charge more than that – most charge much less.

We need to be entirely frank with our members and explain that, given the hostility of the environment in which we operate, they need to pay a minimum

---

5   Phone survey of unions. Annualised rates are developed from the most commonly charged rates. Again, in many of these unions, substantial proportions of members pay much less than these rates.

of $9 per week if we are to have any real hope of ensuring that Australia's economy delivers for the citizens dependant on it.

The process of increasing fees

We need to examine carefully how to go about introducing this kind of increase in fees. We need a careful program of explanation and endorsement by members, if a backlash is to be avoided.

A number of unions have gone through this process and their experience is worth examining.[6]

NSW TWU

Like the LHMU in South Australia, the NSW Branch of the TWU under Secretary Tony Sheldon was one of the first unions to try to make the shift towards organising. They have made many of the organisational changes that are now quite commonplace and they continue to be among the first to experiment with new organising and campaigning techniques.

The problem was that they didn't have enough money to do what needs to be done to build the power of their membership. Most of their members paid their dues on an invoice basis twice per year and the rate of fee was a very low $283 per annum.

The process they undertook has left them with fees that rose to $367 on 1 January 2004 and will increase in the following two years to $428 and $490 respectively.

The process they undertook started with a comprehensive survey of members to find out what they thought of the union – to make sure that the appeal for more money was being made in a context of solid support for the union. Once it was clear that this was the case they set out on a wide-ranging process of informing delegates and staff of the campaigns they were facing and the resources required to make them a success. They got delegates to understand that these campaigns had to go ahead but that without additional resources the union would be "fighting with one hand tied behind its back". They then began a process of member consultation under the slogan – "It's in your hands".

Everywhere the delegates, staff and leadership went they got a positive response from members. Ninety per cent of members wanted the campaigns to go ahead, more than 60 per cent approved of the increase in dues but a substantial group expressed concern about introducing the increase in one year. For that reason, the rank-and-file executive agreed to phase the increase in over three years. What's more, the union set up a union ombudsman to hear

---

6   Only a much-abridged version of the NSW TWU and Finsec case studies is provided here. For a detailed analysis of what they did, please refer to *Running on Empty,* op cit.

complaints about the increase and other issues so that as far as possible, they could respond to members quickly, minimising the possibility of any disunity after the vote was taken. The union leadership was determined that the whole union would move forward onto a new footing as a united group.

Finsec

Perhaps the most comprehensive campaign has been run by Finsec, New Zealand's Finance Sector Union. Distinguishing this campaign from the Australian case studies is the fact that the union took the proposal to a referendum of every member.

Finsec had suffered rapid declines in membership – largely as a result of downsizing by the big four Australian-owned banks. Despite quite aggressive cutbacks in both wage and non-wage expenditure, the union has incurred persistently large deficits so that its asset base has continually eroded over the last ten years.

The union went to its members with three alternatives:

- Merge with another union;

- Reduce costs and activities and gradually disappear;

- Continue as Finsec.

In a series of meetings across the country, the leadership discussed each of these alternatives with its members. Enormous effort was put into getting members to attend these meetings and they attended in very large numbers – over 40 per cent of total membership. The overwhelming majority of these members wanted the union to continue as their union, concentrating specifically on the interests of finance sector workers. The leadership then opened the union's books and showed them just how impossible it was to continue at the current level of dues payment – $NZ273 per year. The union had to grow and to do that it needed more resources to fund that growth program.

They proposed that members agree to increase the dues by 40 per cent – lifting the rate to $NZ390 per year.

This proposal then went to a postal referendum of every member. Over 62 per cent of members voted and of those, 84 per cent voted in favour of the increase.

LHMU WA

The LHMU in West Australia suffered a heavy loss of membership as a result of the Court Government's attack on the trade union movement – particularly those unions like the LHMU who represented workers in government whose employment could be contracted out or who could be forced to accept individual agreements. Their achievement through these years was to survive financially through an aggressive program of expenditure control and a determination to keep the basic union organisation together. Once the Court Government left office, they were conscious of the need to rebuild in a more positive environment. They commissioned an operational review in 2002 which recommended a substantial increase in fees.

The leadership of the union set about implementing the recommendations contained in the report but the staff resisted the idea of increasing the fees – particularly given that so many of the union's members were in low-paying jobs. They were concerned that higher fees would make recruitment more difficult and that existing members would have difficulty in paying the new rate.

Dave Kelly, the Secretary, simply announced to the staff that the Executive had met the previous night and decided to increase the fees. Dues would go up over the next four years from $317 to $525 per annum. The time for debating whether dues should go up was over. The question was how should the extra money be spent.

The staff were quite shocked but, as asked, sat down to brainstorm how to use the money to build the power of the union through a well-resourced growth program. The mood changed fairly quickly as people spoke about what could be done with the extra resources. People got excited as they came up with a highly creative set of proposals built around dedicated organising staff but also a large program of booking members off the job to work as member organisers.

Satisfied, Dave then announced that he had lied. The Executive hadn't met, hadn't approved the fee increase and at present there was no money for any of their brilliant ideas. But their work had revealed so many exciting things for the union to do to re-establish itself as a real force for good in Western Australia that there was no way that they could remain unfunded. He would take their proposals to the Executive. Significant staff resistance ended from that point on. In fact, some hounded Dave until the increase was approved.

The Executive endorsed the increases enthusiastically – if with some trepidation – and the members, after an extensive program of member education, endorsed them. As Caroline Smith, one of the union's assistant secretaries said later, "The process of going to the members and talking to them about the survival of their union and the need for it to grow, was one of the most exciting and humbling experiences of my time with the union".

Queensland Public Sector Union

The QPSU was "running on empty". It had commissioned a report which showed that its capacity to do more with the existing low level of resources was extremely limited. It had one of the lowest fees of any of the public service unions in Queensland – or for that matter in the country.

The Secretary, Alex Scott, went to his council with a program that needed funding. He pointed to the success of the union in the recent past. But he indicated to them how limited was their ability to do the job of representing members and defending public sector employment properly.

He proposed the creation of two new funds:

- The New Strength Unity Fund;[7] and

- The Public Sector Defence Fund.

The first fund was to pay for the creation of an organising team that would be used as a means of building power during the enterprise bargaining process, researching the union's claims and the best means of exerting leverage on employers. It would have the capacity to book off members as member organisers.

The second fund would be used to build the union's political profile as the defender of public sector employment. The activities it will fund would include television advertising in the lead up to elections – but also the resourcing of member to member contact and other personalised communication strategies throughout the year.

Unusually, the QPSU produced in-house a series of videos to be used in educating members about the rationale for these two levies. They feature the honorary officers advancing the cause for the necessary dues increases as well as interviews with Greg Combet and the Secretaries of other public sector unions – the Police and the Teachers' – talking about the necessity of resourcing growth in density and political power.

Will members put up with major increases in union fees?

Union officials are, in general, principled and want to charge the lowest fees possible. The aim, after all, is to make members' lives easier and more secure rather than to add to their burden. This is particularly true of unions representing predominantly low-paid workers.

Officials are also closely focused on the survival of their organisations. There is a fear that increasing fees by any substantial amount will only lead to members cancelling their membership. Far from adding to an increase in income the result may be a reduction of income, as large numbers of members leave the union.

These fears and concerns need to be confronted.

Members will accept very substantial increases in their fee payments – but there are a number of important qualifications.

Fee increases are going to be more acceptable to members if the union is already seen by its members to be successful. In all these cases, the unions made fee increases just the next step in continuing to build the power and success of

---

7   Alex hopes that the SEIU will forgive him borrowing this title.

the union. All could point to tangible success in bargaining outcomes and in organising to get respect at work for union members. All could rely on a very large number of committed union activists who understood the issues and were prepared to help in building support among members.

Members have to be involved in the decision-making process. These are not decisions to be taken behind the closed doors of a union executive meeting. If the first thing that members know about a fee increase is a statement on their wages slip, direct debit notice or invoice requesting payment, then we only have ourselves to blame if they are upset.

Each of the unions had a process for getting to almost every one of their members. They spent time on the process. It became a prime focus for organisational activity. Delegates were first educated because they are the most credible voice for the union. They needed the support of kits, speakers' notes, PowerPoint presentations, briefing materials – and in the case of the QPSU, videos. They needed the arguments and the skills to be able to involve members in a discussion rather than just lecture them about the need for more money. Each of the unions tracked the success or otherwise of their consultation process and used it to identify new activists and problem areas that would require further attention.

None of the unions relied on written material as the prime source of information. Finsec used flyers as a teaser to get members to meetings. The TWU used kits to resource delegates. All these unions knew that the best form of communication is face to face and they set up a process for that to happen.

None of the unions characterised the increase simply as a cry for more money. All of them linked the need for more resources with delivering tangible benefits for members.

Conclusion

We do members no favours at all by running unions that are unable to deliver because they can't defend themselves from employer attack and because they can't build power in their industries by increasing their density. We need to tell them the truth. They are the owners of their union and they need to know what it will take to create unions that can do what they are supposed to. Unions need to be capable of training their delegates, providing members with a voice, evening up the bargaining power between employers and workers, getting good bargaining outcomes, having a say in how their industry is run, ensuring safe and secure working environments. For the reasons that I have outlined above, that task has become far more expensive in recent years.

What Tony Maher of the Miners Union (CFMEU Mining and Energy Division) said at the 2003 Australasian Organising Conference is surely correct:

"Members don't leave their union because it charges too much. They leave because their union is pissweak".

The fear of mass resignation is real if membership is based purely on the purchase of a service. If that is the case, we will indeed need to get the economists in, find out what the elasticity of demand for the union service is – and members will resign once they make the judgment that union membership is not worth the expense.

But most union members don't see their union membership as just another service. The union is about giving them some power in their workplace. It's a statement that they are prepared to stand with and for their colleagues. It's their commitment to each other. Their union will usually be an organisation that they see as theirs – an organisation that they own.

Our experience is that in unions which have done the work over recent years of getting their members to see the union as something other than a service provider, very few members resign as a result of an increase in fees. They see their union as successful, and as an organisation that involves them in its work. They want it to grow and become more powerful. They understand that paying more money is likely to give them more power – and on that basis they are quite prepared to contribute more.

One final point needs to be made. Every process I have described above has been time-consuming and complex. It can generally happen only once in a generation. That means that once such a process is started it had better be for an increase in resources that will really make a difference. The process can't be used just to catch up with the rate of inflation. Having been consulted, having made their decision, understanding the crisis unionism faces, if members don't see their increased fees achieve any improvement, then the union will deservedly suffer a significant loss of confidence from its members.

19

Finding additional resources to win

Employers are increasingly aggressive and it is inevitable that we need to develop the kind of strategic intervention I will propose in the following section. Many of our national offices will need increased levels of resourcing. We need to hire and train a whole generation of researchers and campaigners – in much the same way that we hired and trained organising works trainees. We need to spend money on political activity in different ways.

It doesn't stop there. Once we accept the need to exert pressure beyond the individual workplace, we also need a media strategy that will give us the chance of informing the public of what is going on behind the closed doors of these employers. We need lawyers to make sure that we are not infringing anyone's rights as we seek to pressure the employers to do the right thing.

Employers will react aggressively. Their habit has been to use the legal system to make the job of representing workers as expensive as possible. The law firms that favour these aggressive tactics have a vested financial interest in encouraging the employer community to be legally aggressive. That will continue. We need the resources to match their strategy. We cannot afford to back down in the face of legal intimidation.

I have argued in the previous chapter that we need to reform our expenditure patterns to eliminate waste and increase fees to fund organising.

The savings made and the additional income raised will rarely be sufficient to resource campaigns of the kind I have outlined. They allow single unions to maintain density in existing areas of coverage. They resource teams of organisers to reach new members within a union's traditionally organised industries. The NSW TWU can advance into labour hire employment in the main areas of the transport industry. They can take on middle-ranking contractors competing on wages with the major employers. The South Australian LHMU can move into Aged Care. The FSU has the money to organise the Bank of Queensland, a company with a thousand employees.

But to get a surge of membership across a range of sectors of the economy will require investment of quite a different order.

Amalgamation revisited

In the 1980s we set out on an amalgamation strategy that was aimed at creating 20 large unions that would have the economies of scale sufficient to cope with the demands of a more hostile and decentralised environment. Many of the current generation of leaders have gone through that process and most will be reluctant to spend any more time on it.

The result of all that amalgamation activity is that of the biggest unions, around 16 result from amalgamations. Of these, around half have not used the merger process to achieve significant economies of scale. That is, they still have duplicate officers' positions, separate offices, some have separate membership systems. A few can even be characterised as amalgamations in name only. They are amalgams of unions with a vestigial federal structure tacked on at the top. In these cases, arguably, the merger process has done nothing more than increase the costs of administration. As I have said to some of them, they have all the problems of amalgamation without realising any of the benefits.

The first step in getting serious about improving expenditure efficiency lies not in getting mobile phone costs under control (which is important!) but in achieving the economies of scale that the amalgamation strategy was designed to achieve.

Let's review for a moment what amalgamation was supposed to do for us. By having larger unions, the cost of administration per member was to fall – instead of having three different membership systems, we would have just one. One photocopier in a single office would replace three. By negotiating with suppliers as a large purchasing entity we could get cost reductions not available to smaller organisations. Instead of three federal secretaries we could have one. Indeed, the idea was that, over time, the whole superstructure of senior officers could be thinned out so that more resources could be put at that level of the organisation actually in contact with members.

Even in those unions where a genuine merger is in place, I suspect that many have not been sufficiently ruthless in finding the savings that are avai-lable. Do we really need all those assistant secretaries or would we be better served with industry coordinators or Lead Organisers? How ruthless have we been in merging offices?

In the half of unions where the merger agreement simply papers over what are in fact a series of semi-autonomous unions, the amalgamation process started in the 1980s must become a reality. Dual positions must come to an end. Offices must merge. The cost of administration must fall. It's easy to say and harder to do but each of the unions still coping with a hangover from the amalgamation process must set a date in their rules by which the merger must be complete – even if it is some years into the future – and move towards that date step by step.

It is no coincidence that some of our biggest problems of union survival are found in some of these unions who have failed to merge in the full sense of that word.

In some unions, smaller sections fear being swallowed up by a larger partner should the amalgamation become reality. The reality is that smaller sections have less to fear provided that at the time of integration they are growing and doing the work of representing their members in a self-sufficient fashion. Adjustment for those union sections that are suffering declining levels of income can indeed be brutal. The larger section will impose on the smaller the economies that are necessary to ensure that the integrated whole survives as an economic entity.

More importantly, if the smaller section has developed its own successful way of organising its members and potential members, the chances are that it will be seen as a storehouse of successful strategies. It will wield a disproportionate influence on the larger entity.

The next wave of amalgamation?

Further amalgamations are necessary – beyond just making the current mergers a reality. The motivation has to be more than simply saving money. The amalgamations of the 1990s were defensive in nature. What we need now is a set of amalgamations that aim to aggregate power and resources so that unions can project their power within targeted industries.

Given the importance of white collar employment, it may be time for the movement and the relevant unions to look at the formation of a major private and public sector white collar union. Our experience with organising call centres points to the sense of such a merger. Call centres that do the work of a semi-privatised entity like Telstra span both private and public employment. Such call centres may then take on contract work entirely in the private sector. Both private and public white collar unions have an interest in organising such an entity and any conflict between them will result in the failure of the organising effort. This much is well known and accommodations between the relevant unions have been worked out.

The issue is broader than that. If sufficient resources are to be deployed on targets such as these across the whole industry so that wages can be removed from competition, it will take the combined resources of both unions acting in concert to be able to have an impact.

The same is true of the finance sector. The major financial institutions are gradually outsourcing significant sections of their work to a non-finance industry workforce. To ensure that wages are not in competition it will take concerted action by all white collar unions to ensure that workers doing this work get and retain power over how they are treated. Again, it is not just a question of sorting out demarcation arrangements. Unions need the force of combined resources and expertise to be able to tackle such large tasks as these.

The same can be said for the Health Services Union and the LHMU. It makes no sense for one union to represent non-nursing staff in WA, Queensland and SA and another to represent the same workers in the other States. If we are serious about getting power for workers across the country, then the resources and expertise of a united union needs to be applied nationally.

If we look at the role I have proposed for National Offices, I don't think that effective coordination of organising can occur if the offices are split between two unions.

As they read this, trade union officials around the country will groan.

The problem with amalgamations in the 1980s was that they became all-consuming tasks. Nothing seemed to be done other than negotiate with each other about the details of the amalgamation – who would get which position, what structure of government would apply, what wages would be paid to each staff member.

It's interesting to see what Anja Kirsch, a researcher comparing amalgamation strategy in Germany and Australia, has to say about the difficulty of amalgamation:

> Merger is in reality the least difficult type of change that unions can undergo ... mergers barely touch the core (cultural) features of unions; they are essentially a redesign of peripheral features (structures) ...
>
> The nature of the organisation is something that must be discussed in an organising strategy: is a union a service provider with passive consumers or are the members the active core of the organisation? During mergers, this issue can be safely ignored."[1]

With the benefit of hindsight, I think that's correct. We thought the original amalgamations of the 1980s and early 1990s were very difficult. In fact the changes to our organisational cultures involved in shifting to organising are far more challenging.

We cannot put the union renewal project on hold while we rejig our structures. Organising for power can't wait. That means that the next wave of amalgamations need to be between unions with joint industrial interests but also with a fundamental commitment to organising. Cultures as well as structures need to be aligned.

Some things have changed since the 1980s and we may find the process somewhat easier. Then, we were far less pressured about the future of the movement. Membership decline – as opposed to decline in density – was not then an ever present reality. Our minds are far more concentrated now on doing what needs to be done to get power for our members and potential members.

---

1   Kirsch, "A Union Mergers in Australia and Germany", unpublished Masters thesis, 2003.

Organising needs to be kept in focus throughout any new wave of amalgamations. Merger programs in other countries have had a nasty habit of papering over a financial crisis so that the inevitable day when unions actually have to change their behaviour can be postponed. We cannot allow this to happen in Australia. The basis for merger activity must be to free up additional resources for our growth strategies rather than simply to allow us to continue doing what we have always done.

Further, the purpose of the next wave of amalgamation will be something more than simply lowering the per-member administrative cost. We need to amalgamate in order to get industry power. The last amalgamations took place often not with the industrial interests of members at the forefront of our minds but rather as a way of shoring up the factional power of union leaders. The factions are far less important in regard to union affairs now – although they remain important in terms of wielding power within the ALP.

Amalgamations should take place where they make sense industrially. They should concentrate the power of workers in an occupation or industry so that the union is able to commit resources to building power in that area of activity more easily.

The alternative is for unions to try to organise these target areas on a multiunion basis. Our record in this regard is not good. Maintaining internal discipline among a group of unions is difficult as some will want to declare victory and settle with the employer before others. Equally, problems occur with the allocation of resources. Where a number of unions agree to contribute resources, questions arise as to the proportionate benefit and the consequent gain at the end of the process. Further, questions have been raised in the past about the quality of staff that are allocated to these kinds of campaign. In short, campaigns have a better chance of succeeding where a single union takes sole responsibility for its success or failure. Joint responsibility lessens the commitment of each of the union partners.

The hope is that the current group of union leaders, once they are convinced that merging must happen in the interest of survival and growth, will act quickly. The biggest problems have come from mergers that provided for the indefinite retention of joint positions. That perpetuated division within an overarching structure. Unions that coped with this issue successfully made certain that where a joint position became vacant it was not filled – like the MEAA. Alternatively, other unions like the LHMU provided that after a certain date – set in some cases well into the future – all joint positions had to be combined.

We are unlikely to again be caught amalgamating with partners with unrevealed debts and deficits. Financial reporting is of a generally much higher order and the financial position of unions is far more transparent. Amalgamating partners can be required to either put their house in order prior to the merger or agree to the amalgamated body doing it for them immediately after.

Unions know now how to go to their members in order to achieve a consensus about the desirability of merger. With delegate structures in place and improved systems of one to one communication, it should be possible to involve members in the development of the rationale that underpins the technicalities of the merger.

Sharing resources

Some unions will simply not be prepared to amalgamate again. For others it is not appropriate. Yet it strikes me that we waste a crazy level of resources on doing functions which other unions do equally well or perhaps better.

The MUA and the CFMEU Mining Division have co-located their Sydney and National Offices. This allows them to share a wide range of functions – to the benefit of both. They share reception, library and records management and an organising department.

Enormous scope for this to be done exists for unions that may not even have a logical joint constitutional coverage but nevertheless trust each other.

The MEAA has a state-of-the-art membership section in Brisbane that handles membership for every one of their members around the country. Why couldn't unions subcontract that section to handle their membership processing? Yes, there will be worries that it enables unions to interfere in their internal political processes – but is that really a problem for most unions? The MEAA is unlikely to want to take over too many other unions after all! If there was any interference, the contract would be ended instantly, a claim for breach of contract made and heavy penalties exacted.

The upside of such an arrangement is that the contracting union has the advantage of a professionally managed body doing the work at a lower cost to the union entering into the arrangement.

The same can be said for both the CPSU and QPSU Member Service Centres. Both are professionally managed and cope with a large array of complex queries and grievances. Both have invested heavily in the start-up costs of their own call centres. Both are perfectly capable of being expanded to handle the calls and grievances of other unions. Why is it that every union has to reinvent this particular wheel? Surely it is not beyond the bounds of possibility for another union to contract them to handle the calls from membership? Surely a contract can be written that guarantees that calls and member issues will be dealt with to a certain standard?

Why is it – particularly in the smaller States – that every union employs a book keeper? Again, this is a service that can be contracted out to, say, a State

TLC, so that the resources freed up can be spent on doing the real work of representing members and building power.

In many ways this kind of approach is even more radical than an amalgamation strategy. There is something about proximity to staff that gives leaders the confidence that they are doing the job well.

My suspicion is that union leaders may not be great managers of the administrative functions of the union. It tends to be neglected in favour of organising, campaigning or politics. Yet it's obvious that administration is critical to success. That surely means that efficiencies should be pursued by batching them with other unions to achieve economies of scale.

Getting economies of scale from national bodies

Economies of scale can be pursued within national organisations as well as looking for them between organisations. How crazy is it that we amalgamate two or three unions to form a Branch of 25,000 members and then fail to get the economies of operating nationally in a union of 120,000 members?

Two unions at least have been quite ruthless in ensuring that they get the maximum benefit from their national organisation.

Both the MEAA and the CPSU have instituted a national system of accounts. All money goes to the national office and all bills are paid there. One audit is done for the entire organisation. One financial controller is employed to manage the finances for the whole – rather than a series of often poorly-qualified bookkeepers in each State. Funds are invested as a whole rather than in dribs and drabs spread around the branches so that the best return can be obtained. Purchasing is done for major goods and services so that savings can be achieved. The result for both unions has been savings of hundreds of thousands of dollars.

Similar savings are available to most other unions.

The impediment is an unwillingness to give up power by State Branches that are semi-autonomous.

I don't pretend that this solution is for very union. Some predominantly State-based unions will never agree to the centralisation of accounts. This connotes far too great a sacrifice of control over finances. But if the States control the National Office through a National Council and they increasingly trust the National Office to coordinate industrial campaigns, why wouldn't the issue of centralisation of accounting be pursued?

Again, the CPSU has led the way in centralising their Member Service Centre. I have talked about this elsewhere. But in simple financial terms, think of the savings achieved as a result of having one team of well managed membership staff rather than a series of membership staff spread throughout the country. The same is true of the MEAA's Membership Centre. Centralisation has meant huge savings for that union – most importantly, it means that the level of expertise is vastly improved. (The MEAA is my old union and when I ring up with a membership query I can't get over the fact that they actually know what they are talking about! It was never like that in my day of running the union.)

Getting economies of scale in membership processing need not depend on a State Branch's willingness to give up control. If necessary, the National Office can set the operation up on a semi-commercial basis and enter into a contract with the branch for the supply of membership services! The key is to act like a union with hundreds of thousands of members rather than a set of six or seven tiny unions loosely allied together.

Part 4

BUILDING STRATEGIC LEVERAGE

We have spent the last section looking at how we can make unions stronger and better suited to their harsh environment by using new organisational strategies. Some unions are yet to start this process but others have implemented a substantial part of the agenda.

On its own, as Weil's analysis in Chapter 9 makes clear, this won't be enough. I think it was the SEIU's Tom Woodruff who estimated that, using only bottom up organising techniques, it would take 300 years for workers to win power in relation to their employers.

We also need to work out what needs to change in the strategic environment so that workers have the chance to exercise their right to freedom of association guaranteed by the Universal Declaration on Human Rights.

Three problems exist.

The first issue is the attitude of employers. Opposition to the collective representation of workers is now the ideological norm within the employer community.

Secondly, some employers are so large and powerful nationally and internationally that they are immune from pressure from one union alone.

Thirdly, the political environment, even where State Labor governments exist, is very largely skewed against support for unions' efforts to increase the power of workers.

We need to use our organisational strength to turn these problems around. Until we do, the scale of our success will be limited.

20

Our strategy towards employers

Of all the points of strategic leverage we need to consider, the most important is our relationship with employers.

The current federal government has changed the workplace environment in three ways.

First, they have signalled to the employer community that unions are fair game and that deunionising workplaces, individualising employment relationships and suppressing collective representation is acceptable.

Secondly, the government has created legislative assistance that helps employers reduce the power of workers to act collectively.

Thirdly, the government has periodically targeted particular unions – the MUA during the Patrick's dispute and the CFMEU during the Building Industry Royal Commission – to demonstrate that workers cannot exercise power in the face of overwhelming state power. To date, and in contrast to the experience in both the US and the UK, they have been monumentally unsuccessful in this.

But despite the government's attempts to require employers to individualise employment relations through the linkage of federal funding with their workplace relations agenda, employers still retain a large measure of freedom in the way in which they relate to their workforce. They can choose whether or not they want to suppress their employees' rights to be collectively represented.

If our aim is to organise thousands of new workers in new industries, then employers' reactions to their options will be of central importance.

The key aim of our strategy must be to persuade employers that it is in their commercial self-interest to allow their employees to make a rational judgment about collective representation free of the intimidatory behaviour advocated by Big Business' political wing.

This next section, then, aims to outline how we must analyse our industries to determine which employers are strategically critical, what kind of pressure will need to be brought to bear and the degree to which we are able to reach a mutually beneficial accommodation with employers.

The need for industry analysis

Industry density only tells part of the story about the ability of unions to deliver power to the workers they represent.

I want to look at arguably one of the most powerful unions in the country – the Mining and Energy Division of the CFMEU – to illustrate this point and to show how every union needs to analyse its level of industry power and plan its strategy accordingly.

The mining industry

The CFMEU sees itself as extremely powerful. It boasts rates of membership density of over 95 per cent in its major area of coverage, Australia's coal mines. It has seen off a bitter challenge to its right to represent coal miners collectively by Rio Tinto at one of the country's richest coal mines, Hunter Valley Number 1.

The union itself is rich. It charges high rates of union dues, levies its members to support a large strike fund, and can rightly point to a very high level of internal organisation across all its mining sites. Lodge Committees run the union and ensure that its fate rests in the hands of members.

Despite this strength, it has analysed its own industry and recognises just how important it is to identify and address its strategic weaknesses.

Mining has been one of the strongholds of union membership and power. In 1993, the industry had levels of density higher than 50 per cent.

However, the metal mining industry has been deunionised and as a result of aggressive employer action, government assistance and deficiencies in union organisation in these mines, most now employ their workforce on either individual agreements or non-union collective agreements.

The remaining 29.1 per cent of workers are almost exclusively concentrated in the coal mining sector.

The gap between the treatment of workers in the two areas couldn't be more profound. In metals, miners occupy their jobs at the whim of the employer. I've asked miners on individual agreements how grievances are handled. They laugh. Their supervisors have a standard response: "If you don't like it, you can fuck off!" Because the safety of coal miners is built on a process of consultation, coal mining is much safer than, say, gold mining. At Hammersley Iron, workers had to put up with seven roster changes in 18 months – with all the consequent disruption to family life. At the coal mines, rosters are changed through a process of consultation.

In metal mining the operational requirements of the company are all important. Coal miners, by contrast, have the power to make certain that their issues are dealt with seriously and that their members are treated with respect.

Metal mining needs to be reunionised because it is objectionable that highly productive workers in one of Australia's major export industries should have to put up with this kind of capricious managerial behaviour.

But it also needs to be organised because the problem impacts on the unionised sector of the industry. For the Mining and Energy Division of the CFMEU, the development of such a large group of non-union miners poses a threat to the continuing unionisation of coal mines.

The union won its battle at Hunter Valley Number 1. Employers now, however, are attempting to ensure that every new coal mine opens with either non-union collective agreements or individual contracts. Workers entered these new mines from open cut, non-union iron ore or gold mines in Western Australia. Used to low, non-union levels of wages, they were more than happy to accept even sub-standard non-union coal mine wages on the east coast.

The problems for the Mining Division go even further. The level of labour hire employment in the coal mining industry is growing. Permanent employees, fully unionised and well organised, have looked with some suspicion on non-permanent workers coming into their pits. They sit uncomfortably outside the union's structures. Too many see themselves as second class citizens. Such a position is unsustainable. The union will need to ensure that this casual workforce doesn't become a source of non-union replacement workers capable of diluting the union's undoubted power.

Strategic analysis of the industry provides the following conclusions:

- Mining workers across the whole industry have to be organised – that will depend on the major unions (AWU, CFMEU (Mining and Energy), CEPU and AMWU) working together to ensure that metal miners are re-organised, as they have done successfully at BHP Iron Ore.

- New mines have to be organised. Employers will continue to set up new non-union mines – as the old pits are exhausted. Left unchecked, the union's reach will erode over time. Retaining strong control over existing sites isn't good enough as every pit has a limited life.

- Labour hire miners have to be organised so that their interests are protected and they feel themselves to be an integral and important part of the union's organisational structure. Pit after pit is making increasing use of labour hire contractors – to the extent where they can outnumber the permanent workforce.

Building industry power

We need to look at the level of power that needs to be built in each industry that will secure fair treatment for the workers in that industry.

Once we have established the level of density required overall and which employers in particular need to be organised, we need to determine what needs to be done to achieve that result and then resource every part of that strategy.

Working as we do now, from where we are – our current resources, strategy and tactics – is safe in one sense. We feel that if we do just a little more, then things should improve.

The problem is that we are lying to workers. We say that if we just do a bit more, more organising, more activism, they can win. But doing more of what we are already doing may not be enough. It may well mean that we can't win. If we go up against major employers or whole industries with their scale, their national and international reach, their unlimited financial resources, their determination to stop the union gaining a foothold, their ruthless approach to workers, we need to know that we can match their determination and resources.

Organising with power

The Organising Centre and the NSW and Victorian Branches of the LHMU agreed to try to organise large residential hotels in both Melbourne and Sydney in 1999. At the time, we did what had never been done before on such a scale. We allocated a significant number of organisers in both cities and freed them up from all other work. Their only task was to organise hotels.

We provided them with two skilled Lead Organisers in Troy Burton and Bernie Dean.

We used organising techniques designed to build workplace committees in each of the targeted hotels. We encouraged them to use escalating pressure tactics and to build power within their hotels.

We targeted particular hotels. Instead of just following hot shop leads, we attempted to build issues and activists in those hotels that we thought were critical to success.

Let's be clear. In those days this was radical stuff and we had some success. We established in the minds of both workers and employers that the LHMU was the Hotel Union. We increased membership substantially. Membership committees were set up in each of the hotels that we had nominated – around eight in each city. The members were excited at finally having a chance to deal with their employers from some kind of position of power.

At no time, however, did we achieve enough power to put the issue of union membership beyond doubt. At every stage it required some courage from members to put their hands up and identify themselves as a union supporter. Delegates were asked to lead their existing members in the ongoing battle for power while also deal with the following up of new starters so that density could be maintained.

From the employers' point of view they were always in the position of knowing that the union was only organising in a limited number of hotels. Indeed, not every hotel in each chain was targeted. Their competitors were free of union pressure. And the only power that was being exerted against them was that wielded by their housekeeping staff and in some places, their kitchen staff. The union could be resisted free of the fear of any serious disruption to their cash flow. Employers knew that any weakening in their response to the union might well lead them to suffer wage competition from the other employers not being organised by the union.

I am happy to defend what we did at that time – and indeed, I need to take responsibility for it as I was involved in the planning of the project. But with the benefit of hindsight, we were never going to win industry power. To continue with such a strategy now in the light of what we know to be the result of such a style of organising, would be almost criminally negligent. Yet that is what we are doing in industry after industry.

Workers can't afford to label themselves as union and then have the campaign fail. We have to have a strategy that has a better than reasonable chance of winning. And that strategy needs to be backed with appropriate structures and a resource base that allows us to do whatever is needed to win.

Let's think first about strategies that are likely to win.

Where employers are large, well resourced and determined to resist workers gaining some measure of power, it is extremely difficult for us to expect workers alone to take on their employers and win. Not all employers, of course, are in this category. Some won't like their workers bringing the union in – but won't deploy the full panoply of anti-union techniques to deny them the freedom to associate together. But an increasing number will. In these cases, we can do everything that we have said already about successful organising campaigns: building a committee, one to one contact, escalating pressure tactics, lead organisers, organising away from the workplace in workers' homes. At the end of the day this pits workers against an aggressive employer. Short of embarking on a major strike to get recognition – testing which side can do the most economic damage to each other – it may not be enough to win. The forces arrayed against us are simply too unequal.

We must then look at what more needs to be done to build the power of the workers.

Companies do not operate in isolation from the community. That's where their customers, shareholders and corporate partners and suppliers come from. They are subject to political decision-making – whether it is a local council making a decision about a development application or a government passing regulations or establishing contracts with the company.

All these relationships provide workers with the chance to bring additional pressure to bear on a company that is determined to deny a human right – the right to organise – to its workforce.

After all, if the company is prepared to take aggressive action against its own workforce – presumably in the interests of short-term profit – then surely it is highly likely to be behaving in a similarly unethical fashion towards others. The challenge for the union and the workers trying to organise is to find these areas of poor business practice, identify those who are affected by the company's behaviour and join with them in educating the company of the clear commercial need for high standards of ethical behaviour in all areas of activity.

If local residents are aggrieved by the impact of a development application on their neighbourhood, why wouldn't the workers help them to make their claim against the company? If customers are receiving sub-standard service because of faulty products then why shouldn't we seek to help consumers get some measure of redress from the appropriate authorities?

If government seeks to give a contract to the company and it is a government that is supposed to be friendly to the labour movement, why wouldn't the workers let the relevant Minister know how the company treats its workforce. More importantly, shouldn't the Minister be carefully examining the bona fides of a company willing to cut corners to such an extent that they will infringe the rights of workers? Is there a danger that they will cut corners in fulfilling a government contract?

Are there issues that market analysts and shareholders need to know about the company's behaviour? Again, if they are prepared to cut corners on labour standards, are they cutting corners elsewhere?

For those employers with direct contact with their customers in the retail sector, we can revive the techniques used by the union movement back in the 1900s. Consumers who are sympathetic to the concerns of workers can be asked to go elsewhere. A public campaign against an employer behaving badly can be a powerful force that gets employers to see reason, as we saw so tellingly with James Hardie. In Australia, with its tradition of a fair go, this may well be the most powerful sanction of all.

This may seem harsh to the employers reading this – but they should understand that workers are serious about having a voice about the way they are treated. If companies act in the kind of aggressive way that is common in the United States then that will provoke a reaction proportionate to the company's level of aggression.

As well as widening our range of tactics we also need to consider the depth of our impact on the company. Are we organising to scale? That is, are we just starting the campaign at one end of a large employer's national operations? If so, we are setting ourselves up for defeat. Winning in one State will not generally be enough to make union membership uncontroversial within a company. And remember that is what winning looks like.

Let's apply this strategy to the earlier example I gave of organising large residential hotels.

What would it take to give those workers power in their industry? Let's envisage what power looks like: a hotel industry where workers had real power would be an industry where wages have been taken out of competition, where it was a natural part of working in the industry to be a member of the union, where density levels – at least as a proportion of turnover – were high and workplace leaders had access to training and time to do their business of representing the interest of members to management.

To achieve that outcome the major chains have to be organised – the Accors, Starwoods and Hiltons – and we need to be able to do that in most of the capital cities. We need to identify the owners of properties and their influence on union neutrality. We need to identify and organise particularly important hotels not linked to chain management. After all, the chains need to know that treating their employees fairly will not make them uncompetitive. We need to know the peaks and troughs of the industry and where they source their customers. Are these chains dependent on foreign tourists, local tourists or are they catering primarily to business people? Can they afford to increase wages and if they cannot, by what would their charges have to rise? We need to understand the industry as thoroughly as do the major employers.

To do that requires that we have our own researchers who can tell us how the industry operates and which employers will make a difference to wage competition in the industry.

To organise the key employers we need to develop a strategy for organising that has some hope of success. Workers need to be approached – preferably in their homes – away from pressure from their employer. To do that we need to get lists of workers and their addresses and we need large numbers of organisers to be able to do that work.

If employers are entirely resistant – as their parent companies usually are in countries like the United States and Canada – we need to find pressure points that will persuade them to be genuinely neutral. Do our workplace leaders want us to let customers know that their right to associate together is being infringed? Do we start to publish lists of hotels where the rights of workers to organise are respected and workers consequently receive decent rates of pay and appropriate conditions?

We need to look at all the hotel chains' corporate and community relationships to see whether there are potential allies who can help the workers get their right to organise.

US unions have developed a collective bargaining technique that we can adapt and use here. Organising a whole industry takes time. We have to do it, generally, employer by employer. If we insist that each of the employers pay higher rates of pay and conditions as soon as they are organised, we run the risk that we make them uncompetitive. They will resist us to the death. Even if we win, the employer will lose market share as their product or service becomes uncompetitive. We can negotiate with them a contract provision that only lifts wage rates to the desired level, once a set proportion of their market is organised. Such a trigger means that they can sign with the union, safe in the knowledge that this will not be used as a mean of damaging their business, which can pay higher rates once the industry moves to that higher rate.

21

Managing the employer relationship

We need to work out ways in which we can encourage employers to agree to deal with their workforce on a collective basis so that unionisation becomes in their commercial best interests. In trying to come up with a mutual benefit argument for union organisation, however, we need to reflect on our own recent experience of such policies so that we don't repeat our mistakes.

Let's first though, go back to the fundamental question. What is the endpoint of organising in a workplace?

At one level the answer is easy. We want working people to have power. With power, they are in a position to demand that they be treated fairly, receive a just reward for their work and are able to have a say in how their whole society operates and is governed.

The strategies discussed address how to achieve that power. But for how long do members to keep this up? After all, organising involves taking collective action of some kind.

Think of it for a moment from the employer's point of view.

Are we proposing that workers be let loose on a program of permanent revolution? Do we expect them, every day, to stick together and continually demonstrate their power through escalating pressure tactics? If we are suggesting that the endpoint of organising is the construction of a workers' soviet which will deliver edicts to management backed up with on-going collective action – then quite rationally, employers will pay any price to keep us out.

And employer attitudes are important to us. At a pragmatic level, we can't afford to fight every employer in the country simultaneously. They have far greater financial resources than do we. Further, if we are behaving unreasonably, we lose public support. In such an environment, we cannot win.

Most importantly, workers won't tolerate a state of permanent revolution. They want to get on with their jobs. Many will want the chance to actually enjoy doing what they do at work – their work is an important part of their lives. Most are committed to delivering a good service or product to the public and they take pride in the part they play in making their society a better place to live.

Our aim in organising a workplace, then, is to spend time in helping workers get power for themselves so that they can build a relationship with their employer that is based on mutual respect and a more equal distribution of power. And then we need to move on to other sections of their industry to build power there. We need high density among the strategically important employers so that we can take wages out of competition. Giving power to workers has to be made safe for employers.

Recognition agreements

The trick is that we must leave behind us a workplace that is relatively self-sufficient and capable of retaining its power. If we move on and the workers we have organised do nothing, we run the risk that, as time goes on, their power disappears.

The aim must be to have the workers enter into an agreement with their employer that is aimed at building a cooperative relationship between employer and employee and thereby make the operation of the union in the workplace uncontroversial. Such an agreement will normally be negotiated alongside the collective agreement because it is an issue about which we bargain along with wages and working conditions. It will act as the point at which the employer recognises that the union represents the interests of the workforce. In some cases it can be a quite separate agreement – entered into even before a collective agreement is negotiated. But both sides must recognise that the workers have demonstrated their power and they want a new relationship that reflects that fact.

Such an agreement can cover a range of areas.

At its core is the recognition of the workers' union as the collective voice of the workers.

It needs to provide for union security. It needs to set out the employer's acknowledgment that workers can and will be represented by the union. The employer must make clear that supervisors and managers must respect the right of workers to joint their union. It follows that union representatives and officials will need access to the workplace and a means of communicating with members.

Further, the employer will need to give the delegates access to any inductions they hold or at the least allow the delegate to meet new employees within the first week of joining the firm. Delegates will need to be given a minimal level of assistance in getting direct debit forms filled out with the correct bank details so that it becomes easy to join the union and contribute financially.

The workplace leaders need to be recognised and given the chance to be released from work to attend training as union delegates, handle grievances and participate in union activities. They need to be given time to consult with their colleagues so that they can be certain that they truly represent the views of their members to management.

While the recent *Electrolux* High Court decision[1] may mean that some aspects of these agreements may not be included in federally certified agreements, the same impediments do not exist in the common law. Some unions may seek to make the recognition agreement a common law contract with liquidated damages enforceable in the civil courts. I don't believe this is necessary, just as I don't think that the *Electrolux* decision deals a fatal blow to union organisation. Such a cooperation agreement represents an agreement between the parties that they will respect each other and agree to work together. If one party breaches it, and the workplace remains well organised, then industrial consequences will flow from the breach. The employer knows that and should act accordingly. Equally, if the union abuses its agreement to act cooperatively by pursuing on-going industrial action to settle disputes, then the employer equally is entitled to continue to resist the whole organising process.

Such an agreement means that the union office can deprioritise the workplace as a place where organising takes place. Organisers can look elsewhere to organise the unorganised. And of course, organised employers want that to happen – as it's the unorganised workplaces that are competing unfairly on the basis of wages and conditions.

Grievances will still exist. No matter how well intentioned management or workers might be, conflict will occur and will need to be resolved. The cooperation agreement should contain a disputes settling procedure that will need to be followed. The union office may become involved as part of that procedure. But the office will not normally be assessing grievances, looking for opportunities to organise and agitate workers to build power.

There are dangers in this of course. As workers are replaced with new employees – and as supervisors and managers change, the memory of how the benefits of such workplace arrangements, and how they were won, will be forgotten, and workers' power will erode over time.

That means that the delegates and their organisers will need to ensure that the collective agreement cannot have too long a term. As it comes up for renegotiation, the union should once more organise around the potential outcomes. Where membership has slipped, it will need to be built up again. Where activists are missing from sections of their workforce, they will have to be replaced. Issues will need to be identified and members asked what action they are prepared to take in having those issues considered by management. Members, all over again, will need to be educated in how their power as a collective is to be built and demonstrated to management.

In many bargaining cycles, it will be likely that agreement can be reached amicably. There will be relatively token escalating pressure tactics that remind

---

1 *Electrolux Home Products PL v Australian Workers Union* (2004) HCA 40 (2 September 2004). The decision determined that issues not directly relevant to the employment relationship couldn't form part of a registered collective agreement.

the employer that workers are not to be taken for granted. Then a deal can be done that satisfies both sides.

But even in the most amicable relationships, it seems that at least once every ten years or so, employers forget that workers do have power and have the capacity to exercise it, perhaps due to a new generation of management.

What then about activity between collective agreement negotiations? It seems to be a long time to keep delegate networks active – if the presumption is that they are not used to organise around workplace problems. Does cooperation mean that these leadership networks are deactivated and must be built from scratch at the time of collective bargaining?

Not at all.

Workplace leaders, as a minimum, will need to be involved in the implementation of the collective agreement. When consultation is required, they are the ones to handle it.

Workplace leaders also need to be asked to look for ways in which they can build the collective consciousness of the workers that do not conflict with the employer agreement. It may be that they spend time in organising a blood bank collection drive. They can involve members in activities designed to build solidarity with workers in other countries – which has the advantage of broadening members' horizons to what is happening elsewhere and builds a sense of collective action. The NSW TWU uses the "Truckies Convoy for Kids" for this purpose. The nursing and teaching unions both have extensive programs of assistance through Union Aid Abroad to workplaces and facilities in other countries.

Above all, the union office needs to involve these workers in the task of organising the whole industry. These activists are the prime labour source for member organising programs. These are the people we can develop to help us in political organising at election time. These are the people to get involved in the demonstrations outside the head offices of companies that are resisting our organising efforts.

Partnership as a union revival strategy

How far can we take this?

If we enter into a recognition agreement with an employer, why shouldn't that also deal with issues of productivity enhancement so that both employers and workers would have a very clear self-interest in the outcome. If workers' voice is taken as a given, then shouldn't that provide an opportunity for them to be free to assist the employer in making the workplace more efficient?

No one should misunderstand the depth of feeling among Australian union officials and members towards productivity agreements with employers – particularly given our experience during the Accord years. Just a year ago, I invited a management consultant to speak to the Union Management course. He had an impeccable reputation as someone committed to working with both management and labour so that the interests of both were protected. He had experienced considerable success in this work elsewhere in the world. The group he was speaking to included a range of State Secretaries and a couple of senior national officials. They came from a range of blue and white collar, public and private sector unions.

He put the thesis to the group that a model of industrial relations that concentrated on nothing but the differing interests of unions and employers was far too negative and that both sides wanted the same things – productive workplaces that provided high profits and secure, well-paid jobs. That meant that unions should engage with employers in an effort to change work practices to the mutual benefit of both sides and that we needed to persuade our members to take responsibility for the economic welfare of their employer.

The response from the union officials was savage. Each of them spoke with real feeling of their own experiences during the Accord years of selling cooperation to their members – often at some political cost – and having their trust betrayed by employers. They spoke of employers taking their willingness to negotiate around work practices as a sign of weakness; of employers using best practice, teams and quality improvement as a cover for introducing downsizing, outsourcing, casualisation; of how productivity improvement became code for work intensification; of how firms would – even in the economic good times – pursue retrenchments in pursuit of a favourable bounce from the stock market; of how unions were put in the position of seeing their best organised workplaces decimated and the credibility of union officials as an independent voice for workers destroyed.

The Best Practice Program

An analysis of the most prominent of these programs of engagement between workers and their employers goes some way to showing why the current generation of union leadership is so wary of engagement over productivity improvement with employers.

The Best Practice Program in the metal and engineering industry was a tripartite initiative which was publicly funded and introduced by a supportive government.

The sites were considered 'leading edge' workplaces and workplace union organisation was universally agreed to be strong by Australian standards".[2]

---

2   Buchanan J and Briggs, C, "Works Councils and Inequality at Work in Contemporary Australia" in Gollan, R Markey and I Ross (eds), *Works Councils in Australia* 2002, Federation Press, p 55.

Many union officials from this period will remember these programs. They spread beyond the metal industry but the leading examples of best practice models were found in that industry – largely because the unions there championed them enthusiastically. The AMWU in particular sought to focus on the long-term interest of their members and their job security rather than short-term gains in wages. It was convinced that the best way forward for their industry was to get away from the bitter confrontations that had become standard and to encourage their members to work cooperatively with employers to develop best practice firms that were capable of competing with the rest of the world. They saw this process as giving their members a chance at helping create a "high road" model of manufacturing excellence – in contrast to the alternative of competing on price where a low-waged, low-skill workforce became the norm. (And surely even now, we should agree that this is correct.) "Unions hoped and expected that aspects of best practice such as teamwork would lead to more satisfied and empowered employees and facilitate the involvement of unions in the negotiation of workplace change".[3]

The researchers concluded that far from achieving these objectives, unions were in fact sidelined. Far from being empowered and satisfied, workers were overwhelmed with the exercise of managerial autonomy and management's drive to secure increased flexibility, downsizing, the elimination of idle time and a strengthening of the monitoring and evaluation of performance.[4] Workers were promised better jobs; instead they got work intensification and job losses.

Partnership strategies in Britain

Despite these concerns let's look at a progress report on the British partnership initiative.

After the bitter Thatcher years and the advent of the Blair Labour Government, the Trades Union Congress (TUC) and a number of its affiliates have enthusiastically embraced the idea of partnership agreements as a means of building their relevance in a modern economy. Their hope is that the union movement will at least maintain its relative position, and at best, grow, as the economy prospers.

We have to remember the context in which this occurs. The accepted wisdom in British society is that the pre-Thatcher years of union power were a time of unremitting misery where unions wantonly damaged the economy's productivity, introduced completely unacceptable rigidities and abused their power in every way imaginable. The perception is a nonsense but in adopting

---

3   Buchanan J and Hall, R "Teams and control on the job: Insights from the Australian Metal and Engineering Best Practice Case Studies" in *Journal of Industrial Relations,* Vol 44, No 3, September 2002, p 415.

4   Ibid.

partnership as a strategy, union leaders have drawn a line under that history, matching the success of the slogan "New Labour" with their own slogan, "New Unionism".

Partnership is not an attempt to introduce a tripartite structure at the macro-economic level in the way that the Accord did in Australia. Neither business nor the Blair Government would contemplate such a thing. Instead, partnership agreements were a mechanism to build cooperative relationships at a workplace level.

They are an attempt to move away from an adversarial relationship with employers – presumably in the hope that employers will lower their resistance to the unionisation of their workforce. Partnership will turn the union into a force that builds workplace productivity – and consequently profitability for the employer.

A British academic, Ed Heery, has analysed these partnership agreements.[5] The detail of these agreements determines their value.

At their best, it is clear that a number of the agreements have the effect of widening the scope of collective agreements. Unions buy themselves into issues of job security, skill development and involvement in the business and they and their members have the chance of getting "fuller knowledge of and greater opportunity to influence, business strategy and management style".

In many firms the agreements seem to have been used as a means of defending the employment of existing members against the threat of competition from other firms both in the UK and abroad. Workers have been encouraged to pursue firm level productivity improvement through, among other things, the increasing use of contingent workers, on the understanding that their fulltime jobs will be protected.

In setting up new issues around which consultation is to take place, new modes of behaviour and new consultative forums, the hope has been that workplace organisation will be strengthened and its scope expanded.

The problem is that it appears – according to even their most enthusiastic proponents – that the partnership agreements that have been entered into have been skewed in their effect to the benefit of employers.

The agreements have included:

- "a weakening or even abandonment of stronger, power based forms of participation, which allow unions to regulate aspects of the employment relationship through collective bargaining";

- "a de-emphasis on the role of effective workplace organisation in advancing worker interests";

---

5   Heery, E, "Partnership versus organising: alternative futures for British trade unionism", in (2002) 33(1) *British Industrial Relations Journal* 20.

- "evidence of partnerships leading to a reduction in the number and range of activities of shop stewards";

- an increase in the incidence of long-term wage agreements so that the "risk of conflict between the two sides (is minimised), effectively by rendering decision-making routine in those aspects of the employment relationship where conflict is likely to arise".[6]

Not all agreements have led to such gloomy outcomes. Some workplaces have used the agreements to increase the number of workplace representatives. Others have seen rises in membership numbers and at least one agreement has allowed the union to have an impact on issues like equal opportunity, family-friendly working hours, performance management, job evaluation and the impact of information technology.

Good outcomes, however, need to be balanced against the threat of job reduction, work intensification and lower earnings growth for members.

A more recent study by Brown and Oxenbridge[7] confirms some of these findings but provides us with another way of looking at the problem.

Brown and Oxenbridge analysed 11 different companies but looked at cooperative strategies in general, rather than simply formal partnership agreements. They identified a group of firms with high trust relationships with unions that had built a co-operative relationship to the satisfaction of both sides. A second group of firms had entered into written agreements that had the apparent aim of limiting union activity rather than anything else. These used at least one or more of the following kind of clauses. First, they "explicitly limited union rights and activity in the workplace; second, refusing to deal with 'difficult' trade union officials, and dealing only with officials perceived to be compliant; third, endeavouring to reduce the number of unions with which the company dealt; and fourth, taking steps to reduce union control over communication and consultative structures and to increase management control of both".[8]

It is apparent that in each of this second group of cases, the employer tended to be negotiating with a group of unionists that had been taken over or outsourced to the company and the aim was to "handle" the fact that a non-union company was suddenly confronted with a group of unionists in its midst. Interestingly, in most of these cases, unions were not given rights to talk to any other employees in the company – other than those bound by the partnership

---

6   Heery, ibid, p 23.

7   Brown, W and Oxenbridge, S, "The development of co-operative Employer/trade union relationships in Britain", in *Industrielle Beziehungen, German Journal of Industrial Relations*, 2004, p 143.

8   Ibid, p 152.

agreement. In fact, the primary aim of the agreements was to "contain collective bargaining" rather than enhance the power of the union.

The first group of firms however, may give us some clues as to where to take the issue of building a cooperative relationship with employers. Here the aim of the relationship was to "nurture collective bargaining".

These relationships, at the time the interviews started, had not been reduced to writing but "centred on harmonious management-union relationships, high levels of unionisation, and active workplace representatives. While disputes occasionally occurred, these co-operative relationships represented the continuation of a tradition of employer-union relationships, combined with threats to company survival".[9]

In other words, these were workplaces where the union had the strength of good workplace level organisation and dealt to a far greater extent as equals with the management. Above all, the firm's track record with the union was one based on very high levels of trust. In a number of these firms, the relationship was eventually reduced to writing – for a range of reasons. Some wanted the principles to be extended to other firms in the group, others had a change of management or union representative and wanted to enshrine the principle of co-operation, and one wanted to limit the range of issues over which bargaining might occur.

The British experience on the whole will at least reinforce Australian unionists' wariness about rushing down the path of engaging with employers on projects designed to increase productivity. But the later study does provide scope for exploring relationships between employers in certain circumstances.

Cooperation agreements in Australia

Why are so many of these partnership agreements of such questionable value? I suspect that it is at least in part because unions have bargained their partnership agreements, in most cases, at a time when the employment of their members is under threat and, for that or other reasons, their power is at a low ebb.

The whole tenor of what we have suggested so far is that no agreement can be entered into without workers organising to get power. Surely that solves the problem? If these British unions had organised first, surely the outcomes would have been better? If workers build their workplace organisation to such an extent that they can bargain with their employers as equals, they can then work out ways of truly sharing responsibility for the management of the enterprise so that productivity and competitiveness can be enhanced at the same time that their interests are protected.

---

9   Ibid, p 153.

But since collective bargaining in Australia began, from the 1850s on, employers have vigorously defended their right to manage their business. Despite all the perceived power of Australian unionism at various times in its history, despite the interaction of Labor governments with unions, high density, arbitration commissions and protection, we have never succeed in shaking management's conviction that they have an absolute right to manage. Despite all the evidence to the contrary, they cling to the belief that they alone know best.

The Business Council of Australia provides us with the following telling quote:

> (CEOs) acknowledge that a more cooperative atmosphere has prevailed in most workplaces in recent years ... Nonetheless, concerns remain about the opportunity costs of the system, especially its capacity to obstruct, deter and delay change, innovation and improvement ... The special status of unions within the system remains an issue in that context.[10]

To that extent, Australian businesses are quite different to the German and Scandinavian employer communities who have built their economic success on a close and mutually beneficial interaction between labour and capital. These employers accept that in relation to some issues – like wages – there will be conflict but that a settlement will be reached that will be mutually acceptable. They accept that on other issues they can allow their workers' representatives to become involved in every aspect of their firm's operations to the mutual benefit of both parties.

That conclusion has been reached – particularly in the case of Scandinavian unions – on the back of unions being entrenched in every level of their society, with rates of density of between 80 and 95 per cent.

The situation of unions in Germany may be changing. Despite their very successful model of industrial relations based on principles of co-determination rather than our model of contest, the power base of unions is becoming increasingly more tenuous. Union membership levels are declining. In 1991 they had 11.8 million members and just 7.7 million in 2002.[11] Density has dropped from 35 per cent in 1980 to 25 per cent in 2000.[12] This is despite very strong continuing levels of institutional support and the existence of a dual system of industrial relations – sectoral level bargaining and plant level works councils, giving real privileges to collective organisations. The incidence of collective bargaining coverage and plant level structures is undermined by the shift in employment to the lightly unionised service sector and the proportionate growth in smaller employers.

---

10   BCA, Managerial leadership in the workplace, BCA, 2000.

11   Tarrant, L, *Unionism Around Us*, Briefing paper for LHMU National Council, 2004.

12   *OECD Employment Outlook,* OECD, 2004.

Nevertheless, in well-organised industries, social partnership tends to be associated with a strong union and network of shop stewards. Bosch describes hearing employer leader Mr Hundt "at a conference of the Bertelsmann Foundation, defend his notion of a social partnership against neo-liberal hardliners with the statement that, 'as long as I am active, I will not get past a strong IG Metal'".[13]

But IG Metal is typical of the weakening position of German trade unions. The number of their elected shop stewards declined between 1982 and 1997 by 30 per cent – at a time when employment in the metal industry remained steady. The union lost almost 25 per cent of its membership between 1990 and 2000.[14]

In Australia, it is difficult to imagine that the Business Council will rush to adopt an industrial relations model based on co-determination or cooperation or even a model involving a requirement to consult.

Yet I have come across employers whom I trust and who see their competitive advantage in cooperating with the union. I stress in saying this, that my experience was in an industry where my union was considered to have considerable power and where union membership was not an issue. In many areas, that position still exists. Unions do have power in some industries and some workplaces – despite our overall fall in density. How then can trust be developed?

Trust is learned only on the basis of experience. If both unions and employers behave in a predictable fashion, then trust between the two sides can grow. If one side abuses a position of temporary advantage, then trust will be diminished or destroyed. One of the earliest lessons I learned as a union official was the importance of the continuing relationship between employers and unions. Saving the employer's face was important because we had to negotiate with him tomorrow or the next day. Taking a cheap shot was to be avoided. Securing a victory by questionable or unethical means was not beneficial because our opponents would then simply wait to take retribution at some time in the future.

There are some employers who continue to recognise the importance of that continuing relationship and see competitive advantage in having a good and open relationship with their workforce. No matter what our experience of the Accord period and its role in promoting one-sided workplace co-operation, we need, in these circumstances, to avoid behaving in a doctrinaire fashion. We would be crazy to turn our backs on engagement with employers where we are

---

13 Bosch, G, "The Changing Nature of Collective Bargaining in Germany" in Katz, HC, Lee, W, and Lee, J (eds), *The New Structure of Labor Relations*, ILR Press, 2004.

14 Hassel, A, "The Erosion Continues: Reply" in *British Journal of Industrial Relations*, June 2002 pp 313-314.

confident that they do not aim at our destruction or at damage to the fundamental interests of members.

Peetz is surely correct:

> If for reasons of prosperity or survival, employees generally support the agenda
> proposed by management, then unions run a risk if they frivolously seek to derail
> that agenda. Employees might engage in 'wildcat cooperation' and employers might
> freeze unions out of the relationship with their members.[15]

A good example of productive interaction between union and employers is
found in the ACT cleaning industry. There, a group of employers was persuaded
to get the support of government to insist on the use of a code of conduct for
government cleaning contracts. This has meant that to get market share,
employers need to match the industry standard for wages and cleaning rates.

We have to keep open the possibility of such an engagement process taking
place. Workers don't want to be at war with their employers. If we can manage
to pull it off, workers want to have increased levels of job security. Our country
needs our firms to be highly productive and competitive with the rest of the
world. Our public services need to be of the highest quality. Excellence is
rewarding for workers at every level.

There are a number of preconditions that need to be kept in mind.

The first is that the relationship has to be dependent on workers achieving
relatively high levels of power. There are employers who prefer to work cooperatively with workers and their unions. They will never be heard within the
employer community unless – like Mr Hundt and IG Metal – they can point to
the presence of workers with real power who, if consultation does not take place,
have the capacity to force the issue.

We must not call the process "partnership". With all due respect to our
colleagues in other countries who use this term, there can never be a partnership with employers. The term implies equality in all things – including
ownership. That will very rarely happen unless we believe that distributive
socialism is just around the corner. Employers will always have more money
and information than their workers. Using the term almost guarantees that
workers will become disillusioned with the agreement that they have entered
into. We can go down the path of cooperation – but it will necessarily fall short
of partnership.

We ask for recognition and union security – it is for the employers to
approach us with requests for cooperation. We cannot afford to be placed again
in the position of championing cooperation when the employer holds so much of
the power in their hands. We run the risk that union leaders, both externally

---

15   Peetz, D, *Unions in a Contrary World, The future of the Australian trade union
     movement*, Cambridge University Press, 1998, p 15.

and in the workplace, lose credibility with those they represent as cooperation falls apart in the face of wavering employer commitment.

Successful co-operation agreements will come out of a long-standing relationship of trust.

Agreements must be negotiated with very detailed levels of consultation with the workers concerned. They must own it. If we fail to do this, we fall into all the old traps of third-partyism. Workers will see unions as an external force doing things for them and to them.

Ideally, cooperation should take place at an industry level – in those industries where we have successfully entrenched our power and taken wages out of competition. Employers will find it difficult to engage with us on these questions if they are constantly worried about being blindsided by a competitor undercutting their market share and profits by cutting wages. Workers need to know that their willingness to negotiate on these issues will not be taken as an opportunity simply to drive wage costs lower in order to get a jump on other workplaces in the industry.

Above all, everything we have said elsewhere about maintaining levels of workplace activism must continue to apply. Workers must continue to understand that their ability to enter into cooperation agreements comes from their collective power – and that power needs to be maintained through some form of activism. My fear is that – even in those countries in Europe with very high rates of density (particularly when their subsidiaries operate in the United States on a non-union basis) – if their activist structures atrophy, the temptation will always exist to adopt American models of industrial relations and abandon a system which has worked well for everyone concerned. Short-term profits are extraordinarily seductive for shareholders and those managers with a vested interest in short-term share price gain.

22

The need for scale in organising

The role of the ACTU and the State Labor Councils

The peak councils of the movement have a long history. Arguably, given the high level of institutional support for unionism and the existence of the Labor Party, they have been far more important in Australia than in other comparable countries. All of them have been central to the resourcing of a multitude of small unions and union branches that lacked the resources to run expensive industrial commission cases. They have acted as the voice for unions as a whole, to the community generally and to government – particularly Labor governments. In some States, NSW for example, they have been among society's most powerful extra-parliamentary institutions. During the Accord period, this was certainly true of the ACTU and its leadership. For all these reasons, the peak councils have been, in practice, independently powerful and at times capable of overriding the interest and concerns of individual unions.

That was the past, what of the future?

Amalgamation, the decline in the importance of the State and National Wage cases and the end of the Accord have all led to a perception of declining relevance. Some unions have even decided to disaffiliate from their State Labor Councils altogether. A sense has grown that unions now have far more freedom to act independently of the peak council. Union autonomy is paramount.

The peak councils have responded to this. When Greg Combet wrote *unions@work* together with eight senior union leaders, he quite consciously expressed peak councils' recommendations as just that – recommendations. The document was not to be seen as prescriptive.

The work that the ACTU Organising Centre does is in large part, on a cost recovery basis. Unions can opt to subscribe to its operations. They choose whether or not to involve the centre in their work or send officers to its courses.

The threat that faces us now is of such magnitude that I want to argue that every union needs to think very carefully about its relationship to the movement's central organisations. I want to make the controversial suggestion that some part of individual autonomy needs to be exercised at the centre. I say this because our opponents – big business – are organised as never before and we must unite in order for workers to get and keep some measure of countervailing power.

Let me explain what I mean.

It strikes me that the peak councils have five main functions:

- Leading the union movement overall;

- Expressing a political voice;

- Maintaining minimum employment standards through the industrial commissions;

- Coordinating solidarity action between unions;

- Providing a strategic reserve of resources.

In the case of State Labor Councils, I suspect that we could add the role of coordinating action on a geographic basis. Because they are located so emphatically in their local community, these councils have a powerful role to play in getting unions to examine their interaction within their community. They are charged with the need to get their affiliates to take up issues of relevance to union members in the community and to give teeth to commitments for mutual support made to community organisations.

When a union decides to affiliate, it transfers some authority to the peak council. Rather than speak to every individual union leader, on the big issues, the Labor Party leader will negotiate with the ACTU Secretary or the Trades and Labor Council Secretary. When unions during the Patrick's dispute agreed to assist by taking responsibility for a part of the picket line roster they were surrendering some part of their autonomy – their ability to deploy their resources as they saw fit – in light of the overall need to express solidarity with the MUA. When a union pays affiliation fees to the peak council, those funds are no longer available to be spent on members – they are deployed to the greater good of the movement as a whole.

The argument then becomes not whether unions give up some part of their autonomy of action, but rather, *how* much.

I want to suggest in this section that unions – both leadership and membership – must begin to focus far more consciously on the problems afflicting the whole workforce rather than just their own membership. Every union must deliver for its own membership, of course – but with one eye fixed on what is happening to workers more generally.

This happens now in theory of course. Unions listen respectfully at the Executive of ACTU or Labor Council as a single union describes the attack made on it by government or employer. A resolution will be passed and the officers of the council urged to render all assistance to the affiliate concerned. With the notable exception of the Patrick's dispute, that's it. A meeting of unions may be convened. The council officer may attend negotiations. A press release may go out. The union is on its own.

Some parts of this may be changing. I have seen workers stand up and tell their story of worker oppression at the weekly meeting of Unions NSW. They can move the audience of largely union officials to action. Money can be collected or union offices will empty over the next week to support a rally in the workers' defence.

The fundamental problem for the peak councils is that – even more than the individual unions – they have no money.

The ACTU affiliation fee is $2.50 per member per year. The TUC charges $5.35 pa and the AFL-CIO, $9.71 pa (including a mobilisation levy of $1.27 cents per member).[1]

Greg Combet has dramatically reduced the number of industrial and policy officers since he took office and quadrupled the amount spent on the Organising Centre to some $700,000. Yet, the simple fact is that if any union asks for direct organising assistance, the organisation has nothing much to give apart from the spare time effort of already busy officers.

The same problem afflicts the State councils – with the possible exception of Unions NSW which is blessed with substantial assets. Most of them have one or two officers. They have very little capacity to make an impact on the large challenges which should dominate the concerns of the movement at a local level.

The issue goes beyond money.

We saw the power of a peak council during the Patrick's dispute. It was able to deploy movement wide resources to achieve victory. If the numbers on the picket line needed boosting, the labor council or ACTU officers could activate the telephone tree to deliver bodies to the picket line. Various labour councils have tried to emulate that success since and set up an activist register of people willing to be called out a set number of times per year to dramatise wide support for the workers involved. In every case these efforts have been stillborn. Unions are not willing to give up any of their authority and if members are to be mobilised it must be through the union. And we all know what that means. It never happens.

I contrast that with the willingness of the American unions – a movement far more fractious and disunited than ours traditionally – to hand over their membership lists to the AFL-CIO for use in elections. Yes these lists are strictly hedged around with conditions as to their use and not every union participates – but the fact remains that the union movement in that country starts each election with a database containing 16 million names – and it will get bigger as the families of union members are added to it.

---

1   All amounts expressed in Australian dollars.

If the 2004 election taught us nothing else, surely it showed us that our political activity needs to be far better and that there is a need for some central control of resources if we are to make a difference.

The labour councils too, lack the ability to deliver real assistance to community organisations which need help today – who have helped us in the past and are likely to be capable of helping us in the future. Again, unions need to be willing to allow these locally-based peak councils to call on them and their members for the kind of practical help that builds relationships with community allies.

At 23 per cent density we need to promote cooperation between unions on a geographic basis. Power will come from industry or sometimes occupational organising but we also need to project our power regionally. Employers need to know that if they want to set up shop in a particular city or town, they will have to deal with the local unions. If they don't then there will be consequences.

No one can do that job other than the local labour council.

But the big change that I think needs to be made is in the area of organising.

Exercising power as a movement

Two problems have to be addressed by the whole movement.

The first of these is our inability to support workers who are locked out or forced to strike to secure a reasonable level of compensation. The second is our inability to ensure that large employers or whole sectors of employment previously not unionised are organised.

The escalating pressure tactics I have talked about earlier are just that – pinpricks to demonstrate to employers the commitment of the workers and a reinforcement of the workers' sense of solidarity. But increasingly we are faced with ideologically-driven employers who resist the very idea of collective representation. They feel free to lock their workers out for long periods. Alternatively, the only way to drag them to the bargaining table is to inflict real economic damage through strike action so significant that the demands of the workers have to be addressed.

We have been moved from an arbitral model of industrial relations to a conflict-based model. Yet we don't have the strike funds that unions working in other countries in such an environment have spent years to build up and most unions don't have readily available liquid assets to be used for such a purpose.

Faced with a lengthy stoppage we have to rely on sausage sizzles and collections. They raise small amounts of money that can only ever provide assistance to put food on the table of families struggling desperately to survive. If a sausage sizzle is our response to the overwhelming economic power of employers, it is surely more rational to simply surrender.

The second problem is that we must organise in those industries outside our traditional areas of union strength. If we continue to organise mainly in industries where employment is declining, over time, we will disappear. Worse, whole legions of employees getting work in the growing industries will lose any hope of fairness at work, decent living wages, or having a voice.

As the authors of *Fragmented Futures* have pointed out:

> For the most part, the jobs that have been lost have been permanent, reasonably well-paid, and with access to training. On the other hand, the jobs that have mushroomed – with some important exceptions – have been casual, less well paid and with less access to training opportunities.[2]

The unions that have coverage in the industries that are expanding have extremely limited resources. Tourism, and the service sector generally, is the area of job growth. The burden of getting power in these areas falls on unions that already have a limited membership base and a limited capacity to organise huge numbers of new members.

Are we to say that this is a problem that can't be fixed? That our reach is confined to those areas organised during the first half of the last century? Are we to say to the workers concerned "Sorry, but you have no hope. You will just have to take any damn thing that your employer dishes out. He is just too big for us to take on." For a movement that seeks to represent all workers, that is surely completely unacceptable. Just as the craft unions of the 19th century did when confronted with vast masses of exploited, unskilled workers, we have to meet that demand for voice.

The thing that distinguishes our movement from many others is that we have always acted on the basis of solidarity. In the early years of the 20th century, unions formed Organising Committees and their whole purpose was to help newly-forming unions. Older and bigger unions lent their expertise and resources to give them a leg up. The skilled helped the unskilled. The men helped the women to organise. The movement raised money to fund organising. It coordinated campaigns designed to steer consumers towards employers that treated their workers fairly.

It didn't end there. Throughout the past 100 years, the militant unions have helped the weaker. To go back to the accident make up pay dispute, the building union deliberately moved their claim through the Commission. They knew that while it might make it harder to settle with their employers in the immediate future, a Commission win would mean that all workers could benefit – irrespective of their industrial strength.

That spirit of "reaching down and giving others a helping hand up" needs to be called on now. The strong must help the weak. The well resourced must help the under resourced. The organised must help the unorganised.

---

2   Watson, I et al, *Fragmented Futures*, Federation Press, 2003.

Some occupations are well organised and their unions have limited scope for growth – the Maritime Union, coal miners, rail workers, nurses, (at least in the public sector) public school teachers, police, firefighters. In some sectors of the economy, we are losing jobs in those industries where we are relatively well organised. Some of these unions are part of that trend. We need far fewer coal miners or wharfies than we once did for example. And we are failing to organise workers in those industries which are expanding in employment. Remember that to increase density overall we need to recruit more members than the number of workers entering the workforce. If we are not present in the areas of significant employment growth, it is highly unlikely that we can get an appreciable rise in economy-wide density.

These new areas must become the responsibility of the relevant union – but the union needs to know that it will be backed up by the whole of the union movement.

Of all movements, our history surely shows that we are predisposed to "solidarity organising".

Unions have already risen to this challenge and many have loaned their organisers to house-calling blitzes in a number of States. That activity will continue – the organisers enjoy it and they know that reciprocal help is more likely to be available if they make the effort to help now. That gives us very large organising teams for big targets for a few days – particularly if most of the time spent is on a weekend in the organiser's own time!

However, we need to do much more than this.

The responsibility for organising new industries or major employers is a collective responsibility. And there is a payoff for us all if we take up this challenge. If we organise new industries or major employers, our credibility with the employer community grows. They will recognise that denying workers freedom of association is no longer an option. We will meet any challenge presented to us. We are not going away.

More importantly, workers throughout the economy will know that the union movement is actually moving. We are organising. That they can expect any day that a union organiser will be knocking on their door asking for their help. That, in itself, will ensure that more and more workers become union-ready and our organising campaigns will have more impact.

Collective support for individual unions will give us the best chance of emulating the surge of union membership that led us to have the highest rate of union density in the world in 1912. Workers knew then that the movement was again organising following the Great Strikes, doing it cooperatively and achieving real gains for workers.

How can other unions back the efforts of individual unions in the massive way that will be necessary for success?

I suggest that we ask our members to help in two ways.

First, we must ask them to help pay to build the power of the whole Australian workforce rather than just those workers falling within the coverage of their own union. If every union member agreed to pay 50 cents per month ($6 per year) to a centrally-held organising fund, (The Unity Fund) we would have $10.8 million to help unions organise new areas of unionisation! That's over 100 new organisers and researchers available to unions trying to take on large targets the way they should.

Secondly, unions in Australia need a system of self-protection in the event of lengthy strike or lockout. We need to ask members to contribute an additional $6 per year to go into a fund to be used for such a purpose (The Mutual Support Fund). The money collected each year could gradually build up and act as insurance against the time when access to the fund was necessary.[3]

This is a big ask. Some unions rarely go on strike. Others have overwhelming density and a limited need for new member organising.

Yet it is particularly these unions who should most seriously consider support for these two funds. Their members exist in families and communities that are affected by the loss of worker power. Members of powerful unions have an investment in the growth in power of the whole movement. They and their unions need the security of operating in a society that accepts as the norm the idea that workers will have power through union organisation. A society that determines that the market will not be a dictator.

My hope is that this will be the imperative that drives these unions not at immediate risk. Their job is to mobilise their members financially and in action, to help build a movement of workers that can have a say in how they are treated.

These unions, together with the significant number who are open to many of the ideas set out in this book and who have gone a fair way down the path of building organising unions, may well be willing to participate in such a program. I think that we should be prepared to test whether we can achieve sufficient buy-in to make it worthwhile.

I propose then, that every union be asked to raise such a levy. At $12 per year, it is set at a level that makes it almost obligatory for a union to go to its members and discuss with them why the leadership feels it is necessary. This is important. Union members need to know why movement-wide organising must take place and why they should help provide funds for the mutual support of others. They need to know that they are part of a movement. We should get them thinking beyond the immediate concerns of their own union.

---

3   The terms governing the operation of both funds would need to be worked out by those contributing. Obviously safeguards would need to be developed so that organising funds were spent where they would have most strategic impact for the movement. Equally, access to funding from the Mutual Support Fund would need to be contingent on the union satisfying the governing body that support could be justified.

Where unions agree to go through such a process and a majority of their members agree, the extra $12 will be collected from every member. That then forms the basis for both funds. Not every union will participate but I am confident that we can get unions representing 500,000 members to participate. That yields $3 million for each fund and in the case of the Unity Fund, allows us to employ the organisers and campaigners to make a start on the task before us. If we can't get unions representing 250,000 members to participate we shouldn't waste everyone's time. Expenditure from either fund would only, of course, be available to those unions making contributions. My hope is that as the funds are successful, their coverage will eventually embrace every affiliated union.

These movement-wide projects should not just be collective in the sense of collecting money. We want to build a force within the community that supports organising. We want to build the unity of unions across union structures. By agreeing to concentrate on particular strategically important campaigns we have the chance to involve much wider groups of members in the struggle.

Think how powerful it would be for employers to be confronted with hundreds of workers from worksites across the city – if everywhere they went, they found union members united in support of the workers trying to organise.

Think how empowering it would be for the members trying to organise to see support being given to them from so many other unionists in their State – to see that they didn't have to do it all on their own.

Think of the impact on the activists who are involved – the organising skills they take back to their workplaces. When the victory is won, imagine how proud they will be that they played a part in achieving that victory.

Again, by taking collective responsibility for organising the large sectors with the most aggressive employers, we maximise our chances of winning. Most importantly of all, we build the perception that organising is the natural and right thing to do. We build a demand across the whole community for workers to get power and for organising.

Organising internationally

Australian unionists have always been internationalist in the best sense of the word and that kind of sentiment continues to this day. We have fought Apartheid, we campaign for fair trade, we participate in Global Union Federations' activities, we support boycotts of companies treating workers unfairly around the world, our ACTU President, Sharon Burrow, is the President of the International Confederation of Free Trade Unions.

Most importantly, the ACTU set up APHEDA – Union Aid Abroad in 1985 and that tiny organisation now has some 50 projects in 15 countries.

But something more is required now.

Constructing a global union?

Our employers are increasingly branch offices of multi-nationals. Even our home grown companies, as a matter of course, look for opportunities to expand internationally. If that is the case, we must build the capacity to organise to scale on an international basis. If organising against the State branch of a national employer makes little sense, equally, organising the Australian branch of a multi-national employer only exposes local management to career-threatening head office criticism.

Some way must be found to coordinate and resource international activity so that real organising and campaigning resources are allocated to action in those countries which are of particular importance to the most significant of our multi-nationals.

Most Australian unions are members of their relevant international organisation, their Global Union Federation (GUFs). Indeed, some are members of a number of these organisations. It seems logical that they are the place to locate the coordination and resourcing of international organising efforts.

However, GUFs have varying levels of commitment to the need to organise. Some are dominated by unions who fail to see the need and consequently allocate few resources to the work of organising. Many GUFs have done good work for many years in representing the interests of their affiliates at the various international organisations so that union members benefit at a national level. Some have negotiated codes of conduct with multi-national employers. But their representation work takes as a given that workers are organised and have power. And too often the codes of conduct are negotiated without any potential or actual economic pressure being brought to bear on the employer.

For Australian unions some hard decisions may have to be made. Our loss of power is so significant that nothing can be allowed to get in the way of organising to scale. If the GUFs are unable to meet that challenge, some alternative must be found.

The experience of the American unions, SEIU, UNITE and HERE, in beginning the task of organising Sodexho – a large multi-national French contracting company – may provide a clue to what we might do. They saw this company as a global target and organised accordingly. They built ties with the French unions and sought their support. They built links with the Transport and General Workers Union in Britain and they placed staff in both these countries and a range of others in order to pressure the company in whatever market happened to be important to them. The result was the company eventually agreed to grant neutrality to the unions' organising effort with the result that tens of thousands of American workers will shortly enjoy the benefit of a union contract.

In looking for organising targets we need to be conscious of the chance to expand the reach of our endeavours. We need to talk to those unions in other countries prepared to invest in international organising. We need to be prepared to commit real resources to back their efforts against companies with branch offices in Australia – even though those companies might not be – for the moment – a prime target for organising in Australia. In return, we can then expect them to back our campaigns in their own countries – as they did both in the Patricks' dispute[4] as well in the action coordinated against James Hardie.[5]

A potential problem arises in that every national union already fully commits its resources. Two solutions are possible. Unions wishing to cooperate could strategise together and plan in advance their year's activities. In this way, staff can be coordinated and allocated to targets felt to be of international concern. The alternative is for unions to allocate resources in advance to a Global Union that would then have first call on the resources and put them at the disposition of the international campaign as it arises.

If the latter path is chosen, unions will then need to decide whether there is scope to create an on-going organising Global Union of like-minded unions with real resources at its disposal in the various countries that are a priority. By having resources that are not primarily committed to national campaigns, such a union could have the ability to drive directed organising activity at a pace that suits the international campaign rather than be constrained by the competing requirements of national unions.

These resources should be no match for the organising efforts of the national union. But relatively small numbers of industry analysts, communications officers and lead organisers could bring real and unexpected pressure to bear on corporations in every significant part of their empires.

In some industries GUFs could fill this function – where they have the capacity. But we can't be held back by bureaucratic inertia. It is urgent that we begin this work immediately. We can no longer sit back while employers extend a low labour cost, exploitative economic model to every country where we are unable to build countervailing power.

We need to think carefully about where our international program of organising must be directed.

The United States

The prime target for our help must be the United States' union movement. This will of course raise a laugh. They have 16 million members, are enormously wealthy in comparison to us and they operate in the richest country in the world. Yet they have just 12.5 per cent overall density, 7.9 per cent private sector density and their model of capitalism is being exported to the whole world. The

---

4   Where action was coordinated by the International Transport Federation.
5   Where pressure was brought to bear on the company and its investors in the US by the AFL-CIO and SEIU.

particularly nasty ideology adopted by Australian big business and their parliamentary representatives has a number of names – and one of them is the "Washington consensus". The US unions, with their incapacity to combat their loss of density, have trained a generation of employers to operate and compete with the advantage of being non-union. American companies have made the working poor a fundamental part of their business planning.

We need to find real resources to help American unions organise US based multi-nationals. It is critical for us, given the influence of American business theory in our country, that they organise their employers. American employers have to be made to understand that treating workers as a low-cost commodity is unacceptable in civilised societies – and will harm their business.

New Zealand

Equally, we need to be focused on the fate of the New Zealand union movement. We have a long history of acting in solidarity with each other and we feel free to poach each other's organisers. The Kiwis are closer to us than any other country. Our two economies are already linked by treaty, the relationship will become closer as time goes by and our firms and institutions mesh at every level. We offer open borders to each other's citizens.

The problem is that our employers use New Zealand as a testing ground for all their worst ideas. CRA's deunionisation strategy in iron ore was a development of a strategy put in place at the aluminium smelter at Tiwai Point. The Australian banks – owners of all the major New Zealand banks – first tried de-unionisation in New Zealand. The savagery of New Zealand's *Employment Contracts Act 1991* acted as a formative influence on the designers of our own *Workplace Relations Act*. Our survival is intimately linked with the survival of organised labour in New Zealand. If unionism were to collapse there, given the impact of our open borders, a low-cost competitor would exist on our doorstep.

That means that we must continue to assist our colleagues across what they call "the ditch". We must strategise with them, and above all, learn from their experience. The models of the Service and Food Workers Union and Finsec in particular and their commitment to organising were among the most important factors in the development of these organising concepts in Australia during the 1990s. We need to repay that debt now as we rebuild our strength by making sure that we bring these allies with us.

They need to be (and generally are) involved in our training programs. The Australian Transport Workers Union is helping fund the re-organisation of drivers in New Zealand. The MEAA – at the invitation of the New Zealand unions – is hoping to set up a branch over there. We need to be open to the possibility of lending key resources for short periods of time. Our inter-union relationships should be close enough that teams of organisers could be exchanged between the countries for blitzes. Let's face it, an airfare from Australia to New Zealand is cheaper than an airfare between almost any Australian capital city.

Developing countries

Our obligations go beyond just the US and New Zealand. Just as we need to take wages out of competition in Australia, so we must help workers in other countries organise so that they have the chance to build power for themselves. We have campaigned around the slogan "Fair Trade not Free Trade" – and that is a powerful statement of what should happen. It is one thing for an Australian worker to lose a job as a result of the removal of trade barriers that discriminate against the production of goods or services in a poorer country. It is insupportable for the worker to lose a job to workers who are themselves denied the right to organise to get decent wages and conditions.

What can we do about this problem? In one sense, isn't this time of renewal in Australia – a time when we are grappling with decline, a time when we are experiencing the danger of a long-term systemic loss in power – precisely the moment when we must contract into ourselves and do nothing but concentrate on our own survival?

Unfortunately, capital is international and the owners and managers of capital have organised the rest of the world far better than have we. They have persuaded governments in developing countries that foreign investment is impossible unless these countries are free of labour standards. They, in their turn, now believe that the exploitation of their own citizens is essential if their countries are to be capable of developing. Worse, middle classes have been created who consequently perceive that their self-interest lies in ensuring that workers are oppressed.

Consider the situation of workers in Indonesia, China, Thailand. We at least have the chance of rebuilding our strength from a base of 23 per cent density. We have some assets. We have paid staff. We have 1.8 million members. There is no real threat of our police using tear gas or guns against unionists. Yet unionists in countries to our north are organising with nothing except their own thirst for justice. The level of resourcing available to them is minimal. It will take them hundreds of years at the present rate of progress to get to even our level of union development.

Their progress is part of our project of union renewal. We have to make available to them our organising expertise – which is now considerable. We are successful in training organisers and delegates. We are skilled in getting a whole movement to understand how to have a conversation with someone who is not a member. And we can show others how to build a workplace organisation from scratch.

We therefore need to find the resources to help APHEDA do more in the area of organising education. We will never have the money to subsidise union organisation in other countries on a large scale but we can have a quite disproportionate impact on those union movements through the agency of our education.

There is one other way in which we can help unions to organise elsewhere while increasing our power in this country.

Australian companies are increasingly multi-national. They look for new market in developing countries where they see the potential for profit. Indeed, in some cases their international activity is in fact the outsourcing of work that they no longer wish to do in Australia because of our cost structures. They will be resistant to any attempt by us in our collective bargaining to confer rights on unionists in other countries. But we should try.

We need to make contact with those overseas unions who attempt to organise Australian companies. And where companies refuse to enter into binding contracts that give our colleagues in other countries the chance to organise, we should be prepared to loan organising resources to those unions to help them apply pressure.

Where will this money come from?

First, APHEDA needs to receive a boost, at least from individual union officials. APHEDA has just 1200 members. Of these just 1000 contribute to its planned giving program. Perhaps it's time for union officials around the country to put their money where their mouth is and make a real contribution to the organisation's work.

The Unity Fund proposed above should allocate 50 cents from every $6 contribution to support actions designed to ensure that Australian multi-nationals live up to their responsibilities as corporate citizens. Where rights are not given to sister unions allowing them to organise, the funds can be allocated to pay for organising assistance to those unions.

That kind of activity strengthens local unions. They know that they are not alone. With our help they have a much better chance of winning.

It also strengthens us. Let's face it, many in our community are suspicious of our campaign for Fair Trade. They suspect that this is nothing more than narrow protectionism. Our practical help is clear evidence that we mean what we say. Our campaign is about how workers are treated. We will accept free trade if it means that the workers who benefit from increased trading opportunities get a chance to share in the increased wealth that is generated.

Fair Trade can't be achieved simply through WTO or ILO regulation. That has its place, but it will never happen until workers are given the freedom and the resources and the skills to organise workers to demand, achieve and enforce fairness.

23

Doing politics differently

With the re-election of the Howard Government in 2004 – and with its control of the Senate – we should understand very clearly how limited our leverage is.

Yet Australian unions have no equal in molding our political environment to the benefit of working people. We formed the ALP, secured the world's first Labor Prime Minister in 1904, and had a majority Labor government by 1910.

Our commitment to the setting up and resourcing of a political wing has paid off. We have used the interaction of industrial militancy in some areas, with the all-embracing coverage of legislation, to ensure a higher standard of living for every worker. The decency and civilisation of a society which provides universal health cover, workers compensation insurance, superannuation, annual leave and all the rest, are due to the success of such a model.

Yet relations between the political and industrial wing are at an extremely low ebb.

We have always complained about the Labor Party and its politicians, and the current era is no different. There are a range of examples of the fraying of the relationship between the political and industrial wings of the movement:

- The way in which the dispute over Workers Compensation in NSW in 2002 was handled.

- The bitter resistance of the ALP to adopting into its trade policy the need for labour standards. Its position put it to the right of the Bush Administration.[1]

- The resistance of the federal party to policy proposals which were designed to end the worst aspects of the conservative government's industrial relations legislation.

- The fight to "reform" the party by reducing union voting rights at annual conference.

- The failure of the new Leader of the Labor Party in his opening address to the National Conference in 2004 to mention the word "union" once.

---

1   See Anne O'Rourke and Chris Nyland, "AUSTFA and the Ratcheting-Up of Labour Standards" in *Journal of Industrial Relations*, forthcoming.

- The election of a Labor Party President at that conference who was not a member of a union.

Most telling are the personal examples cited by union officials of their inter-actions with Labor politicians around the country. They report almost a contempt for the views of union officials advancing the interests of their members. Their suspicion is that the same politicians would never dare be so open in their contempt for business leaders.

For unions of course, the frustration is that in government, the conser-vative parties have no compunction in displaying their ideological commitment. On every issue they stand wholly on the side of business. The best we can hope for from the ALP, it seems, is some form of spurious even-handedness.

So serious is the situation that increasingly unions talk of disaffiliation and non-affiliated unions scorn the thought of affiliation. Others recognise no difference between the parties. Some have begun to give financial support to the Greens. Many unions report difficulties in motivating organisers to help at elections.

In seeking to analyse why unions have suffered so badly in the past 20 years, we also play the blame game. The finger is often pointed at the ALP. It was the Keating Government who first allowed non-union collective agree-ments. It was the Keating Government who promoted enterprise bargaining and began the trend of privatisation.

It is true that the relationship is at a low ebb. But that has to be put into perspective.

Unions have complained about the performance of almost every Labor government from the Fisher administration on. The only exception has been the Watson minority administration of 1904, which demonstrably did not have the numbers to implement the Labor platform as it wanted.

We revere the memory of Ben Chifley and his "light on the hill" but it was the Chifley Government that called out the troops to break a strike by coal miners.

The Whitlam Government is seen now in a golden glow of progressive action – but Whitlam lowered tariffs by 25 per cent overnight and then set up the Industries Assistance Commission. His relations with Bob Hawke and the ACTU were, by and large, poisonous.

The electoral strength of Labor – where it has existed – has always been that it has had a core of working class support on which it could rely. And there lies the danger for the ALP currently. To the extent it moves away from its traditional base – working people and their families – so does it run the risk of losing their votes. This is precisely what happened in 1996. Workers, parti-cularly blue collar men, voted for anyone except the Labor Party. We sank to our lowest level of support (38.75%) since the Scullin Government lost office in 1931.[2]

The image of John Howard surrounded by blue collar workers from the CFMEU Forestry Division in the dying days of the 2004 campaign struck once more at the Labor Party's ownership of its working class heartland. Workers were again reminded of what many see as a drift by the Labor Party from their core concerns. This is despite the fact that, overall, at the last election there was no contest between the two parties as to which spoke most directly to the interest of Australia's working people.

Labor needs its traditional rock solid foundation of working people. The problem is that to secure government – even at a time when we enjoyed 50 per cent density – the ALP has always needed to secure the votes of more than unionised workers. Our membership has never voted en bloc for Labor and never will. That means that accommodations with other sections of society have to be made. To the extent that our density falls or we fail to persuade our members to vote for the Labor Party, so the party needs to adjust its policies in an effort to garner even broader support. The more it accommodates other sections of society, the greater is the danger of disaffection between the party and the unions.

The one thing that the ideological radicalism of conservative governments should have done is to convince us that our members need Labor governments. But Labor politicians know that there is no realistic alternative and they believe that unions add nothing – or at least very little – to their prospects of electoral success. They feel free to treat us as irrelevant. Unlike business – which appears able to mobilise money and support against the prospect of a Labor government – we are not a force to be feared.

Let's imagine the relationship between the party and the unions through the eyes of a Labor Prime Minister or Premier.

Unions were once powerful. They no longer are – they represent 23 per cent of the workforce.

They have little capacity to use the industrial relations system to flow breakthrough gains to every section of the economy meaning they have little significant impact on the country's economic management.

Little evidence exists to demonstrate that union members vote for Labor to any greater extent than the rest of the population.

Unions have a 50 per cent share of the vote at ALP Annual Conference – yet the Hawke and Keating Governments showed that policies set at conference level could easily be circumvented.[3]

---

2   Faulkner, J and Macintyre, S (eds), *True Believers, The Story of the Federal Parliamentary Labor Party,* Allen & Unwin, 2001, p 157.

3   See Steketee, M, "Labor in Power 1983–96" in Faulkner and McIntyre, S (eds), op cit.

Unions potentially have a say in pre-selection. But they never vote as a bloc. Instead, their numbers are divided between two factions or indeed increasingly, between four "factionettes".

Unions could potentially get their members to join branches of the party, and at least get parliamentarians to report back to them. But they don't – and in fact, in every State, the party is little more than a shell of supporters. Parliamentarians are not called to account for their actions nor do they have the opportunity of consulting a representative slice of the community. The numbers attending meetings are just too small.

Unions have been important financially in the past. As corporate donations and public funding increases, union contributions are less and less significant.

Throw into this heady mix the fact that unions – egged on by those radicals at the ACTU Organising Centre – have succeeded in building activism among the public sector workforce. Far from the compliant group of workers of the past, these people march down the street, camp outside Parliament and demand that spending on the public sector be increased.

Given all this, is it any wonder that the relationship is strained and that government ministers are less than responsive to our requests for action?

Yes, they like our money. Yes, many have a sentimental attachment to unions – some even worked for unions. It is still true that many are motivated by high principle – they believe in the things we believe in.

But we don't act in a way that makes us indispensable to the ALP's success. Instead, we give our politicians every opportunity of doing just enough to keep our members quiet at election time and very little more.

The fact is that we need to make the relationship between the two wings of the movement work. That's important for our members but it is particularly important for the nation as a whole. To restore a measure of strategic leverage to us, it is essential that we once more get a Labor government prepared to engage with our agenda. We want an economy with high but sustainable levels of productivity, that is, productivity based on real improvements in the productive process rather than just work intensification or cuts in effective wages. We want the wealth generated by a successful economy to benefit everyone – not just the privileged few at the top of the pile. We need to reconstruct the industrial relations framework in favour of the collective representation of workers. We need to give workers the right to have unions in their workplace and make that right enforceable. We need to have a Prime Minister prepared to say the word "union" in a speech and admit that unions are a good thing and that the collective representation of workers is the only way in which workers will be treated fairly. Indeed, it would be a change to have an Australian Prime Minister who came out and said that he believed that every citizen should have equal opportunity, that wealth needs to be shared.

I am convinced that many Labor politicians are desperate to do all that but we have failed to provide the countervailing force to Big Business in constructing the terms of debate within Australian society. As Helen Clark said to the New Zealand trade union movement immediately prior to her election:

> We need unions in New Zealand to keep campaigning – even after we are elected – just as we can be certain the employers will do. Unions need to keep the pressure on a labour government if they are to match the pressure that will be exercised on us by our opponents.[4]

Many of our unions have done the work of building their organisational capacity. That capacity now needs to be put to work building our strategic leverage. One way of doing that is to show the Labor Party that they need our support in order to get into power. They need our campaigning pressure in order to make a progressive agenda a viable option prior to and after they are in government.

A new style of union campaign

Union leaders actually spend a great deal of time in party political activity. They may sit on the party's administrative committee or the relevant policy committees. They may play a prominent role in faction meetings. About two-thirds of unions are affiliated to the ALP and pay an amount per head of membership as an affiliation fee. Unions have a 50 per cent say in what happens at the ALP's annual conferences. That means that they turn out large numbers of organisers and industrial officers to go to conference to make up the numbers. The leader will generally make speeches in support of resolutions that have the backing of their faction.

At election time, organisers are freed of their usual work and allocated to an election campaign. The union Secretary will write an editorial in the union magazine that urges a union vote. The union may also give a large cheque to the campaign which will often be handed over at a union meeting to the party leader – and he or she will then make a speech to the members or officers who have been gathered together.

None of this strikes me as very effective in terms of changing the voting behaviour of anyone or of building influence over the way in which Labor gets government or the way they govern.

The LHMU surveyed its delegates a couple of years ago and asked "How often do you talk about politics in your union?" The answer was clear: "All the time." When they asked where they talked politics, it was revealed that this only occurred at executive meetings or at meetings of delegates – never in the workplace.

---

4   This statement is my recollection of what she said at that meeting.

That is typical of the vast majority of unions.

We don't talk to our members about politics or their political choices – except in a remote and cursory way.

Do they want to hear from us about who we think they should vote for? Almost certainly not. Their view overwhelmingly will be that how they vote is their business. They want us to act in their interest industrially but their political views are a private matter. (After all, it was Australia who invented the secret ballot.)

Neither do we have credibility anyway. The perception is that unions are "in bed" with the Labor Party. We do whatever it wants. Union officials are seen as self-interested. Workers complain that their leaders are only interested in getting a seat in parliament.

How can we do things differently to make ourselves indispensable to Labor?

How can we make a difference in the voting behaviour of our members? We represent 1.8 million workers – many of whom live in swinging seats. Influencing a proportion of them to vote for Labor and a more progressive agenda may well make the difference between Labor victory and defeat.

Our members may not take kindly to us telling them how to vote. But we do have high credibility when we talk to them about issues that we know about. People believe nurses, ambulance drivers, doctors and health care workers when they talk about the health system. They believe teachers or university teachers when they talk about education funding. They trust the union officials closest to them[5] – delegates and shop stewards – when they talk about issues within their competence – policy in their industry or the industrial relations system.

The CPSU surveyed its members to see what they thought about the union getting involved in politics. After all, the union represented largely public servants, it was not affiliated to the ALP and it had, for a long time, taken a non-partisan position in relation to political activity.

The result was quite clear cut: "97 per cent agreed that the CPSU should lobby political parties on issues of direct importance to members. 77 per cent thought the CPSU should NOT tell members which party to vote for and 91 per cent thought that the CPSU should provide information and analysis on relevant party policy".[6]

What do we know about communication? One on one communication works best. And it works best of all where there is a high level of trust or credibility.

---

5   Peetz, D, *Unions in a Contrary World, The future of the Australian trade union movement*, Cambridge University Press, 1998, p 43.

6   CPSU website <www.cpsu.org.au>.

Where one on one is not possible, then communication works best when it is as personal as possible. That means that an editorial in the union magazine from the union Secretary is probably not worth much.

Let me then try to map out a way in which we can achieve high levels of one on one discussion with our members about political issues and failing that, at least improve the credibility of our written communication with them.

Limiting our political activity to the election campaign period sets us up for a fundamental loss of credibility. Given compulsory voting, we don't need to encourage others to actually vote the way people in comparable countries may have to. Our role is to educate our members about the issues that matter to them. If we only do that during the election campaign we become just like every other spruiker.

Immediately after the 2004 election, Hugh MacKay – who had correctly predicted the outcome of the election from the moment that campaigning started – said that the six-week campaign made precious little difference. Voters made up their minds based on their perceptions formed over the whole of a government's term. The party who will win the next election is the party that starts campaigning the day after the declaration of the poll in 2004.

That means that our political activity must be sustained over a much longer period than it is at present.

We can quite accurately describe our campaigning as education for our members. Given the facts, a large proportion of them will vote for one of the progressive parties. The problem is that they are submerged in a sea of contradictory information delivered by the media either as "news" or as advertising.

The most powerful way to educate members is by personalising the process as much as possible. Ideally, it means that we know what issues are important for the individual member. With that information, we put that member together with someone they respect so that he or she can become more informed about the decision they will have to make on election day.

(To do that requires real resources – which will be discussed later.)

We should start by asking members which issues are of most concern to them. If health and education are primary concerns, then those are the issues we should deliver information about. There is no point educating a member about an issue in which they have little interest. We then need to have a person build a relationship with that member over a significant period of time so that they trust the source of the information.

The questioning phase and the one on one contact should be done on a residential basis. If we do it on a workplace or union wide basis we waste our limited resources. Our impact is maximised to the extent that we become important in mobilising voters in the seats that count – the swinging seats, where just a fraction of a percentage point swing will mean the difference to victory or defeat for a prospective government.

That means that the member contact needs to be done by either phone or face-to-face contact at their homes. The same person should be the contact throughout our period of political activity. In this way, a relationship is built up and trust can develop. When the member has questions, it is their particular contact with the union who gets the answers and follows the member up. The information given must be objective. We have to break the perception that the union is just a spokesperson for the ALP. The union cannot be seen as merely endorsing the policies of the Labor Party. If their policies on the issues of importance to our members are not the right ones, we have to allow members to come to that conclusion for themselves.

This form of member education was carried out on a pilot basis during the 2004 federal election. A limited number of unions nominated swing seats where they had reasonable densities of membership. They used their members and activists to call members in these seats and survey them on what issues were important to them. They followed up these contacts with printed material setting out the various parties' positions on the issues. They then contacted each of the members to make sure that they had received the material and to discuss their response to it. At no time did the unions tell members how to vote but instead made sure that they understood where the parties stood. The response we received from members was extremely positive. They appreciated the fact that their union was taking the time to contact them and discuss issues and thought that was entirely appropriate.

The power of this kind of one to one interaction was demonstrated to me most clearly when I got on the phones one night in the ACTU call centre in Melbourne during the 2004 election. I found myself talking to a union's members in one of the far Northern NSW swinging seats. The members were delighted to speak to me. They nominated health and education as their top two issues. More than a third of them indicated that they would be voting Liberal or were swinging but leaning towards the Liberal Party.

In previous elections, these enthusiastic members of their union may well have attended a workplace meeting and been spoken to by the organiser. They would never have had the courage to speak up and reveal that they were voting Liberal at such a forum. Yet in their own home, talking over the phone, they were prepared to discuss their voting intentions and get information on the respective party's policies. Once we can talk to them in a non-threatening environment, we have every chance of having an impact on their voting behaviour.

At the same time that we concentrate intensively on the swinging seats we also need to ensure that we have some impact on the broad mass of our membership – 1.8 million workers. Even though many of their votes are locked into safe seats for one side or the other, the 2004 election demonstrated how important it is that their votes for the Senate or the State Upper Houses go to a progressive destination.

If the union Secretary's editorial doesn't work – what form of written communication does? Again, the more personal the interaction, the more it involves people that the member trusts, the more effective the communication will be.

A pamphlet that is aimed at the member at work, badged in such a way that it is written specifically for that workplace, has a much better chance of having an impact. If it is personally delivered by someone else at work, the impact is increased. If the content of the pamphlet informs members about the relative positions of the parties on issues important to them, then it has a chance of having a real impact. If a recommendation is made about which party to vote for – after considering their policies – it had better be in an area where the union is seen to have real expertise. We are qualified to say that the industrial relations policies of the conservative parties are a disaster for workers. Workers may not see us as an authority on issues of national security. If we stray outside our area of immediate expertise, workers will suspect that we are not separate from the Labor Party and that our appeal is self-interested.

One pamphlet in a sea of advertising, electoral addresses on television, media commentary, letterboxed flyers, will be lost. The contact we have with our members must continue throughout the government's term. At every turn, our communications need to become a commonsense corrective to the confusion of messages being delivered through all other media.

Financing political activity

In the last Presidential election the SEIU understood very clearly just how bad the administration of George W Bush was for working people. They spent $63 million mobilising their own members and supporting like minded community groups.

Most of that money was spent on the kind of one to one communication I have specified above. Very little of it could go to the Democrats for mass media advertising, because of the US electoral laws. The money was raised through the union donating money directly from its dues income and from the voluntary contribution of members to the union's separate political fund.

$63 million buys an awful lot of one to one contact – and we can only imagine, buys a lot of clout with John Kerry.

The Australian union movement – taken together – is the same size as the SEIU. Yet our investment in political activity is a tiny fraction of $63 million.

In Australia, even in those unions where dues have been increased, most of that money has been allocated to organising new members. We need to establish a source of income that allows us to spend real money on ensuring that our members have a good and detailed understanding of the issues of concern to them in elections. I suggest that we set up a separate political organising fund that members can contribute to – at least on a voluntary basis.

The teacher unions – and in particular the NSW Teachers' Federation – have led the way in this regard. They have asked their members to contribute a set percentage of their annual subscriptions, amounting in the case of NSW to around $18 for most members, to a fund that can then be used to support campaigns in support of public education. This income can only be spent for that purpose and in keeping with the non-political stance of the union, cannot be spent on the support of one particular party. The fund is administered by a special committee which implements a set of strict guidelines on how the money is spent. The funding is raised in NSW and it attracts some $1 million each year, funding large billboard campaigns, television advertising, as well as the enormously successful Vinson Report into the future of public education in NSW. Access to these funds has enabled the union to lift the profile of public education as a political issue throughout NSW and is clearly seen by members as one of the most successful activities that the union has undertaken.

The QPSU's Public Defence Fund will have, over a full electoral cycle, as much money as the ALP spends in Queensland on its entire election campaign.

Every union can do the same. Most members understand that their union needs to resource campaigns designed to ensure that employment in their industry is protected and that the industrial relations system is fair to workers. By asking them to donate a small amount additional to their dues to fund campaigns of this kind, we should be able to generate very large amounts of money to fund political activity.

Building activism among members

We need more from members than just their money. We want their time.

The most credible person to ring up at night or go door-to-door for the union is another member. They know what it is like to work in the industry, to have the same level of income, to suffer the same kind of pressures both at work and at home. The difference is that the union has given the activist member the skills to be able to educate another member about the political issues that are most important to that member. That credibility puts the activist way ahead of anyone else touting for the member's vote. The others are just self-interested politicians – this is a real person.

The other advantage for the union, of course, is that this kind of political organising is a tremendous development opportunity for the member. They go back to their workplace with additional training and a huge boost to their confidence. They can do the hard work of talking about politics to other members, they are good at it and they will be far more likely to take a more active role in union work at their workplace.

Building influence with the Labor Party

This kind of activity has the potential to deliver government to the Labor Party. More importantly, it may well allow them to stay in government. That should make unions pretty influential.

As we found at the party's inception, politicians have short memories. Within five years of the party's foundation, many unionists had written it off as a failed experiment. The politicians had forgotten where they came from.

One constant theme running through the history of the party has been the tension between promise and performance. Caucus solidarity was one part of the solution developed early in the 19th century. The socialist objective and party policy generally was another attempt at ensuring that politicians lived up to the ideals of the party.

Policy prescription – the platform – has some impact but the problem is that there is now little sense among politicians that they are responsive to a local constituency. They talk about being answerable to the rank-and-file in the party's branches but by and large the party's branch structure is so hollowed out that it scarcely exists.

The ALP's decline is far more serious than that of the union movement. Unlike unions, there is little effort to restore the representative base. The ALP has become a shell, dominated by its political class, responsible to no mass base. It needs the involvement of unions desperately, because only they are able to provide a connection with a huge number of workers.

We need to remember how the branches of the Labor Party were originally formed.

> If you joined a union and it was affiliated to the Labor Party you were automatically accepted as a full member of the Labor Party with all the rights of voting at Labor Party forums and standing for Labor Party positions.[7]

That ended as unions grew larger and achieved closed shop protection in whatever form. It was clearly not appropriate to have conscripted members able to vote in pre-selections. Nevertheless, "in most States up until the 1950s, if you were a local member of an affiliated union but not of the branch you still got a vote in the local plebiscite to decide the local candidate".[8]

Any move by unions to take over branches by encouraging large numbers of members to join, will set off a panic among politicians. Indeed, it may not help the union to encourage large numbers of members to attend branch meetings that are, by and large, unremittingly boring. But we do need to look at ways in which we can get politicians to be responsive to the concerns of real

---

7   Schacht, C, "How to Make the Labor Party Work in the Twenty First Century" in Hacking, J and Lewis, C (eds), *It's Time Again: Whitlam and Modern Labor*, Circa, 2003, p 397.

8   Ibid.

workers. The tension that was once traditional between rank-and-file and politician needs to be reestablished. At present politicians are under little or no pressure over compliance.

The more we give ourselves the ability to campaign effectively in each seat, the more we build our ability to ensure that the local politician is responsive to the concerns of our members. For the politician, whether they win or lose their seat is an intensely personal consideration. In Parramatta, in Sydney, a marginal seat at the 2004 election, the Finance Sector Union had 1400 members. The way those members voted had a big impact on success in that seat. The FSU in a short period of time built an impressive contact program with those members and can surely expect to get the support of the local member for its concerns about industrial relations and the regulation of the banking industry.

Capacity in a range of seats will mean that the party as a whole and its leader will become far more sensitive to its union base.

The contrast with the American movement – far weaker, industrially, than ours – could not be more marked.

In the 2000 Presidential campaign, Gore talked constantly in speeches about unions and the importance of their work. He appeared on picket lines and was always willing to talk to workers about the difficulties they were experiencing.

In the 2004 election, every one of the presidential candidates for the Democratic nomination supported the following union agenda:

- Legislation which made organising easier (they supported "card check" meaning that the employer had to recognise the union as soon as 50 per cent of workers signed a card);

- Arbitration of the first contract where an impasse was reached;

- Harsh penalties for anti-union employer behaviour;

- Support for universal health care.

They knew that they couldn't win an election against Bush unless they had the active, committed support of the union movement. In 2000, Gore would have lost the election by a very large margin if unions hadn't campaigned for him. He received the votes of 66 per cent of union members while only 44 per cent of non-union members backed him with their votes.[9]

---

9   Meeting with Stewart Rosenthal, former AFL-CIO Political Director, May 2004.

The role of factions

One of the impediments to unions rewarding and sanctioning members of parliament is that so many of our leaders are very important players in the factional system. I want to spend a little time reflecting on what might happen with the system so that the interests of union members are advanced.

For unions, there is now virtually no ideological content to the factional divide. Unions of left and right are militant or not, irrespective of faction. They believe in roughly the same things. Their commitment to organising – or lack of it – is not factionally determined.

In recent years this has resulted in a breakdown in the divisions between unions. Unions strategise together, share staff on campaigns, support each other, attend training together – even in some cases socialise together – irrespective of faction.

The one remaining place where factional activity is important is in the ALP, where pre-selection depends on factional attachment.

It is common among union reformers to deplore factional activity of any kind. But the reality is that unions wield whatever limited power they have within the ALP as a result of factional control of pre-selection and the administration of the party. That represents real power and they will be very reluctant to give this up – lest it widen the breach between unions and party even further.

If we are trying to build unions that are organising-focused, then the interest of the members of those unions comes before anything else.

The unions in the ACT have responded to that imperative. They have decided to caucus together, cross-factionally, before annual conference and determine the union agenda that they will support. The result has been real progress in getting the ACT Labor Government to become aware of the issues that matter for union members. Unions get the help they need to build their density and effectively represent the interest of workers.

I suspect that the vast majority of union members don't have a clue about the factional orientation of their union's leadership. Certainly, they are completely uninvolved in which candidates for pre-selection or party office the union and its faction supports or opposes. If we are serious about building a new kind of union, then we need to work out a way for members to become involved in this decision-making.

Limits need to be made on the degree to which factional allegiance controls the behaviour of the union's leaders. Let me give one example of a place to start.

The kind of activity I have proposed at a local level lends itself to an institutional change in the way in which pre-selection is reviewed by unions and the potential this has for feeding into factional decision-making.

At present, incumbents are very rarely dislodged. Once elected, the member of parliament is largely safe from challenge at pre-selection. The faction will protect him or her and if that fails, very often the central organisation will intervene in the interests of "party stability". Ministers generally cannot be challenged. It has to be said that none of this is good either for the party or for unions and their members. It means that the local member can prove in office to be entirely unsympathetic to the concerns of working people and the concept of implementing the party's policy.

If unions come together to campaign among their members located in a particular seat, they should feel some ownership over the candidate they have elected. He or she is there to do a job and if the job is not done then some sanction must be applied.

Union members living in the electorate should be encouraged at least once a year to form a caucus and come together to hear a report from the local member. The member should be available to be questioned by the union members who attend. If towards the end of a parliamentary term, the members are dissatisfied, they should have the ability to express their dissatisfaction and ask the union's leadership to review its support for the candidate. This can be done is such a way that a factional brawl is avoided. Unions are not trying to upset a pre-existing factional balance. But they do want a candidate that represents the interests of working people. The deficient candidate can be replaced with a member of the same faction.

At a minimum, the candidate will know that if the union members are unhappy, they will not be voting for him or her at campaign time. The union will not be contributing resources. And the union leader needs to make clear that his or her factional allegiance to the candidate – where it exists – will not override the views of the union members.

I don't suggest that this will have a huge impact on Labor members of parliament. If unions can succeed in organising large groups of their members to attend an annual meeting, and the member is skilled politically, they will be able to make the most of their parliamentary achievements. The meeting can become a means of energising the natural support base for a candidate. Members will be able to give the local member feedback on community concerns in a way that is difficult at poorly attended Labor Party branch meetings. But where the local member has performed poorly, is clearly not in tune with the concerns of working people and their families, there is a very real sanction available to them.

Helping create strategic institutions

Even if we succeed in making the Labor Party responsive to the concerns of working people, we need to do more to give voice to the Australian community's fundamental concern that workers be treated fairly. It is too easy for employers to dismiss what unions say as the self-interested arguments of a special interest group and portray our legitimate concerns as an attempt by union officials to feather their own nests.

Our situation stands in stark contrast to that of the United States. There, a range of institutions support the right of workers to organise. These range from Jobs with Justice, to United Students against Sweatshops, the Interfaith Coalition for Worker Justice and American Rights at Work.

The sheer size of the US permits this kind of disparate development. We can't expect to duplicate all that but we do need that kind of assistance if we are to make the public impact that is needed. We do have allies in the churches, who stand on the side of the poor. Students tend to be natural allies and many ordinary Australians know that denying fundamental rights to workers is a disaster for the country as a whole.

We need to publicise what is being done to workers. It needs to become a public issue. If and when our allies show interest in forming a coalition that can give these issues an independent voice, we should be prepared to do whatever it takes to assist them to get started. In helping them, we have to do so in a way that preserves their independence. The more at arm's length from unions, the higher their credibility.

The advocacy of independent groups is a powerful force in the forum of public opinion. Employers depend on their good reputation to be able to compete. Most employers doing the wrong thing can't withstand intense public scrutiny over a lengthy period.

24

The closed shop and the future

Once unions reestablished their power early in the last century, one of their first demands was for union members to receive preference in employment – by and large the closest we ever got to a true closed shop. If we are talking about regaining the strategic leverage we enjoyed for much of the 20th century, perhaps compulsory membership should once more be one of our aims.

The fact is that the employer community has comprehensively defeated us in regard to the maintenance of the closed shop – to the extent that it existed in Australia. They fought against the principle in the strikes of the 1890s and won it in 1996 when the Howard Government claimed that to compel someone to join the union was to breach their freedom not to associate. (If only the government was as assiduous in supporting the freedom *to* associate!)

Part of the problem is that closed shops have a bad name with many Australian unionists. They are seen as one of the reasons why so many Australian unions have atrophied. They removed the pressure of having to be responsive to members in order to maintain their membership.

Perhaps the problem was that once a union achieved some form of closed shop protection – be it preference clause, pre-entry closed shop[1] or post-entry closed shop[2] – the provision was virtually unreviewable. Actors got it as a result of the actors strike in theatre in 1944 and no one ever after queried whether that should have continued.

The Commission could delete preference clauses, and threatened to do so when unions misbehaved by going on strike in defiance of a Commission order, but this was very rare.

Members themselves did not have a clear process for removing the provision – in the way that American unionists can withdraw union recognition through de-certification. If 30 per cent of workers in a bargaining unit file for decertification, a ballot on the question must be held, subject to restrictions as to the time when it can take place.

---

1   A pre-entry closed shop prevents anyone not a union member applying for a job. It has always been very rare in Australia.

2   A post-entry closed shop is more appropriately referred to as a "union shop". Workers are required to join the union within a set period of time after commencing employment.

Before we abandon closed shops to the mists of history, perhaps we need to revisit why it is that unions have fought so strongly for them.

First, they guarantee unionisation. Once workers have been organised, the union doesn't need to stay on top of labour turnover. The employer does the work for the union – new entrants to the workforce are signed up as they are employed and the card is sent to the union office. The union can then focus its resources on organising workplaces where the union is not present.

The other key advantage is that it is much easier to recover the cost of initial organising. Organising a majority within a workplace that forces recognition and then having that followed by the introduction of some form of compulsion means that every worker pays for the cost of organising.

There are real disadvantages to compulsion however. Compel any worker to do anything and you will experience resistance. Those who have been conscripted union members in the past often have a predisposition against the union as a result.

Compulsion also means that some union officials, I'm afraid, abused their power. I was there when Old Sydney Town was first organised. The official who led those negotiations was asked at a meeting of the workers once the enterprise agreement had been entered into, whether she had to join? In the crudest, least sympathetic way, she was told that she had to and that she could get another job if she didn't like it. I wouldn't like to be the organiser today who comes across this woman and tries to persuade her to join!

Many employers liked closed shops. It meant that the union didn't develop a shop floor organisation and union officials paid less frequent visits to the workplace. Indeed, some employers actively sought membership agreements with unions (eg, banks and insurance companies) Apart from anything else it gave another weapon to the employer – "Behave or I will tear up the membership agreement".

By giving unions a guaranteed income source, it also meant that some unions went to sleep. Workplaces were never or rarely visited, members were not involved in the formulation and negotiation of Awards – and we have seen that most workplaces were without delegate structures. As Peetz points out, "on balance in Australia, union compulsion is associated with lower union responsiveness, protection and participation".[3] Certainly, it meant that even the best-intentioned unions could get away with offering an insurance-style service rather than connecting members with the source of their power.

I don't want anyone to think that this was always the case. Quite a few unions that benefited from some form of compulsory membership were nevertheless activist driven, democratic and concerned to continually promote the interests of their members.

---

3   Peetz, D, *Unions in a Contrary World, The future of the Australian trade union movement*, Cambridge University Press, 1998, p 13.

On balance then, not too many people are pushing hard for a return to the closed shop. We don't want conscripts and it is one of our strengths that the overwhelmingly majority of our 1.8 million members are volunteers.

There are nevertheless real pressures from our members about what they see as the freeloading behaviour of non-member workers in well-organised workplaces. Why should they get all the benefits of union membership without paying a cent to get them? Neither does it help that quite a few of these workers are quite open in their contempt for those who shell out for union membership.

An even more serious problem exists in those industries with high levels of temporary employment. Approximately one in every four workers is a casual. Some are long-serving casuals but the rate of turnover in many industries is very high. The SDA reports that in supermarkets on the Northern Beaches of Sydney in the middle of summer the rate of turnover is 25 per cent per month!

Casual employees tend to be lowly paid and by definition have very few rights. Most importantly, they have no power. Complain about your treatment and for some strange, unknown reason, no more shifts are available to you.

Clearly, these are precisely the kinds of workers that unions are designed to protect. They desperately need the power that collective organisation can bring. Yet pure open-shop organising makes it virtually impossible. Unions have to allocate huge resources to build power within a temporary workforce and attempt to "freeze" the workforce for enough time to persuade them to sign cards and demand recognition and get an improvement in their wages and terms of treatment.

Even if such a campaign is successful and the employer can be persuaded to sign an agreement and recognise the union, in a few weeks, the organisers have to start again as turnover in casuals reduces density to dangerously low levels. The problem can be dealt with through access to inductions and the creation of a strong delegate structure but this depends on there being a core of permanent employees willing to take on this work. At the least, there will always be a heavy investment of organising resources just to make sure that density is maintained – before the union even starts the work of representing its members.

It is for these reasons that the introduction of "fair share fees" becomes crucial. The term means that an agreement is reached between the workers and their employer for every worker to be compelled to pay a "fair share" of the cost of representation. The fee is usually set at a rate of around 80 per cent of the union fee – on the understanding that a substantial proportion of the union fee (20%) is spent on things other than negotiating and enforcing the industrial instruments that cover a particular workplace.

The method of implementing such a provision is critical to how it is regarded and to whether it allows for the creation of strong, relatively self-sufficient workplace union organisations.

There should be no push whatsoever for legislation from friendly governments that requires everyone covered by an industrial instrument of one kind or another to pay money to the union. That ensures that workers see it as a tax and allows the union to collect the money without building the organisation that will deliver benefits to members. It also means that it is non-reviewable by workers. They have no power to bring it to an end if they are unhappy about the work that the union is doing in their workplace.

It cannot be an amount that is set at a punitive level as a means of forcing a back-door closed shop. That fools no one, is politically unsaleable and has all the disadvantages of a closed shop.

Instead, it must be bargained for. Workers must be able to get majority support for such a provision that can then be set out in the enterprise agreement or where that doesn't exist, in a separate recognition agreement. At present of course, the government has outlawed the practice, but we should consider the issue now in readiness for when we once again have a say over our legislative environment.

If the law is changed in our favour in the future, unions have to maintain their sustainability. Payment of a "fair share fee" must never be used as a means of bridging the gap between unsustainably low rates of union fees and the needs of a modern, decentralised bargaining environment. Conservative governments will always try to remove legislative backing for these kinds of provisions. If unions rely on the income from bargaining fees as a fundamental part of their financial underpinning, they will be gravely exposed to failure with a simple legislative change. The answer must be that fee income should be separately identified and only non-recurrent expenditures incurred to the value of that income.

I should finish this discussion by putting the issue of union shop in perspective. Getting freeloaders to pay their share of bargaining costs is important – if only to satisfy our members who are offended by the practice. It is not the prime focus for our effort in relation to a change agenda in Australian unions. The core of our support must come from those employees who volunteer to be members of unions and agree to participate in our struggle for power. Far more important in that process is the removal of wage competition from industries where we are trying to organise. Wage competition affects every single worker being organised, because an employer facing that threat will move heaven and earth to stop any of his workers being organised. Freeloading, hopefully, affects only a minority of the workforce. In only one area does the issue of bargaining fees become a first order issue – that is where employment predominantly involves casuals. It is difficult for unions to organise these workers – despite the often exploitative relationship that casualisation promotes – without some mechanism for ensuring that the costs of unionisation can somehow be recovered and that ongoing organisation can be assured.

Part 5
DRIVING COMPREHENSIVE CHANGE

25

Leadership

Even I am fairly intimidated at the change agenda I have outlined! How the hell are we going to pull it off while simultaneously fighting for survival every day of the week?

The key is found in those unions that have gone a long way down the path of shifting to organising. Every union that has taken a substantial shift towards building an organising culture since this project began in the mid-1990s has been led by an individual determined to drive change through his or her union or union branch. There are no exceptions.[1]

Many unions have marvellous organisers, honorary officials, delegates and members trying to drive change from below. But if the union's leader doesn't lead the change process, the process fails. The good organisers find themselves isolated and unable to shift any but those few most closely allied to them. They either hibernate until a leader comes along who gives them permission to flourish – or they go to a union that wants their skills.

Conversely, we have seen unions with a staff resolutely opposed to change, which have nevertheless shifted dramatically towards involving members in the work of the union, building activism, concentrating on a growth in density and power. The difference has been a leader determined to change, to build an institution capable of exercising power through the activity of its membership.

The only times that we have experienced success have been where a union leader has said: "This is where we are headed and nothing will be allowed to get in the way of our success."

Why is leadership so important?

We can see empirically that leaders matter. But why is this the case?

Members gain hope from the aura of confidence that the leader projects. Without that hope, action won't follow.

---

1 That seems to be the experience in the United States too. See Voss, K and Sherman, R, *Breaking the Iron Law of Oligarchy: Union Revitalisation in the American Labor Movement*, in *American Journal of Sociology* Vol 106 No 2 (September 200) p 303.

In the vast majority of unions, the leader has the ability to determine the future of every staff member there. Promotion, work assignments, remuneration, job satisfaction – all depend on the leader's attitude towards a member of staff.

Most union staff – despite their protective veneer of cynicism – are at heart idealistic. They want their union to win. They want their members to have better lives as a result of their work. Staff know that without a leader with vision and a clear idea of what needs to be done, it's just not going to happen.

That means that staff are finely attuned to doing what the leader wants. This can't be emphasised enough. Staff watch the leader closely on a day-by-day basis for any shift in the climate at the top. They are sensitive to the slightest change in attitude. If you think of the minute attention the Kremlin watchers used pay to the order of precedence of generals and apparatchiks standing next to the Soviet leader on the top of Lenin's tomb when he took the salute on May Day – you are starting to realise just how closely a leader's behaviour is analysed!

The prospect of change tightens the level of scrutiny. Staff know that this is the time when they can be given new assignments or that reward systems can change. Where once the measure of success was a 5 per cent wage increase for members, the new measure can now be the level of density in a workplace. Every pronouncement, joke, sign of good favour, budget allocation, access to training – who the leader drinks coffee with – is sifted to see whether this denotes a change in attitude. That intensity of scrutiny doesn't let up.

Union leaders have form in relation to change. Experienced staff have seen leaders come and go and have seen union management fads do the same. They may question whether organising is just another fad that will pass– like Best Practice or work teams or the amalgamation strategy – or if there really will be a fundamental change in the way in which the union operates. How soon will it be before the ACTU comes up with a new way of doing our work and the union's leadership pays lip service to that bright idea?

Effective leadership

What kind of leader do we need?

The need for a transformation of our culture and structures means that our own dominant paradigms of leadership are unlikely to be of much use. This is a critical problem because normally, union culture is passed down to the next generation of leader through the example of those who have gone before.

In a relatively benign environment, leadership was rarely challenged at the ballot box successfully. Incumbents were only defeated as a result of proven corruption or financial impropriety and/or the grossest forms of industrial incompetence. There were, over the 80 years of the Arbitration era, some exceptions, but these tended to be leadership challenges based on intense political activity – by either the industrial groups or Communists.

The point is that it was rare for someone to lose their job as a result of their incompetence as a leader. Given the failure of the democratic process to remove poor performers, most officials with length of experience can point to some pretty appalling role models.

Some leaders have confused leadership with their managerial function. This kind of person obsessed over the smallest detail, involving themselves in the minutiae of office management, while ignoring a major challenge to the organisation's existence, for example, concentrating on a minor point of expenditure while failing to maintain the level of dues in line with the rate of inflation or criticising staff for attending work late, while ignoring their victory over a strategically significant employer.

There have been examples in our history of leaders who have left the union to run itself. These tend to be incredibly conscientious individuals who load themselves with such a heavy industrial or organising workload that directing the activities of the union becomes a part-time activity.

Some unions have been afflicted with the problem of the "Great Man". (It's rarely a problem of the "Great Woman"!) In this case, the leader is so brilliant , so personally touched by God, that he can sit in his office, divine the wishes of members and determine strategic direction, without any need to consult or involve anyone else at all.

Of all the old models this strikes me as one of the most dangerous.

Let's presume for a moment that you are one of those rare people who are far brighter than the rest of humanity – and there have been a few of these in leadership positions over the course of our trade union history. These people do perform at a higher level. They can carry complex information in their heads and as often as not get to the correct solution to a problem more quickly than every one else.

The problem with the Great Man running things is that such an individual quickly becomes impatient with the lesser mortals underneath him. Impatience means that dissenters get very short shrift in raising objections or alternative solutions to the problems that will present. All too often, impatience seems to go hand in hand with irrational bursts of temper that reinforce the idea that underlings should comply unquestioningly.

What the Great Man thinks of as strong leadership is more often simply authoritarian control. Behaviour is controlled through fear. What is seen as inappropriate staff behaviour – that is, when staff don't agree with the leader – is met with an outburst of anger – the leadership tantrum – or alternatively with consignment to "outer darkness", the recipient no longer involved in interaction with the leader as part of an inner group.

If dissent is not welcomed, then underlings get the message very quickly indeed. (Remember how closely leadership behaviour is monitored.) Staff and the honorary officers learn not to disagree with the leader. No matter what idea is put forward by the leader, staff try to implement it.

So what's wrong with that? If the leader is bright enough this will surely mean that the union performs well, as that capacity is put to the service of the union.

Crushing dissent means that the leader is cut off from the signals that need to be received: policy prescriptions are not working, ideas need reworking, additional resources need to be deployed, more information needs to be sought, different skills are required. Such a leader hears what staff think he wants to hear. Staff mouth the rhetoric without necessarily doing the hard work of implementing policy. It means that the bright ideas of the leader are not tested by those who will be responsible for implementation. It means that the leader will have passed up the opportunity of getting consensus around a desired course of action – staff won't buy into the strategy as if it was their own – they just do it in order to stay away from trouble. If it fails, that's not their problem – it was the leader's idea after all.

Despite the brilliance of our Great Man, if the bright idea turns out to be a mistake, then the leader takes the fall entirely on his own.

Two other problems exist.

First, it is simply not rational to think that a single person is brighter than a group. The best leader must surely be the person who is capable of getting the best ideas from a range of intellects and then moulding them into a strategy for action.

Secondly, the change agenda facing unions needs to take place across a very wide range of unions. I don't want to unduly offend all the existing union leaders – but I have my doubts that we can expect that every one of them fits the description as a "Great Man"! Unfortunately, most of us are mere mortals and we have to come up with a model of leadership that fits that reality.

The days of being able to tolerate these models of behaviour are surely coming to an end. Unions are in competition – not generally between each other – but certainly, in the minds of members, between a state of union and non-union.

The risk is clear. Ineffective leaders may well continue to avoid electoral challenge. The temptation for dissatisfied members will be simply to walk away from their union rather than participate in finding and electing a new leader. The danger exists for unions and union branches to survive as a shell, empty of membership, but continuing to hold legally enforceable coverage rights.

So what is a model of leadership capable of delivering a program of change and breathing life into a faltering union? Not all our past experience of leadership has been negative. It is possible to identify many who provide very good role models of leadership. Very often for them, their environment felt anything but benign. It was often these leaders who are associated with periods of union reform. They set down the union culture which would succeed in delivering benefits to members and provided inspiration to succeeding generations of union officials. These are the leaders who are still revered by those who have come after them.

Some will argue, of course, that good leaders are born, not made. There is some truth to this. The greatest leaders will often come to the task and perform at an incredibly high level without giving a thought as to how they do it. Good leadership is a function of personality. If the leader is not a well-adjusted person, then they will feel threatened by those of their colleagues who are capable and they will seek to bully them into submission.

It is possible for union leaders, however, to reflect on the job they are doing and adjust their behaviour to make their performance more effective.

Leadership versus management

Leaders need to consider the difference between management and leadership. Leaders are required to set out a union's vision, develop its strategic direction, inspire its staff and members and ensure that the organisation is well managed.

The role of management, if need be, can be handed to a professional manager or the job delegated to another elected officer. A manager, though, cannot hire someone to provide vision or inspire staff and members.

Building a coalition of support

Almost all union success comes from the application of combined effort, expertise and knowledge. That means that the central function of a leader embarking on change must be to build around him or herself as large a group of like-minded thinkers as possible. The leader needs enthusiastic, capable allies if success is to be achieved. In particular, allies at every level of the union – staff, delegates in key workplaces, honorary officers – need to be sought out who already command respect – leaders in their own right.

If that is the central function, it means that effective leaders don't need to have all the answers. They will inspire staff and members the more they involve these stakeholders in helping to map out the future direction of the union. By giving them ownership of the way forward, the leader binds them into a unified whole. Even where some of these lower level leaders are uncertain about the direction of change, they need to be involved and listened to, so that they at least have the opportunity of contributing to the union's success.

I will often be asked to sit in on strategy sessions with union leaders and their staff or inner circle of leadership. I can see very quickly the quality of leadership. Are people willing to have their say? Are their contributions ridiculed – even when what they say is dumb? Do people argue with each other on the basis of personalities or are different opinions respected? Above all, is the leader really listening to what is being said? Are the staff members telling the leader what he or she wants to hear or do they have the courage to actually say what they think?

At the same time, we need to be clear in this context about the difference between consultation and collective decision-making. In quite a few unions confronting the need for change, we have come across instances where staff, for example, expect to be able to determine the pace and kind of change to be undertaken. In the worst cases, the union has been captured by its staff – the union exists to serve their interests rather than those of the members. (This happens more often where organisers are elected but also happens where staff are appointed.)

Leaders are elected to take responsibility for the union's direction. If they choose unwisely, at best they are blamed for their union's loss of power and at worst, they lose their jobs.

They can therefore, neither hide behind the decisions of a staff collective, nor can they allow themselves to abrogate responsibility to their staff. The benefit and burden of leadership is that the leaders get to take responsibility for the union's success or failure.

Communicating the vision

"Vision" is one of those phrases – like "mission statement" – which is regarded with deep suspicion by most union staff. It has become, in corporate hands, a term devoid of meaning – and more importantly a piece of nonsense designed to pull the wool over the eyes of workers.

But it is important in a union sense – because we need to have a vision about what our unions are for. We don't exist to make money for shareholders or owners. We don't exist simply to perpetuate an institution that may well have passed its use by date. We are there to fight for the right of working people to have a say about how they are treated at work and in their community. We are there too, to get some measure of justice from a market economy rigged against their interest. The union is the machine we have set up to make sure that capital pays a fair share of society's wealth to those who generate the wealth, and so that workers can work safely and get the time off to attend to their needs and those of their family.

Effective leaders are those who are going to, over and over again, remind our stakeholders – members and staff – that that is what we are about.

A change framework

John Kotter is a professor at the Harvard Business School. He sets out eight steps to transforming an organisation and they make a useful framework for union leaders when thinking through their change program.[2] The eight steps are as follows:

1. Establishing a sense of urgency;

2. Forming a powerful guiding coalition;

3. Creating a vision;

4. Communicating the vision;

5. Empowering others to act on the vision;

6. Planning for and creating short term wins;

7. Consolidating improvements and producing still more change;

8. Institutionalising new approaches.

Such a leader needs to remind us that there is a vision about the way in which we are going to bring it about. Our aim is to unleash the inherent power that all workers have – to combine together to release their collective power in pursuit of the common good. We aim to organise workers so that they have the power to stand up for themselves and the values in which they believe. We aim to put in place a union of the kind that can get the ordinary individuals who sign on as members to combine together to do extraordinary things.

None of this is easy. That is why the leader who embraces the change agenda set out in this book needs to spell out, repeatedly, what we are about and how we are going to get there.

Kotter tells us that in corporations, failure in the implementation of an agenda for change most often comes from leaders who 'underdo' vision by a factor of ten. And that is surely the case for unions.[3]

Being Australians, I suspect that we are a bit embarrassed about talking continually about our idealism, about the reason we do what we do. But we have to do it. The most important function of the leader is repeatedly to get us back on track.

---

2   Kotter, J, "Leading Change: Why transformation efforts fail" in *Harvard Business Review* March-April 1995, p 59.

3   Kotter, JP, *Leading Change*, Harvard Business School Press, 1996.

We want more members because we want more power because we need workers to get a fair go.

We need more activists because activists give us power and protect us from de-unionisation. That's important, because without us, workers will be left defenceless against the chill winds of capitalism.

I saw this demonstrated perfectly at the second of our Organising Conferences in Sydney. Greg Combet give an address to 800 organisers from just about every union in the country as well as many from New Zealand. He spoke passionately about what the union movement stood for– our values and why they needed to be defended – and about his determination to win. Nothing was going to stand in the way of building a better society and that our values stood at the centre of that vision of a better Australia.

He had the group standing up cheering – yes, he had a bunch of inhibited, largely Anglo-Saxon union officials chanting "Union" and generally carrying on like a bunch of evangelical Americans!

He was doing what leaders do. Reminding us why we have to win. Why we need to go the extra mile, house-call at night and on weekends, work intensively throughout the working day to produce what the union needs from us.

Living the vision

Words are not enough.

Staff and members have to see that their leader does what he or she says should be done by everyone else.

I thought of this just recently when I ran into Jeff Lawrence – National Secretary of the LHMU – one Saturday in Queanbeyan, the country town next to Canberra. He was out house-calling potential members – cleaners – with one of the Canberra organisers, along with the rest of the national officers. I heard later that he top scored that day with eight signed cards.

He was doing what he expected his staff to do – whatever it takes to make sure that his union grows in strength.

Australian leaders need to have the humility to recognise that many of us don't have the skills of the greenest graduate from the Organising Works program. We have never had to house-call, we don't know how to "equalise an objection" if our life depended on it and some of us have never had to sign a member up in our life. We can't fudge this. We have to get operational credibility. We need to know how to do it if we are going to be able to provide feedback to our own organisers. We have to be able to recognise good organising if we are to give praise when it is merited.

It is a sign of the importance the leader attaches to organiser training if he or she participates in the training. Hell, they can pretend they know it all if there is a need to save face! At the same time, it's not essential that they sign in to an organising program – but they need to find someone in the organisation – or out if it – to show them quietly how it is done, what the young organisers learn in training – and then to have a go at it.

I don't underestimate the difficulty of this. Once we get to be leader we have generally spent years earning our stripes – doing the long hard slog to build the union's power. The temptation is to enjoy the benefits of office.

I don't think that we have the luxury of using our time in senior office to take a breather. Now we are desperate to rebuild our power and now is the time to lead by example. We need to show our organisers that we can house-call, that we still have the energy to put the hours in, that we are living the vision we have of unremitting effort in defence of workers and their families.

Instilling hope

Every union member, every staff person, understands what happens if we fail. We see the effect of unbridled employer power every day of the week. Most of us have a pretty fair idea of what needs to be done. The big question is – can we get there? Hope needs to be continually nurtured if we expect staff and members to keep fighting for the renewal of our unions.

Instilling hope is the job of the leader.

We need to hear from him or her about the victories we are achieving. We need to have the program that will lead to victory spelled out for us. We need to sense inevitable victory, invincible optimism from our leaders.

Of course we all suffer setbacks. Employers and anti-union governments win often. The odds are stacked against us. But despite all that, the effective leader is going to outline the way forward. Defeat should be seen as only a setback in the long path to victory.

Michael Newman, the labour educator, tells the story of Tas Bull, leader of the Waterside Workers' Federation, confronting the issue of waterfront reform and the loss of thousands of his members' jobs: "Tas talks of waking in the early hours of the morning wondering whether the union would 'last another day', and then going to work and acting and speaking in a way that would lift the morale of everyone around him".[4]

I was at Port Botany the day the hooded thugs and their dogs locked the wharfies out of their jobs. John Coombs (National Secretary of the MUA) got up on the back of a truck and spoke to the pickets that had already assembled. The government and Patrick's CEO Chris Corrigan held all the cards and the whole process was obviously carefully planned. The speech he gave that day was all about how we were going to win. How goods would not move from that dock. How lawyers were moving, as he spoke, to take action in the Federal Court. How

---

4   Newman, M, *Maeler's Regard*, Stewart Victor Publishing, 2000, p 101 .

nobody could get away with this kind of action in Australia. How the Australian people would get behind the union and its members. How the crowd from every union in Sydney present that day was just a taste of what the government and employer were up against. Even the most cynical of us felt hope at that point. We had a chance and we were going to take it.

Much later, I spoke to John about that day. He remembered the speech and his frame of mind. It would have been all too easy then and there to have acknowledged defeat – he knew the odds were stacked against him. But he knew that wasn't an option.

We destroy the union's hope when we lose it ourselves: when we let staff and members know that we can't see the way through; when we lose faith in our ability to win; when a defeat is so shattering that we give the impression that it is too much for us to bear.

Hope is lost when we succumb to cynicism, when we allow our disappointment with individuals to affect our own belief in the idealism of our cause.

Hope comes from thinking through what needs to be done: from encouraging good behaviour from those we supervise; from matching our behaviour to what we want from staff and members; from celebrating wins along the way; from constantly pressing for better performance; from providing context for setbacks and for the ultimate victory; from accepting defeat but learning from it; from being enthusiastic about the task ahead; from challenging staff to come up with the ideas that we need to win; from drawing strength from the work of the wider movement as it gradually rebuilds its strength.

If that is no longer possible, if the leader is mired in hopelessness, the time has come for them to leave – for their own sake and for that of the unions' members. Without hope, such a leader can never achieve victory for the union's members.

Personal values are important

> The strength and vulnerability of unions has the same source: the trust that members place in their representatives.

> Jean-Gerin Lajoie[5]

Personal behaviour is important. None of us are saints, but leaders have to be people that our staff and members can admire.

A group of Canadian educators has written:

---

5   Quoted in Burke, B et al, *Education for Changing Unions*, Between the Lines, 2002, p 18.

activists have huge expectations of union leadership, and the range of forgiveness for error is small. That's because people put their hearts into their unions, and there is a smaller margin of tolerance for human frailty.[6]

I've heard Tom McDonald – the former National Secretary of the construction union – talk each year to the organising trainees. He points out that despite the reputation for profanity among construction workers, he has never sworn at a public meeting in front of them. He makes the point that workers expect their representatives to be different from them. As union officers we are no longer simply representing ourselves.

So far, corruption is not a problem that we have had to worry about in Australia – with a couple of exceptions. It needs to stay that way. Members and staff need to know that our idealism is not fake. That we believe in what we are doing and that we are not using our period in office as a time to rip members off. When corruption comes to light it destroys the good faith members and staff have in their union.

Some unions have had a culture of hard drinking. That has, by and large, died out. But make no mistake, getting drunk and behaving objectionably is death to a leader's credibility.

Treating people fairly is also critically important to successful leadership. Unions are like all other organisations. People get irritated with each other and rumours spread about the perceived incompetence of this staff member or the other. Leaders have to be incredibly careful that they act on the facts and not prejudice.

Every union leader will have enemies – both within the union and outside it – people who don't like the leader, oppose their policies, undermine their leadership. No matter what the provocation, at a personal level, it is important that even these people are treated fairly and with respect.

Mike Newman tells a great story about a course he was running at the Clyde Cameron College. Tension on the course was running high as a result of inter-union conflict and at one moment the whole course boiled over and two of the participants were about to come to blows. The fracas stopped instantly as one of the other participants intervened and reminded them – "Hey, cut it out, we're all union here!"

We have to be better than employers. It's expected of us.

We can hate the dirty deals that other union officials do, but we can't stoop to their level. We will be demoralised as another union raids our jurisdiction – and we need to defend the coverage rights of our union with all our strength. But we need to set a standard for good union behaviour.

If our behaviour is of a high standard then we can have equally high expectations of our staff.

---

6   Ibid, p 18.

Consistency

Chopping and changing expectations will lead to a completely dysfunctional union.

If you decide to go down the path of union renewal then you need to be prepared to settle in for the long haul. If you limit yourself to just dipping your toe in the water, then staff and members will pick that up – you're not really serious.

If you speak about organising one week and the next you respond to the member complaint about a failure to rush out and deliver service in the way it has always been delivered, then expect your credibility to drop.

Crash through but prepare a soft landing

Leaders may be prepared to take radical action to drive change through their unions – but forget everything they know about organising principles as they do it, relying only on the force of their oratory at critical meetings.

It's difficult to believe that we would be so cavalier with a mass meeting of new members or potential members. Surely in that case we would talk to our activists? Build a consensus among them and make sure that they were prepared to speak in support of the position being put? Wouldn't we imagine the likely objections and prepare answers that will satisfy the questioners? If we do that for workers, why wouldn't we do it for the critical union meetings?

There are many ways to get the entire union behind process for change.

The SEIU under John Sweeney famously did it by setting up their "Committee for the Future" – a group of leading branch leaders who were given the job of devising a survival and growth strategy. By involving a wide group of leaders in the process, they had buy-in across a broad range of decision-makers. That model has been used repeatedly by the current President of SEIU, Andy Stern, to build a consensus around the direction and intensity of change.

Some unions have used the Organising Centre as an outside expert to validate the changes that are proposed to be made. We write a report on what needs to be done and we consult with every member of staff and key honorary officials to make sure that they have input and buy-in to the conclusions.

At the very least, you can ask senior officials from the ACTU to attend the relevant meetings and speak in your support.

Briefing the key decision-makers and forming a guiding coalition is the minimum required to ensure broad support for the strategy. Considering the likely objections – and who will be objecting – is a basic piece of preparation that should never be overlooked.

Giving credit

Union success depends on the leader being able to inspire staff and members to perform at an extremely high level. No matter how personally competent the leader may be at the work of the union – without the staff, activists and members playing their part – the leader can make little difference to overall success.

The key task must then be to ensure that the union's stakeholders get a feeling that their efforts are appreciated and that they receive the credit for the success they have achieved.

This means that the union, if it is of any size at all, needs to have a process for drawing good performance to the attention of the leader. It needs an accountability system. Praise from the leader of the organisation can be of critical importance to future commitment.

Just as leaders don't realise how closely their performance and attitudes are monitored by staff, so they underestimate the power of their praise.

I see this particularly with members. For members, the State or National Secretary is a big deal. Members don't often get the chance to shake the hand and have a few personal words with someone so important. When the Secretary goes out to a meeting of delegates or drops in on a training session or takes the time at a mass meeting to circulate beforehand and talk to individuals in the audience – it has a completely disproportionate impact.

When the Secretary nominates an individual in front of his or her peers and talks about their achievement – it's something they talk to their family about that night, the instant they get home.

American unions do this far better than we do. My colleagues and I travelled to Philadelphia six months before the 2004 Presidential Campaign. We were there to see the way in which the SEIU had turned out 2004 volunteer canvassers to spend up to nine months full-time on the road, door-knocking potential voters and persuading people how to vote on the issues that were of concern to them. The SEIU – in their usual over-the-top style – had called them the "2004 Heroes", given them flash bomber jackets and every one of them had a purple mobile phone. Being Australians of course, we rolled our eyes at all this. We laughed to each other at the thought that we might ever call Australian delegates, "heroes"!

Then we met the members.

Here was a bunch of ordinary delegates who had left their homes and their families to live in cheap hotels for up to nine months, door-knocking strangers, in the hope that they could make their country a better place to live. Of course they were heroes! And the SEIU was just telling it like it is when they used the term.

Just ask yourself this question. When was the last time that an Australian union leader described the work of delegates – to their face – as heroic? I haven't heard it in 29 years working for the union movement. Yet these are the people in many cases who risk their jobs, put up with daily harassment from their employers, give up precious time from their families, defend the union to their workmates, get stuck with the job of defending workers in the most difficult of situations. And all for no reward. Of course they are heroes!

Yet we so rarely acknowledge them.

We need to start emulating the Americans and give them stuff: a jacket when they get to 90 per cent density in their workplace; a commemorative pin when they have served as delegate for ten years. At the very least, the handshake and the word of congratulation from the leader of the organisation.

We have started in small ways. It works marvellously. I watched an LHMU meeting of hotel workers in Sydney a few years ago when the ACTU President, Sharan Burrow, attended. She was there to hand out delegate badges to the new shop steward in each hotel. As the Sheraton shop steward came forward to receive the badge and have a photo taken, every one of the members at the Sheraton stood and cheered their leader. And so it went for every hotel.

Sharan of course is quite a humble person. She doesn't think it's a big deal to shake a member's hand. But I will bet each of those delegates still talks to their families about the day they shook the ACTU President's hand and got their delegates' badge.

I can remember the 1999 ACTU Council. We showed a video that described what we were trying to do in organising large residential hotels. The house-keeper from the Sheraton stood up on the stage – nervous as hell – and when she finished speaking raised her fist in solidarity. The place erupted. That kind of honour paid to workers is good for them and good for the union's officials.

Giving praise to staff, where it is due, is also of critical importance.

The best way of getting staff to perform at a high level is to make sure that they receive acknowledgment when they manage to achieve high performance. It's so obvious I know – but we so rarely do it. We work under intense pressure. The day is full of stuff to do and they tend to be very long days. But giving positive reinforcement to those who do well is imperative.

Praise in private is important but it also needs to be public. Any reporting to members either at a meeting or in the union magazine needs to acknowledge who was responsible for the union's success. And I don't just mean the vague, generalised "Thanks to all those who contributed!" Staff and members need to know that you know exactly what they did that was exceptional and worthy of notice. It's not hard!

How hard is it when you introduce staff to an outsider, to mention what they have done recently for the union. "Can I introduce Joe Bloggs. He's famous around here because he organised such and such a workplace in just two months."

Validation by third parties is also something that needs to be handled care-fully. I have seen a few examples over the years when a journalist writes a story on a successful campaign. The leader gets the credit and the people who have done the work are ignored. It may be the fault of the journalist but the damage is done.

All this is of more importance to Australian union leaders than leaders in any other country. More important because we have such a well developed "tall poppy syndrome". Maybe it's our convict heritage, but we just love to cut those over-achievers down to size. We don't approve of leaders who take the credit for everything that happens in their organisation. Leaders who do that tend at the very least to become a standing joke within the organisation or worse, end up with their heads lopped off!

Of course, leaders like to think that they in fact have played an important part in their union's success. And of course they have. But it doesn't need to be explicit.

Most important of all, if we do deflect praise, I suspect that we get a double whammy of credit. Outsiders recognise that we are being generous and we go up in the estimation of our staff and members.

Deflection of praise is important because it is a demonstration of a leader's confidence. If he or she doesn't need praise – that is taken as a sign that they feel confident about their position – and that helps build confidence in the organisation as a whole.

Ensuring effective succession

Good leaders can be judged by the quality of those who advise and ultimately succeed them.

All too often, the "Great Leader" will kill off any competitive pressure from below. Capable deputies are a threat not to be tolerated. This is a crazy attitude: "If I surround myself with idiots I will be okay"? Freedom from electoral challenge comes from the success of the union – and that is in large measure a function of the quality of staff. Above all, the institution has to be greater than the ambitions or the job security of one individual. A key part of the evaluation of a leader is the degree to which he or she ensured that the union prospered after their departure at just the same level as it did while they were in office.

Able lieutenants will be attracted to and serve happily under a leader who involves and consults them and diverts credit to them in the event of success.

The example of the Accident Make-Up Pay case I have referred to earlier[7] provides a useful insight into the quality of Pat Clancy's leadership. He had an able deputy in Tom McDonald, and was happy for Tom to run what was a highly significant campaign for the union. At the same time, at the moment when the dispute's success hung in the balance, he was prepared to take responsibility for

---

7   See <www.actu.asn.au/organising/>.

the outcome. The fact that Clancy promoted someone as talented as Tom – rather than someone who would pose no threat – was again a tribute to the quality of his leadership. The payoff of course is that Clancy will always be a revered figure in that union.

Ensuring an effective succession is important but there are traps here too. We shouldn't rush to nominate a successor – and certainly not do so publicly. Such a person needs to be tested to see whether they are up for the job. Responsibility will often reveal that a seemingly talented person will not make the best leader. Early nomination is also likely to create political difficulties for the elected leader. As the end of the term draws near the leader becomes a lame duck and the work of the union suffers. It also has the disadvantage that it discourages other talented people who may have harboured leadership ambition. Either they work at less than their capacity or look for alternative employment where their ambitions have a better chance of being satisfied.

26

Women in leadership

In the previous chapter I have set out the qualities I think go to making a good leader. It is also true of course that good leaders need to be people of substantial capacity to begin with – not everyone is cut out for the role. If that is the case, I want to think through for a moment our attitude to women in leadership positions – in the interests of making sure that we get to see the most talented individuals running our unions.

We have a lot to be proud about in relation to the openness of our movement to the involvement of women. Half the ACTU Executive is female, we have a female ACTU President and the union movement has developed – quite deliberately – a program designed to ensure that a majority of the new organisers being hired are female.

These developments mask a problem in getting women from the ranks of organisers and other staff into senior positions. In looking at the list of State and Federal Secretaries it seems pretty clear that there are fewer women in those positions than has been the case in the recent past and there are certainly far fewer women there, proportionate to either the organiser workforce or the union member population.

If that is true, it is not fair to the many talented female organisers, specialist staff and industrial officers who should aspire to take leadership positions. More importantly, it is damaging to our hopes of reviving the union movement and protecting the interest of workers.

We need the best people that we can get to hold leadership positions. It is not rational to suggest – particularly as our staff become more evenly balanced between male and female – that only males are talented. Yet that is what we are saying if we believe that the best leaders are getting positions and they just happen to be all male! Quite clearly, we are failing to make the best use of some of our best people.

Further, if workers are to be attracted to an organisation, if they are to be confident that it will welcome their participation, it needs to look like them. If we need women to join, they need to see that they are welcome and that the union is likely to understand their issues. If women can't see other women in senior positions, they will perceive that the union is somehow foreign and that its leadership is a stranger to their concerns.

What can we do about this?

I don't believe in quotas when it comes to finding the right people to take leadership positions. Unions are hard pressed and will be for the foreseeable future. We can't afford to have any but the very best people running our unions. Appointment or election except on the basis of merit is unsustainable. But that means it's doubly important to remove whatever roadblocks exist that are preventing the promotion of female candidates of merit.

The first thing that we need to do is to look at the basic factors that lie at the heart of injustice affecting women in the society. We have to check how we judge the performance of women. Are we using standards that are unfair – a bloke can be tough, but a woman is aggressive? And do we provide a safe environment for women where they can do their work free of the problem of sexual harassment? If we can't even do that, then we shouldn't be all that surprised if they are not rushing to stay in the union and pursue a leadership role. In other words, the starting point for what follows is that we don't make all the same mistakes that bosses make.

Beyond the fundamentals of treating women fairly, we need to go back to the way in which men get themselves on the promotion track for leadership positions. I suspect that what happens almost as soon as a talented man gets a job in a union is that he is evaluated – perhaps unconsciously – for leadership potential. Of course he may find himself cut down as a potential competitor but in many unions, some ambition will be welcomed as a means of increasing the size of the leadership gene pool.

Union leaders, having identified a person with potential, will then imperceptibly put preferment his way. He will be tested with more and more challenging jobs and get the opportunity of being trained. He will receive the chance of going to meetings of the national body – perhaps go to meetings of the ACTU, ALP Conference or other bodies of significance. He might be given the task of representing the union at a faction meeting or negotiating with other unions about issues of importance. Responsibility for delivering an important report at a membership meeting or a meeting of the union's council will be his. Members across the union will get to know him as he moves into leading important campaigns. All the time his reputation will grow as someone to keep an eye on – someone who will go a long way.

Eventually, a talented individual will be given preferment for subsidiary leadership positions. His name will be put forward for positions of team leader, lead organiser, Assistant Secretary.

All this is entirely appropriate. The union and its leadership are taking care of succession by testing a potential leadership candidate and giving that person the opportunity of developing their skills. If they fail in the tasks allocated, the union will know that the person may not be capable of holding higher office and someone else can be tried. Because all this is done on a relatively informal basis, if they prove not to be up to the challenge, no great harm is done to the self-esteem of the individual or to the organisation.

The problem is that this process is too rarely directed to the testing and skilling of female candidates. There are two reasons for this.

First, women don't put themselves forward. They generally don't come into the organisation thinking from day one: "Gee I wonder could I ever get to run this union?" I suspect that many men on the other hand are hot-wired to ask just that question.

It is also a question of women's lower level of self-esteem.

It constantly amazes me that so many of our female officials are far less certain of their capabilities than are their male equivalents. In my work within unions it is clear to me that men are characterised by very high levels of self-confidence. It simply doesn't occur to them – as a rule – that they might not be able to do a given job. (You can guess, that on occasion, that self-confidence can be misplaced!)

By contrast, women are much less likely to be confident that they can do the job – despite the fact that in many cases, perhaps because of their less threatening attitude to workers and their communication skills, they often have a quite superior level of capability. That leads to far too many women of talent not considering the possibility that they might advance to higher office. They seem to suffer from an ambition deficit.

The other problem that we face is that we tend to replicate ourselves in the hiring and promotion decisions we make. If we think we do a good job as an organiser then when we are hiring a new organiser we look for someone just like us. In the current climate that can be a real problem. I tend to be biased in favour of job candidates who would be good on the stump – a loudmouth just like me. But the job of organiser has changed. What we need now to a far greater extent are listeners, people who can ask questions, people who can move workers to action rather than impress them with the brilliance of an argument.

We increasingly have used new methods of testing job applicants to tease out these skills. We use role plays to find the people who are capable of listening and questioning, rather than arguing. The result is that I have now hired a series of people that would never have got a look in when I was running a union.

That same process of breaking the mold needs to be applied when union leaders look for their successors. We need to accept quite consciously the possibility that the next person to hold senior office will not be like the current incumbent. We need to push women as well as men into testing situations. We need to give them access to the possibility of preferment. We need to challenge their lack of self-esteem and use positive reinforcement to give them the courage to aspire for leadership positions.

Women have little chance of running our unions if they cannot get access to the current process of patronage that exists in unions.

The ACTU and the other peak councils can do some things to help this process. We can ensure that women are represented on decision-making bodies – to force unions to identify their most talented women and give them representational responsibility.

We can subsidise the cost of attendance at significant management training initiatives. We can't allow the situation to occur where males dominate the most expensive of our residential training courses. Unions need to be encouraged to identify women who can benefit from these courses and put their names forward. In some courses, we could do this by permitting a second participant to be nominated provided that that person was female and the cost could then be reduced.

It may also be that the peak councils could develop a secondment program for middle-ranking female officials that would allow them to spend time shadowing a senior official from another union to see how the job is done.

The problem of elected positions

There is also a structural problem for women in the union movement in Australia. Far too many of our senior positions are elected.

In Australia – whether we like it or not – women still bear the primary responsibility for child rearing – and most women starting a union career will want to have children. This means that women are placed in an extremely difficult position. Do they time their child rearing for the period prior to securing elected office? That means that they will be absent during precisely the time that the union wants to test them out with additional responsibility to see whether they have what it takes.

Do they wait until they have an elected position? How then do they fit in the responsibilities of that position with raising children? They retain an entitlement to take maternity leave but taking a year off just after election will give others the opportunity of undermining their security in the job. When they return to work, whether it is genuinely the demands of the job or it's the pattern of leadership developed by males like me, they are expected to work long hours. Again, without a change in the traditional domestic division of labour, that is generally incompatible with raising children.

Many women decide that they can't combine elected office with child rearing. They resign their office, spend the time with the children, perhaps take a part-time job and hope to return to full-time work once the early, most intense period of raising children passes. If they want to come back to their own union or the union movement generally they will find that they have to start back at the beginning. While they were away, someone else has been elected to their position and will be very threatened about an alternative candidate coming back to the union. The same goes for moving to another union. The fact is that most women who have given up elected positions in these circumstances don't come back to the union movement at all. Their skills and expertise are irretrievably lost to us.

Compare the situation with business or the community sector where a senior employee leaves and then comes back into the workforce. Because these top jobs are appointed, she can simply apply to have her application considered alongside everyone else's. These internal labour markets are open to anyone that applies and selection is far more likely to be on merit. That means that these sectors lose the skills of their best performers for a relatively short period. They then come back and make a contribution at the level they should somewhere in the area – even if not in the organisation they left some years ago.

We have constructed a system with large numbers of elected positions. Our labour market is therefore closed to anyone without a long history of service in that particular union. We deny ourselves the chance of selecting the best candidate on merit. We rely only on internal candidates who have never been forced to take a break in service. That means we limit ourselves to male candidates, women who give up the chance to have children or women who, with superhuman capability or an enlightened partner, can effectively juggle home and work responsibilities.

How vital is it then that the most senior of our full time officials are elected? In many circles, this characteristic of Australian unionism is seen as a measure of the democratic control of our unions.

Yet some unions have not gone down this path and are seen quite rightly as thoroughly democratic in their operation. APESMA[1] is a successful union with strong member control of its operation. It has an elected President and Council of Management and hires its Chief Executive who is responsible to that elected body. When John Vines, the current incumbent retires, the board can advertise throughout the whole of the union movement and look for the best possible person to do the job. That person may well be a woman who has held senior office successfully in another union, left work to have children and now can come back and take on the position. After all, what do the members of that union want – an engineer looking for a career change who knows little or nothing about running a union – or an experienced official who knows unionism backwards?

I suggest, in fact, that the current system puts a heavy constraint on the democratic control by members of their union. Direct election of a national or State union leader can mean that such a person can completely ignore the wishes of the elected members of the Council of Management – on the basis that he or she is responsible directly to the members that elected him. These members are disempowered – quite unable to ensure that their vision of how the union should be run can be implemented. In fact, the balance of power is

---

1   Association of Professional Engineers, Scientists and Managers, Australia.

such that most council members are placed on the ticket dependant on the degree to which they will agree to do what the leader wants. That is scarcely an example of a well functioning democracy!

However the argument goes, as more and more talented women move their way through the system, we have to construct unions that allow us to capture their talent for the benefit of the workers that we represent.

27

Conclusion

This book and its prescriptions are hard, I know. The agenda we have been pursuing looks pretty intimidating. But we don't start with a blank piece of paper when we come to rebuilding our movement. Ours is a proud history. We are building on the strength of a movement with a reputation of tremendous achievement for the working people of Australia. And many unions have already gone a long way down the path of reform and achieved significant success.

Unions have reformed their financial systems; set up grievance centres to free up organisers and to deal with grievances efficiently; trained and recruited organisers who have the skills to talk to members and get them organised; developed training packages; identified large numbers of new activists and delegates and developed their skills. They have run campaigns around individual issues and in enterprise bargaining campaigns that have given members a sense of excitement and accomplishment about what collective action can deliver.

It's not enough.

Not enough unions have done the basics. I can't point to whole swathes of the union movement that are building massive delegate structures, hiring organisers to concentrate on growth, ensuring that their bargaining activity is leading to increases in organisational power. We have barely started on the strategic changes outlined in Section 4.

It's true that the work that has been done to date has been successful in stopping the catastrophic union decline that would have seen us out of existence by 2012. From 1999 to the present it looks as if membership is static. In three of the last five years, we grew – but by almost statistically irrelevant amounts.

Union density is still trending downwards – but at a slow rate.

I can now redraw the 2012 graph that I designed in the middle of the 1990s. Instead of the union movement becoming extinct in 2012, it will now take until 2019 before we disappear! The immediate crisis would appear to be over. We can keep what we have got and our unions are not going bankrupt. We are managing our finances much better and it is unlikely that there are too many "scary graphs" around now. The problem is that there is a sense of complacency in a number of unions that the worst is over and we can all now settle down to churn out better outcomes for our existing members and everything will be alright.

The English academic Bob Carter warned us back in 1999 of precisely this:

> If change is born of crisis alone, is simply pragmatic, it can be reversed when the sense of crisis recedes to allow more comfortable institutional patterns to reassert themselves. Pragmatic change is likely to gauge success by short term and quantitative results and is likely to involve only partial structural reform rather than change encompassing all levels and functions.[1]

With membership decline stabilized, where is the urgency for completely changing the way in which we operate our unions?

If unions are nothing more than cooperatively run businesses, there is no urgency. We should all set about fireproofing our unions so that they will survive into the future and continue to do the job that they are doing – delivering benefits to those who are members. That, after all, is the position that was taken by most American unions after the Second World War. It is that idea that allowed George Meany, President of the AFL-CIO to say in 1972:

> I used to worry about the ... size the membership ... I stopped worrying because to me it doesn't make any difference ... The organised fellow is the fellow that counts. This is just human nature.[2]

There are two things wrong with this conception.

First, we can't survive in our present shape. We are sitting ducks for the next wave of anti-union repression. Many unions have done the basics in defending themselves against the most straightforward of employer attack. But our enemies at the HR Nicholls Society and the Business Council of Australia will just work harder at refining what it will take to wipe us from the economy. We don't, after all, fit with their world view – we are an impediment to the free operation of the market. We can only be tolerated to the extent that we add value to their businesses.

Howard's win in the Senate at the last election makes certain that their agenda will be implemented. This is his big chance to do what he has always promised. Anyone who doubts his ruthlessness and the pressure from his business constituency has not been listening to him for the past 20 years.

In the union management course, we spend time on thinking like Peter Reith and Chris Corrigan. If they could run the Patrick's dispute all over again, how would they win second time around? The answer is all too easy. If we can imagine what it would take to wipe us out, so can our enemies.

---

1 Carter, B, "Adoption of the Organising Model in British trade unions: Some evidence from the MSF" in *Work, Employment and Society,* Vol 4, No 1.

2 Buhl, P, *Taking Care of Business and the Tragedy of American Labor,* Monthly Review Press, 1999 p 196.

Next time round, we will have to be capable of even higher levels of performance to be able to win.

Secondly, we aspire to be far more than little businesses churning out benefits and services to our members. We aim to represent every worker in Australia. Every one of them should have a say in how they are treated and receive a much better share – both collectively and individually – in the wealth produced in our country. That takes power and that means that we have to represent 50 per cent or more of workers in each industry.

Thirdly, we are inspired by the principle of solidarity. At its base this means that, I will help you on the understanding that at some time in the future you will help me. But we don't interpret the "understanding" part of that definition narrowly. The Maritime Union and its predecessor unions helped virtually every other union and most progressive causes in the country, without ever seriously expecting that they would need to call on the help of their friends at any time in the future. Back in 1944 when wharfies stacked out the Dress Circle of the Theatre Royal in Sydney and pelted the scab performers with rotten tomatoes during the Actors Strike, they could scarcely imagine that their descendants would want the help of actors on their own picket line in 1998 at Darling Harbour! We interpret solidarity generously. Organised workers in Australia will help any worker organise because that's what we should do.

It is from these understandings of what needs to be done that we must build the urgency for union reform. We cannot rest on our laurels. We have to build power in our industry or industries. And we have to take responsibility for ensuring that every worker has the chance to organise and thereby give themselves power.

It is to that imperative that the members of the LHMU in South Australia were responding when they were considering whether they should ask members to pay more in fees. Yes, they want to make sure that their union continues to deliver for its members. But they know that they are responsible for the deal that is handed to the next generation of workers to follow. They are more than happy to commit their time and their money to making sure that no worker in South Australian is treated with disrespect and that every worker has a chance to at least live in the "frugal comfort" first envisaged by Mr Justice Higgins in 1907.

It is crucial that we remember how attractive the American model of capitalism is to big business and their backers in Parliament. In America:

- More than 90 per cent of the private sector workforce's wages are set on the basis of unilateral employer determination.
- Employers have an absolute right to terminate the employment contract. (Remember the character Peter Parker in *Spiderman 2*? Our hero has a job delivering pizza, makes crazy, comical efforts to get the

pizza delivered on time, is late with reasonable cause and gets sacked with no appeal possible. That's the way it is. Workers are cowed.)

- Unemployment benefits give out after around six months when the workers start to have to rely on charity.

- The cost of vocational training has been almost entirely shifted to the worker.

- Occupational health and safety standards are at an all time low – they can't even get standards on the prevention of repetitive-use injuries through the Congress. What regulations that exist are largely unenforced because of the tiny expenditure on the public servants supposed to uphold the health and safety laws.[3]

- An underclass of illegal immigrants exist who, given the ever present threat of deportation, suffer the worst kinds of sweatshop exploitation.

- Minimum wages are set for the whole economy – either on a State or federal basis – at levels that do not permit a worker to live without the help of charity.[4]

- The laws encouraging the organisation of workers have been so debased that they now act as a positive hindrance to workers trying to give themselves some power.

- The dominant ideology is still that if Americans work hard enough they will become successful – even though there is less chance of this happening in the US than in almost any other developed country.[5]

And the clincher for our business friends is that with all this, they get to be paid – on average – 500 times the average wage of their employees!

That's what Howard and his friends want – and look at how far they've got.

- Collective bargaining coverage in Australia has gone from around 80 per cent in 1990 to around 32 per cent in 2000 – and the trend is for this to get worse.[6]

---

3   See Schlosser, E, *Fast Food Nation: The Dark Side of the All American Meal*, HarperCollins 2002, for the horrifying impact on consumers and workers in the meat industry of the neglect of health and safety enforcement – not to mention a loss of union power.

4   See Ehrenreich, B, *Nickel and Dimed – On (Not) Getting by in America* Metropolitan Books 2001, for a very personal, bittersweet examination of what it's like to try to live on minimum wages.

5   Hutton, W, *The World We Are In*, Little Brown, 2002, p 166-167.

6   Campbell, I, "Industrial Relations and Intellectual Challenges: Conceptualising the Recent Changes to Labour Regulation in Australia", 2001, available at <www.econ.usyd. edu.au/download.php?id=4299>.

- Access to unfair dismissal laws has been restricted and, as soon as their legislation passes the Senate, the government will allow businesses with 100 or less employees to sack people unfairly.

- Eligibility for unemployment benefits has been tightened so that benefit holders have to work incredibly hard just to meet the conditions imposed by the government. Any breach of the conditions leads to a reduction or ultimately termination of benefit for eight weeks.

- The cost of vocational training is shifting to workers as companies cut back on their training budgets and real apprenticeships – while employers are complaining about a skills shortage.

- An attack is expected any day on the regulation of occupational health and safety.

- The system of Award minimum standards in each industry is now fatally undermined. Basic wage adjustments – keeping wages in touch with the increased cost of living – are now dealt with by someone other than an independent arbitrator and minimum wages are undermined in any event by the access of employers to both individual agreements and the use of independent contractor arrangements.

- Government and big business continually push the idea that workers are individuals and they now want to look out for themselves alone and reject the idea of collective representation.

And yes, we all know the increase in Executive remuneration. Our bosses only get 70 times average employee wages – a poor second to the US – but they are trying hard to keep up.

The pattern seems to be pretty clear doesn't it?

The only thing standing in the way of the full-scale adoption of an American model is the union movement with our belief in helping each other out, our commitment to fairness and decency and our determination to make Australia prosperous for all and not just an elite few.

Over and over again, we have to remind our members and ourselves that this is what we are about. We can never limit ourselves to being the service providers that employers and conservative governments want us to be. We are the mechanism that gives workers power. To do that we have to organise. To organise we need to change the way in which our unions operate.

The employers will not stand still while we get our act together.

The ideology of individualism will become more and more persuasive to the extent that we fail to educate workers in large numbers as to how flawed that value system is.

As time goes on, there will be pressure from many in the employer community to deliver a knock-out blow to organised labour. Already we have seen how worried they were by the ALP's minimalist industrial relations reform agenda, just think how they will behave if Labor actually tried to introduce a level playing field into industrial relations!

The force of competition imposes its own pressures on firms. As we lose industry power, so non-union firms gain a competitive advantage and the pressure to be rid of the union grows.

Finally, we have to acknowledge that as we are successful in rebuilding our organisations, some employers will respond with ever more extreme measures, in an effort to get the upper hand once and for all.

What's proposed is a broad-ranging agenda for change. I know that many reading this will see it as something of a menu of options from which selections can be made. "Increasing fees will be difficult so we will leave that to later"; "We don't have people who can be lead organisers so we will just defer that change to a later date"; "Teams of external organisers may be okay in the US or Canada, but it won't work here."

I have to confess, that when I have talked to union leaders contemplating what they have to do, I try to be fairly diplomatic. (I admit that I often don't succeed.) And it is true that I, and my colleagues at the ACTU, can only advise – to that extent we have no power. Union leaders are responsible for their unions, they know it best, it's not for me to superimpose my judgment on their views about what is needed for the future. I have sometimes taken the view that it is better that they do something than nothing.

Let me now, once and for all, climb off the fence.

The ability to survive depends on unions taking all the measures that have been outlined in the section on building organisational capacity. It is not a menu. You can't pick and choose. You can't say that you are an organising union and leave crucial sections of the program out – and then complain when you don't get the growth that you expected and need. The theory only works when it is fully implemented.

Let me take a moment and reiterate the bare essentials.

- Australian unions need more money. If you are not charging somewhere around at least $468 per year (the ACTU Congress policy) you will have difficulty in doing what needs to be done.

- Organising unions need a different style of leadership. It requires a guiding coalition that is determined, involved, skilled and thoughtful. We need a model of leadership that is open to challenge and that is prepared to listen to contributions from every section of the union. We need leaders with courage and vision.

- Grievances have to be dealt with, but unions must free organisers of the grievance load. You don't have to have a call centre, but if you don't, you need to show how you are ensuring that your organisers don't spend their time dealing with grievances.

- Enterprise bargaining is a pre-eminent organising opportunity. We can't continue to deliver good outcomes for members and leave the bargaining table without a marked increase in the union's organisational capacity.

- We have to get cooperation from the employers we have organised. We can't continue to fight every one simultaneously. We have to build bridges to those employers attempting to do the right thing so that we can go after the bosses who are oppressing workers.

- We must have external teams of organisers who do nothing but build the power of the union.

- Organisers must be led by lead organisers who make sure that the resources invested – and workers' money is precious – actually deliver what it is supposed to.

- Union leaders have to manage. If union staff are unwilling or incapable of delivering for members, then they have to go.

- Every union has to have a well-considered education program that is properly resourced. Organising unionism is built around membership involvement and they can't be involved if they haven't got the knowledge, skills and confidence that training brings.

- Finally, the proof that organising is happening and the strength that is necessary for organising to happen is the presence in the union of hundreds and hundreds of passionate activists. We need activists at every level of the union from its national councils right down to its workplace committees. You need to be able to see them at the centre of every one of the union's activities, whether it is in a commission hearing, at a rally, on the doors of an organising campaign, at a delegates' convention. If they are not there, you are not organising and your union will have great difficulty in surviving.

For some, that policy prescription means that the union needs to change everything. These are the unions that have relied on closed shops, compliant employers and an institutional system that delivered what members needed. Some of the unions that have advanced furthest fall into this category. They had no option.

For others, the jump to the kind of unionism I have described appears to be easier. They have a tradition of militant action. Some of their workplaces have had delegates' committees. They have a strong democratic tradition. In practice, these have found the change most difficult. In many cases, their relative strength has allowed them to delay facing up to the changes that are necessary. They have continued to defend their territory at least in their strong areas of workplace organisation. But generally, despite this, they have failed to grow. As time goes on, their strongly organised workplaces will be exposed to wage competition and the struggle will become tougher. They too will need to throw themselves into a comprehensive reform program that builds on their strength but also learns from the experience of what has worked so far in union reform in this country.

It is possible to pilot this program in one section of the union to build confidence and make short-term wins. But that means that the whole program is trialed in one section so that it has some chance of success. Experimentation can't proceed by introducing one reform at a time. The reforms work together and support each other.

The elements will be applied in different ways. Some unions have very high levels of density. Their emphasis on external organising will be limited to the activation of existing delegates' networks. Other unions will rely on industry-wide activists rather than workplace delegates because their members are concentrated in short-term employment. Some unions already charge high levels of fees and therefore have the resources to organise. But all the elements must be applied in some way.

The simple fact is that, without having undergone a thorough reform program, no union I have come across in Australia matches the description I have set out above in all particulars. Where these changes have been embraced comprehensively, unions are winning.

But that just gets us to square 1. Defending our existing membership and helping them to win against employer attack is just the start. We need much higher levels of density. Building density is far more difficult than halting membership decline. To increase density by 1 per cent means that we have to organise an additional 420,000 new members each year.[7]

And more important than getting an additional 1 per cent density overall, we need to achieve massive density growth in targeted industries if we are to hope to be able to take wages out of competition in each of those industries.

That's why we have to build strategic leverage – to build cooperation with those employers open to it, resource movement-wide organising campaigns aimed at major employers and international companies and reinvent our political activity. We have to plan for success – be able to set out in advance how it is that we will organise whole industries. We need whole swathes of the unorganised workforce to demand collective representation and that means that we must give ourselves the opportunity of organising to scale.

Can we win?

---

7   ACTU, unions@work, 1999, p 25,

I am absolutely optimistic – and that optimism is founded on a rational assessment of our position.

Union reform has progressed rapidly and particularly rapidly in the last few years. Until 1999 not one union had adopted this agenda in any form. In five years large numbers of unions have worked incredibly hard to pursue their processes of internal reform.

The organising agenda – at least in its most basic form – is well accepted.

Everywhere I look I see hundreds of bright enthusiastic organisers ready for the challenge to come.

Thousands of new delegates have been identified and are passionately interested in the survival of their union.

Unions have started to increase their fees and everything we predicted about membership acceptance of the need for higher fees has been proved true.

Public approval for unions is at record levels. Of seven public institutions, only the union movement has recorded increased public approval.[8]

Despite the best efforts of our political masters and big business, the Australian commitment to fairness and collective solutions is remarkably enduring.

In every State, I see union leaders anxious to take up the challenge and put their unions in a position to win.

As Peter Ellyard has said:

> The future is not some place we are going to but one we are creating; the paths to it are not found but made; we can only build a future if we can first imagine it.

We must all work to make this the generation that made Australia once more a model for a truly civilised society – a market economy forced to deliver a decent way of life for all those in it. That will only happen if Australia's working people are able to build for themselves power sufficient to counterbalance the power now so dominatingly held by their employers. The process has started. It is up to us now to press on, combining together with courage, to advance a fair Australia.

---

8   Pusey, M, *The Experience of Middle Australia, The Dark Side of Economic Reform,* Cambridge University Press, 2003, p 151.

Bibliography

ABS, Unpublished data, Employee earnings, benefits and trade union membership, 2000.

ABS, Employee Earnings, Benefits and Trade Union Membership, 6310.0, March 2004.

Access Economics Pty Ltd, *Assessment of the Australian Labor Party Workplace Relations Policy Platform*, Business Council of Australia, July 2004.

ACIRRT, *An analysis of the 1996, 1997 and 1999 Newspoll Industrial Relations Survey,* Labor Council of NSW, 1999.

ACIRRT, Survey of community attitudes, 2001.

ACTU, *unions@work*, August 1999, available at <http://www.actu.asn.au/public/papers/unionswork.html>.

ACTU, *Future Strategies*, May, 2003, available at <http://www.actu.asn.au/public/papers/Organising.html>.

Alinsky, S, *Rules for Radicals, A pragmatic primer for realistic radicals*, Vintage Books, 1971.

Australia Council, archival recording, Hal Alexander, 1980.

Berry, P and Kitchener, G, *Can Unions Survive?* Building Workers Industrial Union, ACT Branch, 1989.

Behrens, M, Fichter, M and Frege, CM, "Unions in Germany: Regaining the Initiative?" in *European Journal of Industrial Relations,*2003.

Bosch, G, "The Changing Nature of Collective Bargaining in Germany" in Katz, HC, Lee, W and Lee, J (eds), *The New Structure of Labor Relations*, ILR Press, 2004.

Bronfenbrenner, K, and Hickey, R, "Changing to Organize, A National Assessment of Union Strategies" in Milkman R and Voss, K (eds?) *Rebuilding Labor, Organizing and Organizers in the New Union Movement*, ILR Press, 2004.

Brown, W and Oxenbridge, S, "The development of co-operative Employer/trade union relationships in Britain" in *Industrielle Beziehungen, German Journal of Industrial Relations* 11, 2004, p 143.

Bryson, A and Gomez, R, *Why have workers stopped joining unions?* Discussion Paper 589, The Leverhulme Trust, November 2003.

Buchanan, J and Briggs, C, "Works Councils and Inequality at work in Contemporary Australia" in P Gollan, R Markey, I Ross (eds), *Works Councils in Australia*, Federation Press, 2002.

Buchanan, J and Hall, R "Teams and control on the job: Insights from the Australian Metal and Engineering Best Practice Case Studies in *Journal of Industrial Relations*, Vol 44, No 3, September 2002.

Buhl, P, *Taking Care of Business and the Tragedy of American Labor*, Monthly Review Press, 1999.

Burke, B, Geronimo, J, Martin, D, Thomas, B, Wall, C, *Education for Changing Unions, Between the Lines*, 2002.

Business Council of Australia, Managerial leadership in the workplace, 2000.

Callus, R and Lansbury, R, *Working Futures, The Changing Nature of Work and Employment Relations in Australia*, Federation Press, 2002.

Campbell, I, "Industrial Relations and Intellectual Challenges: Conceptualising the Recent Changes to Labour Regulation in Australia",2001, available at <www.econ.usyd.edu.au/download.php?id=4299>.

Carter, B, "Adoption of the Organising Model in British trade unions: Some evidence from the MSF" in *Work, Employment and Society*, Vol 4, No 1.

Centre for Economic Performance, *Future of Unions in Modern Britain*, The Leverhulme Trust, 2002.

BIBLIOGRAPHY

Cockfield, S "McKay's Harvester Works and the Continuation of Managerial Control" in *Journal of Industrial Relations,* Vol 40, No 3, September 1998.

Cole, M, Briggs, C, Buchanan, J, *Latent trends become manifest: where were the non-members in 2002,* ACIRRT, 2003.

Cooper, R, *Making the NSW Union Movement? A study of the Organising and Recruitment Activities of the NSW Labor Council 1900- 1910,* IRRC, 1996.

Cooper, R, "'To Organise Wherever the Necessity Exists': the Activities of the Organising Committee of the Labor Council of NSW, 1900-10" in *Labour History,* Number 83, November 2002.

Cooper, R, "The Organising Committee of the Labor Council of NSW, 1900-10" in *Labour History,* No 83, November 2002.

Crosby, M, "Running on Empty", ACTU, 2004.

Davies, A and Trinca, H, *War on the Waterfront – the battle that changed Australia,* Doubleday/Random House, 2000.

Easson, M (ed), *The Foundation of Labor,* Pluto Press, 1990.

Ellem, b, *Hard Ground, Unions in the Pilbara,* Pilbara Mineworkers Union, 2004.

Ehrenreich, Barbara, *Nickel and Dimed – On (Not) Getting by in America,* Owl Books, 2002.

Fahey, Charles and Lack, John, "'We Have to Train Men from Labourers': The Agricultural Implement Trade 1918–1945" in *Journal of Industrial Relations,* Vol 42, No 4, December 2000.

Frank, T, *One Market Under God,* Anchor Books, 2000.

Frank, T, *What's the Matter with Kansas,* Metropolitan Books, 2004.

Freeman, Membership and Earnings Data Book (1983-2001), BNA, 2002.

Freudenberg, G, "The Great Strike" in Easson, M (ed) *The Foundation of Labor,* Pluto Press, 1990.

Gunness, G and Lewis, A, "The NZAS Experience and the Implications for CRA", Comalco Smelting, 1992.

Hassel, A, "The Erosion of the German System of Industrial Relations" in *British Journal of Industrial Relations,* September 1999.

Hassel, A, "The Erosion Continues: Reply" in *British Journal of Industrial Relations,* June 2002.

Hearn, M and Knowles, H, *One Big Union, A History of the AWU 1886–1994,* Cambridge University Press, 1996.

Heery, E, "Partnership versus organising: alternative futures for British trade unionism" *British Journal of Industrial Relations,* Vol 33, p 1.

Howard, WA, Australian Trade Unions in the Context of Union Theory in *Journal of Industrial Relations* Vol 19, p 255, September 1977.

Hutton, W, *The World We're In,* Little, Brown, 2002.

Kelly, Paul, *The End of Certainty,* Allen & Unwin, 1994.

Kisch, E, *Australian Landfall,* Macmillan, 1969.

Kirsch, A, "Union Mergers in Australia and Germany, A Comparative Study from an Organisation Theory Perspective", Masters thesis, Universitat Konstanz 2003.

Kochan, T, *Restoring Workers Voice: A call for action,* paper to a Washington DC conference on the future of organised labour, 2003.

Kotter, JP, "Leading Change: Why transformation efforts fail" *Harvard Business Review,* March-April 1995, p 59.

Kotter, JP, *Leading* Change Harvard Business School Press, 1996.

Lerner, S, "An Immodest Proposal: A New Architecture for the House of Labor" in *New Labor Forum* 12(2) Summer 2003, p 9.

Lund, J, Giving unions their due: a comparison of union dues for selected unions in New South Wales (Australia) and Wisconsin (U.S.), July, 2001, ACTU Organising Centre.

Markey, R, *In Case of Oppression, The life and times of the Labor Council of NSW,* Pluto Press, 1994.

Markey, R, *The Making of the Labor Party in NSW 1880–1900,* NSW University Press, 1988.

Markey, Ray, "Explaining Union Mobilisation in the 1880s and Early 1900s" in *Labour History*, No 83, November 2002.

Markus, A, "Divided we fall. The Chinese and the Melbourne Furniture Trade Union" in *Labour History,* No 26, May 1974.

Marr, J, *First the Verdict,* Pluto Press, 2003.

McDonald, Tom and Audrey, *Intimate Union, Sharing a Revolutionary Life,* Pluto Press, 1998.

McKay, Hugh, *Generations, Baby boomers, their parents and their children,* Macmillan, 1997.

McMullin, R, *So Monstrous a Travesty, Chris Watson and the world's first labour government,* Scribe, 2004.

Metzgar, J (ed), *An Organizing Model of Unionism. Labour Research Review 17,* Midwest Centre for Labor Research, 1991.   ·

Moreshead A et al, *Changes at Work, The 1995 Australian Workplace Industrial Relations Survey,* Longman, 1997.

Morgan, HM, "The Nature of Trade Union Power", <www.hrnicholls.com.au>.

Newman, M, *Maeler's Regard, Images of Adult Learning,* Stewart Victor Publishing, Sydney, 1999.

Office of the Minister for Employment and Workplace Relations, *Labor and the Unions – A Radical Agenda,* June 2004.

O'Rourke, A and Nyland, C, "AUSTFA and the Ratcheting-Up of Labour Standards" in *Journal of Industrial Relations,* (forthcoming).

Peetz, D, *Unions in a Contrary World, The Future of the Australian Union Movement,* Cambridge University Press, 1998.

Peetz, D, Webb, C and Jones, M, "Activism Amongst Workplace Union Delegates" in *International Journal of Employment Studies,* Vol 10, no 2, October 2002.

Pocock, B, *The Work/Life Collision,* Federation Press, 2003.

Pocock, B, Prosser, R and Bridge, K, "'Only a Casual ...' How Casual Work affects Employees, Households and Communities in Australia", Department of Labour Studies, University of Adelaide, 2004.

Pusey, M, *The Experience of Middle Australia, The Dark Side of Economic Reform,* Cambridge University Press, 2003.

Riley Research Pty Ltd for Labor Council of NSW, *Attitudes to Work and Unions,* April 1996.

Schacht, C, "How to Make the Labor Party Work in the Twenty First Century" in Hocking, J and Lewis, C (eds), *Its Time Again,* Circa 2003.

Schlosser, E, *Fast Food Nation: The Dark Side of the All American Meal,* Perennial, 2002.

Tarrant, L, *Unionism Around Us,* Briefing paper for LHMU National Council. 2004.

Taylor, R, "Social democratic trade unionism. An agenda for action" in *Catalyst* 2003.

Voss, K and Sherman, R, "Breaking the Iron Law of Oligarchy: Union Revitalization in the American Labor Movement: in *American Journal of Sociology* Vol 106, No 2 (September 2000), p 303.

Ward, R, *The Australian Legend,* Oxford University Press, 1958.

Watson, I, Buchanan, J, Campbell, I and Briggs, C, *Fragmented Futures, New Challenges in Working Life,* Federation Press, 2003.

Weil, D, *Turning the Tide, Strategic Planning for Labor Unions,* Lexington Books, 1994.

Weil, D, "A Strategic Choice Framework for Union Decision-making" in *Working USA: The Journal of Labor and Society,* Vol 8, March 2005.

Wooden, M, *Union Wage Effects in the Presence of Enterprise Bargaining,* Melbourne Institute Working Paper No 7, 2000.

WSI Mitteilungen, Special Issue, Industrial Relations in Germany – an Empirical Survey, 2003.

Wynhausen, E, *Dirt Cheap,* Macmillan, 2005.

Zappala, G, *Mapping the Extent of Compulsory Unionism in Australia,* ACIRRT, September 1991.

Index